Valuable Vegetables

Growing for pleasure and profit...

'Dedicated to all the worms in my garden'

First Published in 2003 updated in 2008 by
eco-logic books
Mulberry House
19 Maple Grove
Bath BA2 3AF

Web: www.eco-logicbooks.com

ISBN (10) 1 899233 12 1
ISBN (13) 978 1 899233 12 0

Illustrations by Sue Kendall.
Editing by Marjorie Gibbon.
Design and Typesetting by The Design Co-operative Ltd.
Printed and bound in Great Britain by Cpod, Trowbridge, Wiltshire

eco-logic books publish and sell mail order books that promote practical solutions to environmental problems, organic gardening, sustainable development, permaculture, transition thinking and related topics. For a complete list visit their web site.

The Small Print

Whilst every effort has been made to ensure the accuracy of the information in this book the publisher and author accept no responsibility for any errors or omissions. Whilst we have attempted to identify the common uses for some types of plants described in this book we make no claim whatsoever as to the medicinal uses of the plants.

Contents

INTRODUCTION

Growing and Selling Vegetables
Sustainably 5

GROWING SKILLS

Growing Skills – Introduction 7
Choosing Your Site 10
From Field to Garden 13
Soils and Nutrients 17
Machinery, Tools and Equipment 21
Fertility 28
Rotation 35
Green Manures 40
Sowing Propagation Modules and
Transplants 43
Protected Cropping 50
Storing Your Harvest Through
the Winter 55
Water and Irrigation 59
Weed Control 63
Pests and Diseases 65
Seeds and Seed Sowing 77

VEGETABLES

Vegetables – Introduction 81
Artichokes – Globe 84
Artichokes – Jerusalem 86
Asparagus 88
Aubergines 90

Beetroot 91
Brassicas 94
Broad Beans 97
Brussels Sprouts 99
Cabbages 101
Calabrese...103
Carrots 104
Cauliflowers 107
Celeriac...108
Celery 110
Chicory 112
Claytonia...113
Courgettes...114
Cress 117
Cucumbers 118
Endive 122
Fennel..123
Flowers 125
French Beans 126
Garlic 128
Kale 130
Kohl Rabi 131
Lamb's Lettuce or Corn Salad 132
Leeks...134
Lettuce 135
Marrows and Pumpkins 138
Onions 140
Oriental Salad Leaves 142
Parsnips...143
Peas...145

Peppers and Chillis 148

Perpetual Spinach and Swiss Chard 150

Potatoes...152

Radish..157

Runner Beans 159

Salsify and Scorzonera 162

Spinach - Annual 163

Spring Onions...165

Sprouting Broccoli 166

Squash 167

Swedes 170

Sweetcorn 171

Tomatoes 174

Turnips 178

HERBS

Herbs – Introduction.......................181

Basil 182

Celery Leaf..184

Chervil 185

Chives 186

Coriander 187

Dill and Fennel 189

Lemon Balm 191

Lovage..192

Mint 193

Oregano, Sweet and Pot Marjoram........194

Parsley..195

Rocket...197

Rosemary and Sage 199

Salad Burnet 200

Savory – Summer and Winter 201

Sorrel 202

Tarragon 204

Thyme..205

SOFT FRUITS

Soft Fruits – Introduction 207

Blackberries and Hybrid Berries 209

Blackcurrants 212

Cape Gooseberry 215

Gooseberries 217

Melons 219

Raspberries 221

Red and Whitecurrants 224

Rhubarb 226

Strawberries 228

SELLING SKILLS

Selling Skills – Introduction 231

Finding and Keeping Customers 232

Growing Vegetables for Sale 234

Buying In Vegetables to Sell 237

Selling Vegetables 240

Money 245

Labour and Help 247

APPENDICES

Polytunnels 249

Building Your OwnPropagator 253

Average Monthly Costing
and Content of Boxes 255

Timetables of Plantings for
Succession..259

Sowing and Harvesting Table................263

Useful Organisations 265

Bibliography 268

Index..270

Introduction

Growing and Selling Vegetables Sustainably

G rowing enough vegetables to eat and have a surplus to sell in order to pay your bills can be hard work. To do this as sustainably as possible can be even harder work. However, I find the more I grow and sell my produce sustainably, the easier it gets. This book is about the journey between the planting of the seed and the harvesting and selling of the crop and how to make it a pleasurable, sustainable and rewarding task.

I practise organic horticulture and follow permaculture principles but the more I garden the more it occurs to me that nature intended the goodness in our crops to come from their health, vigour and freshness. Ultimately this is of far more importance than the label that describes how they are grown.

If you follow nature's example, you will nearly always grow good vegetables. Nature is the best model for sustainability and it only takes an awareness of this simple fact for us to begin to replicate nature's bounty. It is also necessary to be aware of nature's limits. Once you exceed those limits you start to abuse its inherent productivity and you will have to rely more and more on non-sustainable energy sources and products. The trick is to capitalise on nature's bounty but not exceed its generosity.

I grow vegetables in the system I've developed because it sustains me and the land on which I work – it is a holistic and balanced process. I grow vegetables to feed myself and in order to sell my surplus through a box scheme. I don't send my crops off to market, to a faceless wholesaler, for the best price I can get. I make a living profit from a living venture and regard this as more than sufficient for most of my needs.

My customers are an integral part of my vegetable production system. I set my prices realistically and know many of my customers by name. They in turn tell me what they do and don't like. I regularly take apprentices who can learn how to grow and sell vegetables and are then able to run a similar system themselves.

There are many box scheme operations that act as middlemen for the large scale growers and whilst

I applaud their efforts in getting more organic food to the mass market at an affordable price, they are still subject to mass-market economics. They have little control over the sourcing and pricing of their product. They cannot hope to know the various production methods of all the growers who supply them via the wholesalers.

There is definitely a large market for organic produce sold under this system and I hope that it continues. However I would like to see more small-scale producers and cooperatives growing the vegetables themselves and selling them direct. This is the only way that the grower and consumer can co-exist without being subject to economic and market forces outside their control.

I have always tried to use second hand and waste materials in my garden for both environmental and financial reasons. I use old windows, tyres, used silage bags, feed sacks (paper and plastic), cardboard, newspaper etc as well as new equipment. I find secondhand polytunnel plastic can be useful and even old fridges can come into use as cloches and store cupboards.

A lot of people don't like the idea of plastic and tyres littering their gardens but I find there are always ways in which they can be hidden, more often than not they become covered in greenery in the summer anyway. Using waste materials wisely you can help to increase their productive life, save money and still have a garden that looks wonderful. I try not be too principled about the materials I use as they are often a means towards a more sustainable end.

I hope that this book helps all gardeners to grow healthy vegetables and encourages them to sell their surplus or even set up a small business. I also hope they do so in a way that gives them immediate contact with their customers either through a box scheme, farmers' market or farm gate sales.

Growing Skills

Introduction

grow a good range of vegetables, herbs and soft fruit on my acre and a half. A couple of years ago I counted the number of lettuce and salad leaf varieties I grew and it amounted to 24; it would have been more if I'd included all the flowers and herbs I use in my salads. I have reckoned, quite roughly, that I grow at least 150 varieties of vegetables alone. Also I allow all sorts of plants to seed themselves in the garden, including flowers, herbs, salads and some weeds.

The result is that I have a huge diversity of plants. They complement each other, attract and deter predators and pests of all kinds, look very colourful both in the garden and the boxes I sell. They also create an interesting mix of work for me and, perhaps most importantly, I never have all my eggs in one basket. If a crop fails for whatever reason, it is easily replaced by a multitude of others. I feel that this diversity is the basis of a healthy garden. If you maintain the health of your environment you will undoubtedly maintain the health of your crops.

Being organic and chemical free

The organic gardener is half way to creating a living and healthy environment. There is a great misconception concerning the word organic. Many people regard it as simply a chemical free system of agriculture, which is a great over-simplification.

Organic agriculture is about creating and sustaining healthy soils, crops, animals and humans. The gardener's approach does not just concentrate on not using chemicals, but must consider how all the aspects of their garden can be maintained sustainably. This will include features such as rotations, fertility, composting, weed control and controlling pests and diseases without reaching for the skull-and-cross-bones bottle. Nature has its own way of dealing with problems and the organic approach copies and enhances nature's example.

The essential element of organic growing is a very simple cycle - feed the soil, the soil feeds the plant, the plant feeds the animal, the animal feeds the soil.

Permaculture

As the word says, this is a system of perma(nent) culture. It is a very simple way of designing our lives and what we do in them to mirror natural systems. In terms of gardening, the perfect permaculture garden in this country is a forest garden. It mimics natural forests whilst providing an abundance of food within its boundaries. It relies heavily on perennial cropping so that the work involved in maintaining the system is minimised.

Although I use an abundance of annual vegetables in my garden I am very aware of using permaculture designs and systems within it. For example, I coppice the hedges around my garden for bean poles and pea sticks, making use of a relatively unproductive (in terms of food) sheltering hedge. In front of my north hedge, which is quite large and sucks the water out of the ground, I grow Jerusalem artichokes under a deep mulch. This is a tall, perennial crop that can withstand a lack of water. Next to the hedge it can't shade any of my other vegetables but creates shade for the soil under the hedge, reducing surface evaporation. I have also put fruit trees around the edges of my garden, and into the hedges, to produce fruit in years to come and to use space that is often wasted in conventional gardens.

Permaculture is a big subject and I could give countless examples of the way I use it in my garden but I would suggest that you look for more information on the subject in other books and magazines (see bibliography). It is a bit of a religion to some and while I find it useful in terms of efficiency and design I will always use techniques that work rather than those that dogma dictates.

Weather

Understanding weather patterns is something I have had to learn. Knowing that clear skies in the spring might result in a frost was something I learned quite quickly. The difficulty is knowing when the clear sky is likely to produce a frost and when it isn't. For this I rely on the BBC weather forecasts. Being in a frost pocket, I know from experience that when they put the temperature over my region at 1° above freezing, it will actually be −1° in my garden. When they point at a front that is coming in from the west, I always look at the weather over the Atlantic to try and get some idea of whether there's going to be more of the same, or showers or if the wind will change direction. I keep an eye on the weather forecasts on a daily basis during the growing season.

Knowing what the weather is likely to do gives you a helping hand with planning ahead. For example, sowing carrot seed in the middle of a wet spell will, hopefully, result in them emerging during a dry spell, making them less vulnerable to slugs. This doesn't always work - sometimes you can't help but think that you may as well have asked the slugs round for dinner. Being aware of approaching cold weather in the spring is essential because you can cover crops with fleeces and cloches to protect them and minimise growth checks. Also, watch out for the first frost in the autumn, which is often light enough only to burn the edges of leaves. Take it as a sign to harvest your frost tender crops quickly. It is usually only a day or two before a following hard frost, which will damage tender crops. And if freezing weather is forecast, enough to freeze plants and soil, dig any vegetables that you will need before the ground gets too hard.

Observation

To take proper care of the vegetables that you are growing you should be constantly aware of their condition and their readiness for harvest. I walk around the garden regularly just looking at what is going on, seeing how much a plant is growing and how well it looks, checking for disease or pests, gauging harvest times and getting work organised for the days and weeks ahead. This means for example that if you plan to clear and muck a piece of ground, but then it rains, you know what other jobs need doing indoors.

Having said all that, I feel my way about the garden. Try and cultivate a 'sixth sense' based on experience. When I started, I didn't really know what I was doing. I would check the temperature in the polytunnels every few hours, worry that my new potatoes would get frosted if I went away, cultivate soil when it was too wet because I worried that planting my peas too late would mean they wouldn't crop in time. In reality, if you follow the weather and wait, even when it's tempting to race ahead, your crops will be a lot happier and so will you.

Choosing Your Site

Your garden will be the basis of your business, and the better it is the easier your job will be. Remember that growing vegetables on a small scale is time consuming. If you want to grow for sale it can be a full time job. The more advantages a site has to offer, the easier your life will be.

Whatever you do, don't rent or buy anything until you have considered all the relevant factors. You are going to be spending a lot of time and effort on this venture over the next few years. It is important to know what you want to achieve. Draw up a checklist using the categories below and award points to positive features. This can be especially useful when comparing two possible sites. If you are buying your site you are much more likely to be able to get what you want than if you are renting.

Location

Beware of living and working in the same place. It can be difficult to 'go home', and customers tend to think that you are available 24 hours a day. On the other hand, if you live far away it is annoying if you have to pop back to turn a tap off or to shut a polytunnel door.

History

Find out the background of your prospective plot. Talk to as many people as you can who live nearby, or have farmed or gardened the plot before. They will have valuable information. For example, if the ground has never been used for vegetables then it may be worth asking why. Conversely if it has been used as a vegetable plot for donkey's years it may have a very friable and light soil, but you might inherit a disease such as club root.

Access

You will need good access for getting materials onto your site and for getting your produce out. Without direct vehicle access you will waste mountains of time and energy moving muck, straw, vegetables and other materials.

Soils

Take samples from different parts of the site and have them tested for nutrient and mineral content and pH. Look at the soil structure and colour, dig some holes a good few feet down to see what the subsoil looks like. To understand what you discover, see the chapter on soils.

Gradient

A slight slope is a bonus because it helps drainage, particularly on heavier soils. However, if the gradient is greater than about 10° you will have to consider erecting some sort of soil retaining structure. These will be costly if you are going to make them look nice and time consuming to keep neat and tidy, and they are a haven for slugs.

Aspect

The aspect must be taken into account if you are on a slope or if there is a tall obstacle such as a building, tree or hedge next to your site. On a slope it makes a huge difference if you have a southerly orientation: the soil will warm more quickly if it is pointing towards the sun. If you choose a site on a north-facing slope you're not doing yourself any favours.

Windbreaks

These are essential on most sites. The northern and eastern edges tend to be the coldest, most exposed areas of your site. Having a tallish hedge or trees on those sides will help protect early, late and over winter crops. If the site doesn't already have protection then plant fast growing hedges such as willow. You can always plant a traditional, slower growing hedge behind the willow to take over later. Do not plant your hedge too close to the growing area as it will rob the ground, and subsequently your vegetables, of water and nutrients. Also take care that any hedges will not shade out your crops. If you don't have access to coppice type wood such as hazel, think about including it in any hedges you plant. Hazel will provide you with bean poles and peas sticks within five years of planting.

Structures

If you find a site with polytunnels/greenhouses and barns/sheds already erected then you are lucky. Barns and sheds are useful for storing vegetables and machinery (which will need to be secure), for keeping vegetables cool and as a possible packing area. If you don't have buildings already you will need to find out if it's OK to erect them. Check with your neighbours and possibly the local planning office. Don't be too precious about building design. If necessary a multitude of sins can be hidden by fast growing willow screens and evergreen hedges.

Water

Considering your water sources is vitally important yet often overlooked. More and more houses, farms and smallholdings are being put onto a metered water supply. The cost of water could become a large factor in the profitability of your venture. Ideally a site would have a free supply of water, such as a spring or a stream (and preferably at the top of the site). If you are on the flat with no water source you must consider collecting water from roofs. It may be wise to construct a raised pond or tank for summer supplies. You could also dig a well or borehole but you will need an extraction licence from the local water company.

Other services

An electricity supply isn't essential but it does help. You can get away with paraffin for light and heat, but supplying the propagation unit is more difficult. If you don't have electricity at the site and don't plan to get any, it's worth considering doing this part of the growing where you live (presuming you have electricity there).

Local resources

If you are going to grow vegetables for sale it helps to have a local (organic) wholesaler for the times when your crops are either insufficient or have failed. Also check out local supplies of organic matter. If you are surrounded by cereal farmers then you will have ready access to straw but little hope of getting any farm yard manure (FYM). If you are near livestock farmers the reverse will be true. You may find there's a mushroom grower down the road who has spent mushroom compost for sale.

Markets for your produce

Find out about any other growers in the area and how they sell their produce. They may want to sell you their vegetables or they may resent you if you start selling into their markets. Find out where the nearest farmers' markets are and where there are any other box schemes running. It's sometimes possible to slot into areas that aren't covered. You may want to try supplying restaurants but check if anyone else is, and that the restaurant is a reliable payer. If you are on a fairly busy road you can also try farm gate sales.

Aesthetics and friendly neighbours

Remember that a gorgeous site won't make your vegetables grow any better but if it makes you happy then it will have a beneficial effect on the way you grow them. Friendly neighbours are a great source of help and support and worth many stars on your checklist.

From Field to Garden

Having secured your site the first thing to consider is any permanent features. If they are not already there you will need to erect polytunnels, sheds and hedges. See the chapter on protected cropping for advice about siting a polytunnel. Remember that good access is of paramount importance for getting materials and produce on and off the site, and if you want to use large-scale machinery.

Soil preparation

Ploughing

Although I tend towards as little mechanical cultivation as possible, I would recommend that if your site is over half an acre you get a big tractor in to plough the whole lot. Ploughing is the only effective way of burying green matter of any sort deep enough to prevent it regrowing. Either find a friendly farmer with a plough or employ an agricultural contractor. It is a relatively quick job on a small area. A small two-wheel tractor is unlikely to have sufficient power to pull a plough through turf effectively.

Whoever is doing the ploughing, talk to them about the depth of your soil. If the plough is set too deep it may bring up subsoil. Also it is essential to make sure that the ground isn't too wet when it is ploughed – not only will the equipment suffer on wet ground but also you are likely to cause more compaction in the soil. The best time to plough is during a dry spell in the winter. Once the ground has been ploughed the natural action of the weather (frosts, snow and rain) will help to break the soil down. Later, get it rotovated. A small rotovator won't be able to get over the ploughed furrows so use a tractor driven rotovator. Level the ground afterwards with a rake or a small rotovator.

Hand digging

This is only worth considering if you have plenty of time, you're very fit and you relish the task. You will need to double dig to prepare the ground properly.

Firstly make a line where you want to start digging. Take the first spit of topsoil out (a spit is a spade's width and depth) and place it to one side. Take the lower spit of subsoil out and put this to one side as well (separate from the first topsoil spit). Take a step back and dig the next line of topsoil out and place this to one side. On this second line you can take the next subsoil spit out and turn it into the first trench. Then take the third line of topsoil out and place it, turf side down, on top of the first trench, which will contain the turned subsoil of the second trench. Work your way backward until you have reached the far side of the plot, and fill the last two trenches with the soils from the first trench. Take care not to dig too deeply, to avoid bringing subsoil to the surface.

A slightly easier method, which I often use if I'm hand digging, is to slice the turf off with a spade to about 5cm deep, then take out a spit of soil. Loosen the soil at the bottom of the spit with a fork to break any possible compaction and to create better drainage. Put the turf from the next section upside down in the first trench and then put the next spit of soil on top of it.

Mulching to clear ground

If you are not in a hurry, mulching is by far the easiest way of preparing soil for tilling. It involves covering the ground with a layer that keeps out the light. Turf will rot down over a period of three to six months under this system. You can then either plant through the mulch or take it off and till the soil in any manner you wish.

All sorts of materials can be used as mulch, from aluminium foil to walnut shells. To clear a large area of ground, black plastic sheeting or carpet, cardboard or newspaper makes a good mulch. Be prepared, though, as you will need large quantities of material. For this reason I would only recommend mulching for clearing a reasonably small site, up to quarter of an acre say. Your mulch must be well secured to stop it blowing around, and if it is plastic to protect it from the elements. Dig plastic sheets in well around the edges, and if you're using more than one piece make sure you overlap the joining edges by at least 30cm. To stop the mulch blowing around, cover it with old wool carpets, any green material or a lot of compost and manure. Plastic sheeting can be held down with tyres and old plastic bottles filled with water (these have smooth edges so won't tear the plastic). Plastic sheeting will degrade if exposed to sunlight so cover it well if you want to be able to use it again. I use a layer of matted straw, which acts as a sun and wind protector.

Put the mulch on the ground in the autumn, while the soil is still warm. It will stop the ground from drying out and getting too cold. In the spring mulches will prevent the sun from warming up the soil, so I take them off about a month before I want to start cultivating the ground. If you have used a layer of plastic you can leave that down for a couple of weeks longer as it will help the soil to warm up. Save the waste mulches to reuse around crops or on paths.

If you have a light soil then you will get away with quite light cultivation before you can start sowing. Heavy soils tend to get compacted and you may need to rotovate, plough or dig by hand. I use a small plough attached to my two-wheel tractor, and finish off with a rotovator.

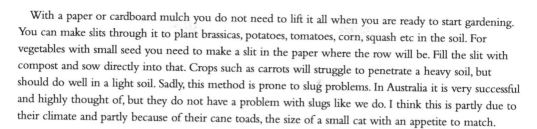

With a paper or cardboard mulch you do not need to lift it all when you are ready to start gardening. You can make slits through it to plant brassicas, potatoes, tomatoes, corn, squash etc in the soil. For vegetables with small seed you need to make a slit in the paper where the row will be. Fill the slit with compost and sow directly into that. Crops such as carrots will struggle to penetrate a heavy soil, but should do well in a light soil. Sadly, this method is prone to slug problems. In Australia it is very successful and highly thought of, but they do not have a problem with slugs like we do. I think this is partly due to their climate and partly because of their cane toads, the size of a small cat with an appetite to match.

Beds and contours

Once your plot has been tilled you are in a position to mark out your beds. If your plot is on any sort of slope it pays to position your beds along the contours. A contour is a hypothetical horizontal line which runs level along the side of a slope, and it is prudent to grow your crops along these lines. Growing your crops downhill (or against the line of the contour) will inevitably lead to soil loss. Even if you have good green cover, when soil is being tilled on a regular basis a heavy downpour is often enough to wash topsoil away.

How to find your contours

If you think you can see the contours on your site with the naked eye, then think again. It's almost impossible to accurately mark out a contour without the use of some kind of levelling device. This can either be an 'A' frame, a bunyip or a simple level. I suggest that you refer to a good permaculture book for details of how to use them. I use a simple level (*see over page*) because it's a quick and easy way of assessing your contours.

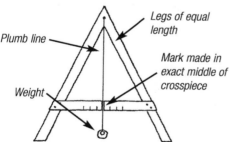

Two points level when plumb line covers mark on crosspiece

'A' Frame

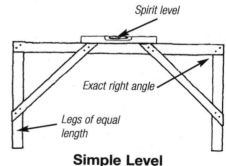

Simple Level

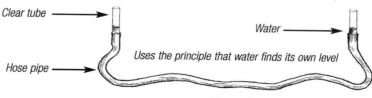

Bunyip

To set out your beds, start at one side of your slope with the level and a handful of sticks. Mark your starting point with a stick and place one end of the level on the ground at the base of the stick. Turn the level about the stick until it is level along the ground, then mark the other end with another stick. Repeat from the second stick and so on until you have a line of sticks marking the contour.

Use your contour line as the edge of a bed, and measure the other side from it. In my garden each bed is between 1 - 1.25m wide, allowing me to weed and harvest from each side of the bed without over-stretching myself or having to tread on it and risk compacting the soil. I can also use my two-wheel tractor with ease on these beds. If you use large machinery then make your beds the right size for the tractor wheels and implements.

Repeat the process across the whole site, marking contours and laying out beds of the required size. The paths can be left to revert to grass, in which case you should keep it cut to limit the spread of seeds onto your cultivated areas. Alternatively mulch the paths, which will be easier to maintain.

Building raised beds can help if you have a heavy soil prone to compaction, or a stony or alkaline soil. Raising a bed by just 15cm can greatly improve drainage. However you cannot work a raised bed with a tractor, and they can be a haven for slugs. This type of growing will result in the build up of soil as added organic matter will increase the soil level over the years.

If you want to garden on raised beds you must consider how these beds are going to be contained. The edging can be whatever you have; wood, stones, logs, bricks or turf. Cedar or redwood is naturally rot resistant but less expensive wood such as pine can be treated with linseed oil to make it last longer.

Don't lose heart

If this is your first attempt at growing vegetables on a large scale then please don't get disheartened by the amount of preparation required before you can start harvesting bumper crops. Think small and take time to get the infrastructure of your garden right. Time spent at this stage of your garden is time well spent.

Soils and Nutrients

Your soil is the foundation of your garden. It is not just where the roots of your plants grow, it is a reservoir for water and nutrients. The ideal soil is easy to work, is not too wet or too dry and has a good balance of nutrients readily available to your plants. Unfortunately most soils are not ideal, and you need to classify yours so that you can manage it in the best way, and in the longer term improve it.

The top layer of soil is called topsoil and this is what we grow vegetables in. The next layer down is called subsoil. Vegetable roots will penetrate this layer but it is low in nutrients and should be left where it is. If the subsoil is heavy then drainage may be a problem: if it is light the soil may dry out too quickly. Underneath the subsoil is parent rock, the basis of the soil. The junctions between the layers are visible as a change in colour and texture.

Soils and soil particles come in all sorts of shapes and sizes but in general the types are clay, silt, sand, chalk, and peat. A mix of soil particles makes up your soil. It is simple to find out which type of soil you have, using the palm test. Take a pinch of soil and put it in the palm of your hand. Spit on it and rub it. If it feels silky smooth you have a clay soil. If it is gritty and dry it is a sandy soil. A chalky soil will be quite grey and silky but will also have small white lumps. A peaty soil will feel quite fibrous and leave a brown stain.

Sandy soils

Sandy soils are easy to cultivate, but are usually poor in nutrients. The particles are large so the soil is free draining. It's possible to cultivate a sandy soil when it is wet without damaging the structure. Sandy soil warms up quickly in the spring, so early plantings are possible. On the other hand, being free draining it dries quickly, and nutrients are easily washed away. Adding organic matter helps a sandy soil retain moisture as well as adding fertility. During the spring and summer a mulch of compost or well-rotted muck is essential, to retain moisture. Green manures will help stop nutrients being leached out in the winter and add loads of bulky organic matter in the spring. It is likely that a sandy soil will have a low pH so you will probably need to add lime ($200g/m^2$) as well as nutrients, in order to grow most vegetables.

Clay soils

The good thing about clay soils is that they are rich in nutrients. On the down side, they feel heavy and cold. This is because the particles are small so there is a large surface area for water to adhere to, making them sticky. The soil will become compacted if it is worked when wet or if it dries out, resulting in poor drainage. Assess the wetness of a clay soil by turning a spit over. If bits of soil crumble away then it's probably dry enough, but if it stays in a soggy mass leave it alone. I plough my patch of clay soil when it has dried out sufficiently, then rotovate it when it has dried some more. This is the only way I can get a fine enough tilth to sow small seeds. Many gardeners suggest digging a clay soil in autumn. When the water in the soil freezes through the winter it will help to break up the soil, making it easier to work in the spring. This does work, but it leaves the soil exposed to flooding and possible erosion. Using a rotation incorporating deep rooting vegetables will help break up a clay subsoil.

Adding organic matter lightens the soil improving drainage, but the added fertility is usually unnecessary. After a couple of years of working in organic matter a clay soil will perform very well, being lighter and much more manageable.

Clay soils are prone to 'capping', forming an impermeable crust on the surface. This can be difficult for seedlings to break through. If you are sowing small seeds fill seed drills with a mixture of compost and sand, which will not form a cap.

Chalky soils

Chalk soils are pale and hungry, usually with plenty of stones, often flints. They are usually easy to cultivate but they tend to be quite shallow. The large particles make it free draining and quick to lose nutrients. Make sure you know how deep your soil is before you start to cultivate so as not to draw subsoil up into the top layer.

Chalky soils are very alkaline, containing lots of lime, so they need their pH checking and adjusting frequently (see below). Adding plenty of organic matter helps to reduce the pH and improve water retention as well as adding nutrients. Retain the nutrients by covering the soil in winter with a green manure and during the spring and summer mulch around crops wherever possible.

Silt

Silt is an in between sort of soil, a mixture of clay and sand deposited by ancient rivers. It feels silky in the palm test. When it is wet it performs like clay, becoming compacted and poorly drained. Treat similarly to clay but remember that drainage is the biggest problem: add as much organic matter as possible to help open up the soil.

Peat

Peat is a very dark and spongy soil. It is made up of rotted organic matter. It's an easy soil to work and quite fertile but it is usually acidic. Water management can be difficult with peat: mulch well in summer to stop it drying out as it is difficult to wet it again, and provide good drainage as it can become waterlogged.

Loam

Loam is the term used to describe a well-balanced soil. You can have a clay loam or a sandy loam, but the balance of clay, silt and sand is fairly even and the soil has a good humus content. A loam is usually the best type of soil for gardening.

Soil acidity and alkalinity (or pH)

The acidity or alkalinity (pH) of your soil determines how well your plants will grow. Most plants do best slightly on the acidic side of neutral, and nutrients in the soil are most available at this pH. Most soil bacteria thrive at this pH too, including those responsible for nitrogen fixation. pH is measured from 1 to 14: 7 is neutral, below 7 is acidic and above 7 is alkaline. Aim for a pH between 6.2 and 6.8 which is the optimum range for most vegetables. For information on testing your pH, (*see 'Machinery, tools and equipment.' page 21*)

Lime

Basically the pH of your soil is an indicator of how much lime is in it. Lime is alkaline and can be added to soils to reduce acidity. For a sandy soil add lime at $200g/m^2$, increasing this amount as you move through loams to clays. It takes time to adjust the pH so do it slowly over the years, according to the results of your pH testing.

To make an alkaline soil more acid is more difficult. Add as much compost and manure as possible, particularly to chalky soils, and try to use raised beds to stop alkaline water draining though the soil. For a quicker result add gypsum at a rate of $130g/m^2$.

As well as increasing the pH of your soil, adding lime helps clay soil particles bind together, increasing the air content and drainage of the soil. Be wary of using it to improve your soil if you do not need to adjust the pH, though, as lime can lock up trace elements making them unavailable to plants. I have never added lime to my soil as its pH is just about perfect and I don't want to upset it.

Avoid using slaked and quick lime, which are prohibited under organic standards. Ground limestone, or dolomite, is the best type of limestone to use because it is slow release and also contains magnesium. As an alternative, calcified seaweed is good. It lasts a long time, contains magnesium and other plant foods but is expensive.

Stones

Stones and gravel will affect drainage considerably. The more stones, the better the drainage, and the more quickly the soil will dry out. The best place to have stones is in the subsoil where they will provide good drainage without making the topsoil dry out too much. A problem with stony soils is that they tend to cause taproots such as parsnips and carrots to fork. The best way to avoid this is to make raised beds of deep soil to grow these crops in. On a large scale this is a bit impractical and the best alternative is to accept that their taproots will be forked. If you are selling them, explain to your customers why they are like that. Invariably they will accept them in any condition once they understand the reason behind it.

Soil nutrients

Nutrients are essential for healthy plant growth, but if there is an imbalance it can cause problems. For example, the flowers and fruits of a plant suffer if there is not enough potassium, but too much potassium can cause deficiencies in calcium, magnesium, nitrogen and phosphorous, causing a whole range of problems. Most deficiencies will be corrected by adding compost, which provides the right blend of nutrients. Also remember that nutrients will be most available to plants when the soil pH is in the range from 6.2 to 6.8. For more information about adding nutrients to your soil see the chapter on fertility.

The main components of a healthy soil are:

■ **Nitrogen,** for the growth of shoots and leaves. A nitrogen deficiency shows itself as yellowing leaves and stunted plants. It can be corrected using liquid muck and nettle teas.

■ **Phosphorous,** for root growth. A deficiency shows itself in stunted plants and a bluish colour in older leaves. However, deficiencies are rare because there is nothing in the soil that locks phosphorus up. It can be corrected by adding bone meal, particularly in the autumn.

■ **Potassium** (*potash*), for production of flowers and fruits. A deficiency shows itself by plants producing small, inferior flowers and fruits, stunted growth and a yellowing around the outer edges of leaves followed by brown scorching. If there is too much potassium plants can't take up magnesium. A deficiency can be corrected with rock potash in the soil or with comfrey liquid to plants.

■ **Magnesium,** a constituent of chlorophyll. A deficiency shows as yellowing between the veins of leaves, which eventually turns blue, particularly common in the lower leaves of tomato plants. Insufficient humus in the soil has the same effect, in which case correct with more compost or FYM. A magnesium deficiency can be corrected with seaweed meal, liquid seaweed or liquid manure. A longer-term solution is to dig in dolomite, particularly if your whole garden is affected.

■ **Calcium,** used in the formation of protein. It also neutralises some acids. A deficiency is particularly likely on sandy soils and results in blossom end rot in tomatoes, tip burn on lettuce, black heart in celery and browning in the centre of Brussels sprouts. It can be corrected by applying lots of compost. On sandy soils annual liming will help.

■ **Sulphur,** a constituent of proteins and important in the formation of chlorophyll. A deficiency shows as a yellowing and stunting of the plant.

Trace Elements

■ **Iron,** needed for the formation of chlorophyll. Deficiencies can be caused by over-liming and are particular to chalky and alkaline soils. A shortage is shown as a yellowing between veins of leaves too early in the year. Acute cases result in hollow centres in the seeds of peas and beans. It can be corrected with liquid seaweed and compost.

■ **Zinc and copper,** enzyme activators. A mottled yellow on young leaves is a sure sign of a deficiency of either of these trace elements. Correct with seaweed meal.

■ **Manganese,** used in the formation of chlorophyll and proteins. Plants with deficiencies look similar to ones with iron deficiencies, stunted and with yellowing of leaves particularly on alkaline soils. Again, compost and liquid seaweed tend to do the trick.

■ **Boron,** used in growing tissue. Deficiencies occur particularly on alkaline soils and can be caused by excessive liming. It can cause corkiness in root crops, fruit spot in tomatoes, crown canker in beetroot, hollow stem in cauliflowers and brown heart in celery and brassicas. Seaweed meal and compost will prevent its recurrence in future crops.

■ **Molybdenum,** important in the production of protein. A deficiency results in deformed growth, usually on acid soils. Raise the pH of your soil with lime and use seaweed meal.

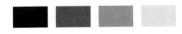

Machinery, Tools and Equipment

arden machinery and equipment can be a big drain on your resources when you start your garden. If you have enough cash you can of course buy new and get exactly what you want. If not, then you need to beg or borrow it from others. Don't forget to save the receipts for any items you buy for work as they can usually be claimed as a business expense on your tax return.

If you are in a position to buy in bulk for things like planting modules you will usually get a better price for your supplies. Perhaps you can team up with neighbours to get a good deal. (*A number of suppliers for garden sundries can be found on page 265*).

I have listed in this chapter the things I need for my acre and a half of garden. Use this as a guide to what you might need. What you need in your garden will depend upon the scale of your garden, your method of gardening, your growing techniques and, to a certain extent, the type of soil you have. Specific items relating to watering are described in the chapter on water and irrigation.

Machinery

Tractors and tillers

If you have more than five acres to cultivate I would suggest using a four-wheel tractor plus implements. On the other hand, if you cultivate less than half an acre you can get away with no mechanisation at all. For anything in between, I would recommend that you get a small cultivator, unless your gardening method doesn't include cultivation.

In my garden, which is about an acre and a half in total, I have a two-wheeled tractor. It has a PTO (power take off), which means I can attach different powered implements to it. I use a plough, rotovator, potato ridger and potato lifter. The plough and rotovator are used mainly in the spring when the ground is dry. I have a very heavy soil which turns to sticky concrete during the winter and needs quite a lot of breaking down before I can grow anything in it. When using the plough I use steel lug wheels. These look a bit like spades welded onto steel frames. They grip the ground much more effectively than pneumatic tyres and are especially useful on heavy ground.

A two-wheeled tractor like mine costs anything from £1500 to £2500 new depending on the make, the type of engine and added benefits. The implements vary in cost, increasing as they get more complicated. A plough that is simply pulled along by the machine will only cost about £200 but a rotovator will cost over £600. You can get them second hand but they are quite rare. Simple stand-alone rotovators are more readily available and much cheaper to buy although they only do one job, rotovating. You can't attach other machinery to them as you can with two wheeled tractors.

Instead of buying a tractor or rotovator you can hire them from garden tool hire companies. This is the cheapest option in the short term but the costs soon mount up. Because I use a lot of different implements on my tractor I do need it on a more ad-hoc basis than hiring one. One way to significantly reduce the cost of buying machinery is to share it with other local growers – great until everyone wants to use it on the same rain-free day.

Mowers and strimmers

Although my garden paths are mulched rather than grassed, there are areas of grass (including the lawn outside my house) that I need to cut to keep the spread of seeds under control. I cut them regularly with an ordinary push mower and the mowings are used as a mulch around all sorts of plants - it is a rich source of nitrogen and fibre for the soil. I do not use a strimmer as I value untidy edges for their benefit to wildlife, more important to me than neatness. I share the use of a heavy-duty mower with two other growers. This can cut very long and wet grass, brambles, nettles etc with ease, and is particularly useful for cutting down green manures. It was expensive to buy new but the cost was shared, and we share the cost if it ever breaks down. If your site is very overgrown a horizontal scythe-type mower will save you a lot of time and effort. It is probably best to hire or borrow such an expensive piece of equipment.

Tools

Tools are quite personal. Some are a must for some gardeners while others regard them with disdain. You have to find out what you get on with.

Acquiring tools on a budget is quite easy. Car boot sales are a really good source of older types of tools and sometimes jumble sales and farm auctions can yield a useful bargain. It is often the case that the older tools are nicer to work with because they are better balanced and have sharper edges.

Consider the length of handle of the tool you are using - long handled forks and spades will take a lot of hard work out of tasks, particularly turning compost and dealing with muck.

Personally I have two forks, one spade, three hoes (onion, swoe and round edge cutting), a mattock, a trowel, pruning saw, bush saw, secateurs, spar hook (a small bill hook), small scythe and loppers. Don't forget to keep any edged tool sharp as it will make your work much easier. I borrow tools that I only use occasionally, including fencing equipment.

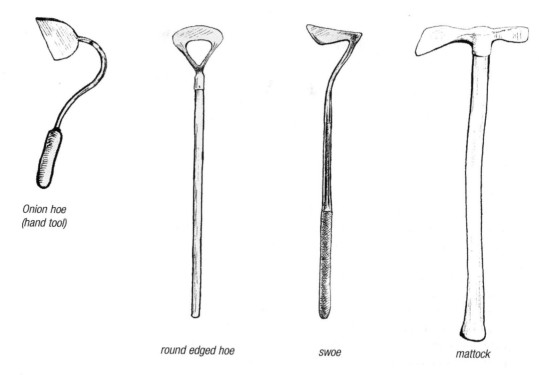

Onion hoe
(hand tool)

round edged hoe   swoe   mattock

Equipment

Pots and trays

There is a huge range of pots and trays that you can use to grow your plants in. I have settled on a few that I find work well. It is general garden practice to wash and disinfect all trays and pots at the end of the season to remove unwanted bacteria, moulds and fungi. I have never done this although I would if I suspected that I had a problem as a result. To my mind it is time consuming and boring and I can't be doing with that sort of approach unless absolutely necessary.

■ **Pots:** I use a range of pots with diameters from 75 to 180mm. I need 4–500 of the 75mm pots for growing runner beans, tomatoes, pepper and squash plants. The larger pots, of which I have about 100, are sometimes used for flowers and individual pepper or chilli plants.

■ **Trays**: I use standard seed trays for vegetables such as brassicas, celery, celeriac and lettuce. You can get clear plastic tops for them, which act like a mini greenhouse. Generally I have a stock of about 15 to 20, not all of which will be in use at one time.

Modules

These are my favourite containers for growing young plants in, particularly the polystyrene ones. Plastic modules don't last very long and it's difficult to remove the plants from them without damaging the root ball. The polystyrene ones are easier, and keep the compost mix warmer too. I use a range of polystyrene modules. The number of cells per tray varies but they are all the size of a standard seed tray, which means I can fit a plastic lid on them. The three sizes I use are 2cm, 4cm and 5cm. The 2cm I use for plants such as basil, celery, celeriac, parsley, anything with a tiny seed, the 4cm for brassicas, spring onions, beetroot, tomatoes, peppers and the 5cm for sweetcorn and any type of pea or French bean. I have about 20 of each type.

Soil blocks

You can buy a tool that makes blocks of soil that stand alone, without any container. You fill it with a compost mix and soil blocks are punched out. Roots grow through the compost until they reach the air. The plants can be planted out without disturbing the root ball, and there is a saving on plastic and polystyrene. I do not use soil blocks because I never get my compost mix quite right so they inevitably fall apart. For propagating thousands of individual plants it would probably be worth working on a compost mix that would stay together.

Root trainers

These are a new type of module which are designed to encourage the roots downwards rather than around the pots. They are deep, square modules with ridges down the sides and are hinged at the bottom so that you can open them up without disturbing the root ball. I don't use them because they are expensive to buy and the only long rooted crop I grow in modules is sweetcorn. These are generally fine in the large polystyrene module. However, some gardeners swear by them and use them for peas, beans and squash as well as sweetcorn.

Labels

Labelling your plants is important. You can slice up plastic yoghurt pots and washing liquid bottles and use an indelible pen on them but I just can't be bothered. It is my small luxury in a large and sustainable garden to buy in new labels. If you use a waterproof pencil you can get away with scrubbing the pencil off at the end of the season and reusing them. I need about 100 a year, costing a few pounds. Wooden lolly sticks make good, sustainable labels.

Row-seeder.

This is a wheeled tool that drops seeds into the ground at set intervals. Sowing small seed at the right density can be a bit of an art, particularly if you are growing one crop on a large scale. If you are then a row-seeder is a useful tool.

String

It seems obvious but when you're starting out it is easy to forget string. I use jute string for tying tomatoes and peppers to stakes and this will rot down in the compost. Nylon string is used for tying stakes in a straight line in polytunnels.

Fleece

Fleece is a fairly recent addition to the gardening trade. It is a very light material that will sit on top of a crop without crushing it, letting in light and water but protecting plants from dips in temperature and from pests. It is sometimes referred to as a floating cloche and it does, in effect, have the same function. It will keep delicate crops several degrees warmer just by preventing wind chill. Fleece is a product of the petrochemical industry so it isn't what I'd call sustainable, but using fleece as frost and pest protection is really essential in my garden. I have different sizes for my different sized beds. Generally speaking I buy rolls of fleece 100 x 2m wide to go on my long, metre wide beds and 4 x 50m rolls for my new potato bed. I take great care with my fleece and reuse it when I can. Any pieces with holes and tears are used to cover young brassica plants to keep the birds off. Smaller bits can be cut up to use as fleece tents around cucumber and tomato plants in the polytunnels.

Mesh

This is similar to fleece but much thicker, almost like net curtain. Being tougher it will last a lot longer. Because it is a much hardier material, I use it on my carrot crop to stop carrot root fly. It needs to be on the crop almost from start to finish and it will withstand a whole season outside with hardly any damage. The disadvantage of mesh is that it doesn't stop frost damage to the crop, although it will limit the effect of cooling winds.

Netting

This is essential if you grow soft fruit. Fleece will bring your strawberries on quickly but will also encourage moulds to set in if it gets at all wet. Netting allows good ventilation as well as protecting the crop from birds. Redcurrants, white currants, blackcurrants and raspberries also need netting protection during their fruiting period. I drape the net across the soft fruit bushes, although it would be much easier to negotiate at harvest time if it was suspended from a cage.

Staging (or work tables/benches)

It might not seem very important but staging is essential for keeping trays and modules full of young and tasty plants off the greenhouse or polytunnel floor, where they are more prone to slug and snail attack. They are also useful for keeping your back straight. They don't have to be anything special so long as the working surface is at a comfortable height and, in the case of greenhouse staging, easily movable.

In the summer when I no longer need it in the greenhouse, I set up the staging under a hedge in the shade. I put my harvest on it during the morning pick on delivery days. It's far easier to pick up a tray of heavy vegetables at waist height than it is from the ground.

pH test kits

There are a range of pH testing devices. The simplest is the type you can get from a garden centre, but they can be unreliable. The general rule is the more money you spend, the better the kit and the more reliable the result. It's possible to spend a lot on a very good pH test kit. If you have the money, it is worth using the kits that professional growers use, which can cost £50 plus. There is also a pH probe. I have used one but it wasn't reliable. The whole of my garden read as pH 7 and I know from agricultural tests that it ranges from 6 to 7.

Propagators

I have three propagators ranging from a standard seed tray type that will fit on a windowsill to a 1m x 50cm thermostatically controlled unit that I built myself. The simple windowsill types cost from about £15 to £40. Larger ones cost from about £80. I spent about £50 on the propagator I made, using second-hand bits of wood and plastic. (*See page 253 for details*)

Heating greenhouses and polytunnels

Although heating a greenhouse or polytunnel seems like a good way of bringing plants on in the spring, it is really energy consuming, costly and not very sustainable. Heaters run on paraffin, electricity or gas, cost a lot to buy and are expensive to run. The alternative is to insulate with bubble wrap or cover plants with fleece tents and cold frames inside the greenhouse or polytunnel. If it is cold enough for the temperature inside a cloche inside a polytunnel to reach freezing, you can use a very simple paraffin heater. Where I live it never gets that cold in the spring but growing vegetables in the north of the country might require this sort of action.

Thermometers

These are essential for propagators, even ones that are thermostatically controlled. It is probably sensible to have a thermometer in your polytunnel and greenhouse but after a while you get a feel for the right temperature and don't need it so much.

Miscellaneous

You will need one or two wheelbarrows, buckets and trays for picking and collecting vegetables and a minimum of two watering cans. Invest in good, non drip roses for the cans.

Wellies

These are another obvious item often skimped on. As a gardener you will spend a lot of time in your wellies so they must be comfortable and warm. I buy a new pair of expensive wellies every year or two and either wear two pairs of socks in the winter or use fleece liners. Beware of cheap wellies – they don't last very long and they are usually very uncomfortable.

Gloves

Most of the time I work without gloves because I find it much easier and I like to be able to feel the plants and the earth. My hands go through a stage in the spring where they turn to sandpaper for a couple of weeks and then become very smooth for the rest of the season. The trick is not to use hand cream, which just stops the skin from hardening.

There are some jobs where gloves are really necessary, such as pruning gooseberries and blackberries and pulling creeping thistles. Get a really thick warm pair for winter work and a couple of thinner ones for summer work.

Wet weather gear

I would normally recommend spending money on anything that keeps you comfortable and dry, but wet weather gear and gardening just don't go together. Waterproof fabrics tear very easily in the garden so I never buy anything expensive. As long as it keeps me dry, that's all that matters. If I'm gardening in drier weather I wear a thick leather jacket or fleece, which don't rip so easily.

Work clothes

These are again something you might not consider but I do have work clothes specifically for gardening because they get muddy and worn quite quickly.

Radios

Solar and wind-up radios have improved gardening work considerably. Sometimes when I'm in the garden the last thing I want is the noise from a radio, but at other times I really like it. If you have someone working with you it's nice to offer them the radio too.

Garden sheds

It is important to have a garden shed to house all the bits and pieces of equipment mentioned above. I keep all of my tools, fleeces, meshes, cloches, trays, pots etc in a standard 2 x 2.5m garden shed. This isn't big enough for the bigger tools such as rotovators, mowers and strimmers. Luckily, I have access to a barn where I can store all these things: otherwise I would probably have to erect a bigger shed. Remember a lock and key or your insurance will be invalid.

Fertility

Maintaining the fertility of your garden should always be uppermost in your mind. There are many ways to add nutrients but you should always aim to feed the soil and not the plant. One thing that I find can be difficult in organic gardening is identifying what is wrong if your plants look unwell. If you have a healthy garden you will rarely get nutrient deficiencies, so you get little practise in recognising the signs. Remember: you can overdose your crops with too much, so beware of the potency of what you are applying, particularly teas and liquid feeds.

Farm Yard Manures (FYM)

If your garden is on or near a farm then grab all the FYM you can get. It has a good humus content which feeds the soil and all that live in it, and provides a good balance of nutrients. In an ideal world, farmers would use their muck on their own farm. If they don't want it then make the most of it!

There are all sorts of manures: cow, horse, sheep, pig and poultry. The first two are the commonest and these are the ones I would use for feeding the soil. Be careful using horse manure as many stables now use wood shavings to bed their animals down. Although this would seem a perfect source of manure it takes a long time for wood to rot down, often robbing nitrogen from the soil. If you are going to use it make sure that it has been composted for a long time first. Pig and poultry manure are high in nitrogen. If fresh I would use them on a compost heap as an activator rather than directly on the ground as it can 'burn' your plants.

When you get your FYM be sure to cover it with a plastic sheet – heavy rain will soon wash out its nutrients. Keeping it covered will also encourage the decomposition process. If you can, turn it every few months to increase its oxygen content, again aiding decomposition. Muck is best left for a year before using; after this time it should have rotted to a fine and crumbly texture.

Once incorporated into your garden FYM will add nutrients as well as helping to retain moisture. In a light soil it will ease drainage and in a heavy soil darken it, helping it to warm quickly in the spring. It also makes heavy soils easier to work. I add FYM to the soil for some crops, put it in pits for others, mulch some crops with it, use it as a scab deterrent in my potatoes – the list goes on.

Muck tea

You can make a good, nitrogen rich plant food by making muck tea. All you do is suspend a hessian bag full of muck in a bucket or barrel of water for a couple of weeks. The resulting brown liquid should be used on heavy feeding crops such as brassicas and lettuce. Also use it on any crops which show signs of nitrogen deficiency. Don't get carried away though – too much nitrogen causes sappy and weak growth, which is very attractive to pests like aphids.

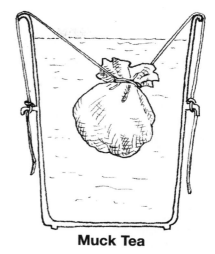

Muck Tea

Compost

This is the food of the soil. You must make compost if you're going to call yourself an organic gardener. It uses up all waste green material and turns it into a friable, light plant food with which to feed your beloved crops.

There are many compost experts who give precise instructions for making compost. I have to admit to being rather more lackadaisical about it. There are some very simple rules that are easy to follow which I have outlined below. If you want to delve into all the complexities of compost making I suggest you buy a book which concentrates on the subject.

Simple compost

I make my compost in a heap in one area of my garden and don't use bins or containers of any kind. (I am planning to make a bin soon for the sole purpose of creating good, easily accessible seed compost, though). To make good compost quickly you need the right balance of carbon and nitrogen (from organic material), air, water, lime and bacteria. It should be turned regularly, it should not be too dry or too wet, and it should be covered.

In order to make compost effectively it is best to add your materials in layers. I use left over plant material, weeds, feathers, muck, wood ash and the remains of my seed compost. Grass mowings are good, they are high in nitrogen, but only add thin layers as they have a tendency to coagulate into a slimy mess that won't break down. Avoid wood or large clumps of one type of material. A few cabbage and Jerusalem artichoke stalks stuck in the heap will help get air in and will break down eventually. Shredded paper sacks and brown cardboard are good and high in carbon. Make sure they are well wetted first and aren't covered in plastic tape. I also use perennial weeds as long as there are no seeds on them.

Start the heap off with an activator such as fresh urine, chicken or pig muck or a shop bought, proprietary activator. Add lime to reduce the acidity, improving the environment for bacteria. Finally add enough water to make the heap not too wet. This is difficult to assess but if you give it a good soak any excess should drain away and if necessary more can be added when the heap is turned. Cover with plastic and it should all begin to heat up.

After three to four weeks, check inside the heap for moisture. If you put a metal rod in the middle at this point and recover the heap, within a week the rod should be too hot to handle when it's drawn out. The heat should kill any pathogens such as undesirable moulds and mildews, and may kill weed seeds too. The compost should, after a couple of months, take on a nice, friable, dark, soil-like composition. In reality, my compost heap is never as organised as this. I pile on anything I can get in layers for a six to twelve month period, then cover it up and leave it for a year. I let the worms do the work. The result is usually patchy – every so often I get clumps of soil in it and only the middle gets very hot – but it is a fine general compost and the top 15cm makes a wonderful (albeit weedy) seed compost once sieved.

As yet I've had no problems with recurrent disease. Inadequate composting does worry me and I have a plan to make three bins for my seed compost and to turn and activate my big general compost heap more regularly. Although I am well intentioned I am very lazy. Turning lots of stringy material with a fork hurts my back so I will probably leave well alone and get on with growing vegetables.

A word on perennial weeds. I'm a great advocate for putting these on my compost heap. Some of their roots, particularly dandelions and docks, contain nutrients from deep in the soil and there's no way I'm going to waste them. My compost gets no light for a year so they are guaranteed to rot down. I find couch grass always rots down but I do draw the line at bindweed, which I burn or put in black plastic sacks until rotted. If you really want to use it you can dry it out in the sun then compost it. Be careful, though, not to put the seeds of your weeds in the heap. They won't rot and will germinate wherever you put the compost.

Vermin

Compost heaps will attract rice and mats even if you're really careful about what you add (don't put any type of grain, meat, fish or cheese on, cooked or not). There is a way to repel them - put chilli, ginger and mustard in their runs. I've yet to try this but my mum says it works and I don't argue with her. Alternatively, make your compost heap/bin rat proof with small gauge (10cm holes) rabbit netting.

Top tips for a successful heap

- ♣ Almost everything that once lived will compost down, eventually.
- ♣ Never add diseased or pest infected plants to your compost heap.
- ♣ Wood (from twigs upward) will take too long to break down so leave them out.
- ♣ Don't add weed seeds.
- ♣ Don't add perennial weed roots unless you are leaving the heap covered for a year.
- ♣ A good source of compost material is your local greengrocer who will bin any unsightly produce.
- ♣ Don't add cooked food as it attracts rats.

Worm compost

Using worms and a little preparation you can compost everything, from bread to meat to any other leftovers, which do not normally go on a compost heap. Most compost and muckheaps contain brandling or tiger worms, which eat compost material. They are striped and dark red so they can't be mistaken for earthworms. To make worm compost the simplest method is just to add these types of worms to your compost heap. They will eat through the compost material and their deposits are full of nutrients. As you will be adding things that will attract rats, the wormery must be vermin proof.

The temperature of the heap is important for worms: it must not get too hot or too cold. A good worm working temperature is 20 - 24°C. The worms will die if it falls below 7°C. For more information on how to make wormeries properly, and a good read, see the worm book in the bibliography!

Green manures

So important they have a chapter to themselves, *page 40.*

Comfrey

This plant is invaluable to the organic gardener for many reasons. Firstly, it contains a lot of potash (potassium) which is the perfect feed for many crops. Secondly, it has deep roots that bring nutrients up from the subsoil, making them available to crops. Thirdly, it can be used as a mulch or as a liquid feed.

The best type available at the moment is Bocking 14, or Russian comfrey (*see page 267 for sources*). It produces sterile flowers so it can't spread all over the place. You don't need a huge number of plants unless you want to use it as mulch. My patch of about 20 plants makes enough liquid feed during the season for all my needs. However, if you want to use it for mulching it would be more realistic to have a patch of 40 to 50 plants.

You need to consider where you want to plant your comfrey. It thrives in damp soil and can tolerate shade. If you have an area of boggy or wet ground, this is ideal. I have some of my comfrey actually growing in the bed of a stream. Choose the site carefully, though, as once established it's difficult to move – the roots snap easily and regrow prolifically. For three years I have been trying to kill a comfrey plant with a layer of black plastic, and it is still happily growing away.

Planting down the side of a polytunnel should be considered although a word of caution – remember to put it far enough away so that you don't have to dig up your comfrey when you replace the polythene on your tunnel. You can also grow it around your soft fruit bushes, which will benefit from the potash. Cut the comfrey in situ and lay the leaves around the bushes, suppressing weeds and feeding the soft fruit at the same time.

Growing comfrey is easy from sections of root. They should be planted about 7.5cm deep and 45 – 60cm apart. Water in if the soil is dry, maybe even putting a mulch over the patch to start with and the comfrey will grow through it. Let the plants establish a little before cutting but once away, there is no stopping them. After the first year you can cut the leaves three times, preferably before flowering.

Comfrey liquid

As well as using the leaves as a mulch, comfrey can be made into a potent liquid feed. It is one of the cheapest and most sustainable feeds of its type - no more buying in expensive seaweed liquids. To make comfrey liquid you need a barrel with a tap at the base. I put a bit of netting in the barrel where the tap comes out – once the comfrey has degraded it can produce stringy bits that can clog up the tap. Getting into the barrel to remove the blockage is a particularly smelly job so a little bit of fruit netting as insurance is well worth the effort. Put the barrel on a stand of some sort, either a pile of bricks or wood or even a table, so that you can empty it either via a hose or straight into a sizeable container – you'll be surprised at how much comes out. Pile in the comfrey leaves until the barrel is full, then put a heavy weight on top. I put a string round the weight so that

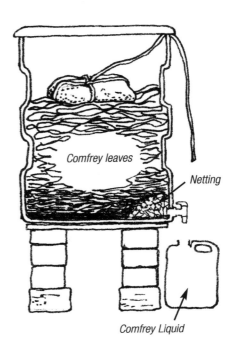

Comfrey leaves

Netting

Comfrey Liquid

once the comfrey has sunk down I don't have to lean into the foul smelling mess to get it out. Put the lid on the barrel and wait for a few weeks.

Once you have drawn off the thick, dark brown liquid you can top up the barrel with more comfrey leaves as they become available. At the end of the comfrey season you must empty the mess in the bottom of the barrel. The best place for it is the compost heap.

To use the liquid you need to dilute it roughly 25:1 with water. It's always a good idea to water it on as a feed after the ground has had a good soaking. I recommend that you wait for six to 12 hours after watering then add the liquid: this way it won't wash straight through the already sodden ground.

You can also spray the diluted liquid onto the plant as a foliar feed, which is said to deter aphids. I think you need to do it every day for it to be effective.

I know that some people just soak comfrey leaves in water and use this as a feed. This seems okay to me but will require many more containers to accommodate the increased amount of liquid. Also the concentration of the solution will be much more variable than with the concentrate method.

I have used comfrey to correct a nutrient deficiency in potatoes. One year some of my early, indoor potato crop began to look decidedly yellow around the leaves and I was at a loss as to what the problem was or how to treat it. I looked up the problem in a book and the nearest I could get was possible magnesium deficiency which, I found out elsewhere, can be corrected with comfrey. I fed the plants with comfrey liquid and within a couple of weeks the potato leaves had stopped deteriorating.

Nettles

These brilliant plants should be an essential element in any organic garden. The first thing to appreciate is that they indicate a very fertile soil, so if you've got them you must consider yourself lucky. The second thing is that they are a source of food in the hungry gap and make a really tasty soup, beer and tea. They also make a good substitute for spinach. In terms of providing fertility in your garden they act in a similar way to comfrey although their nutrient plus is nitrogen rather than potash.

Once cut and wilted for a few hours nettles lose their sting and can be handled easily. Young nettles can be used on the compost heap but beware of older nettles: they have a much stronger sting once they start producing flowers. The seeds shouldn't go on your compost heap otherwise you'll have nettles all over the garden. To make a liquid feed either follow the instructions for muck tea (*page 29*) or press the liquid out of them by the comfrey method (above).

Nettles are wonderful plants for the ladybird and its larvae. In the spring, nettles are home to the nettle aphid (which doesn't spread to other plants) and these make an early spring meal for ladybirds and their larvae, thereby increasing their numbers ready to attack other types of aphid later on. It's always a good idea to leave several clumps of nettles around and treat them with as much respect as you do your vegetable crops.

Leaves from trees

Leafmould makes an excellent soil conditioner, but it can take a long time for the leaves to decompose. Leaves are broken down by fungi rather than bacteria, which require more air to work effectively. Keep them separate from your compost heap, in a wire mesh bin with no lid. Fill the bin and leave it for a year or more. The resulting leaf mould can be used on the soil and in seed composts. Some people swear by it but I must admit to being as lazy about collecting leaves as I am about turning compost.

Other organic materials

Spent mushroom composts are available from mushroom growing companies and can sometimes be had for free. Beware of putting it directly on the ground as it may be a bit alkaline. It is probably better to add it to the compost heap, where any excessive alkalinity will be neutralised.

Seaweed makes very good compost as it is an activator and particularly rich in trace elements. If you live near the sea then use it.

Spent hops are often available from breweries and will add nutrients and organic matter.

General fertilisers

If you can't get hold of muck and you don't have enough compost then you will need to import nutrients, particularly if your soil is light. This is where a soil test comes into its own - it will tell you which of the nutrients you need to supplement. Ask the organisation that tests your soil to indicate the rates of nutrient application they would recommend for an organic soil. Elm Farm Research Centre are one organisation that can do this work. (*See page 265 for details*).

Fertilisers at a glance

- **Blood, fish and bone**: General compound fertiliser, but restricted under organic standards.

- **Bonemeal:** High in phosphates, good for root growth.

- **Dried blood:** Fast acting, nitrogen rich fertiliser.

- **Fish meal:** Check that potash isn't added as an extra because it may have come from an inorganic source.

- **Hoof and horn:** Good slow release of nitrogen.

- **Liquid manures:** Rich in trace elements and contain all the main nutrients in small quantities.

- **Liquid seaweed:** Balanced fertiliser, corrects deficiencies quickly and contains all trace elements.

- **Rock potash:** Good, long lasting source of potassium.

- **Seaweed meal:** More expensive than blood, fish and bone but a good alternative as it has a better balance of nutrients and released them slowly. It also has the complete range of trace elements.

- **Wood ash:** Potassium and a small amount of phosphorous. Content depends on material burned.

Chemical composition of common fertilisers

Fertiliser	% Nitrogen (N)	%Phosphorous (P)	%Potassium (K)
Blood, fish and bone	3.5	8.0	0.5
Bonemeal	3.5	22.0	–
Dried blood	13.0	–	–
Fish meal	9.0	2.5	–
Hoof and horn	13.0	–	–
Liquid seaweed	1.5	trace	2.5
Liquid manures	1.0	1.0	1.5
Rock potash	–	–	10.5
Seaweed meal	2.8	0.2	2.3

Rotation

A rotation is the sequence of crops grown in the beds in your vegetable garden. For an organic grower, a sound rotation is one of the essentials. It will help to avoid soil–borne problems, and make best use of your efforts to add fertility. Growing the same crop in a patch of ground year after year will gradually result in a build up of problems, resulting in poor crops and in some cases complete failure. Pests and diseases can survive in the soil, with the levels increasing each year until the plants cannot withstand them. Once you have a problem in your soil it can take years to rectify unless you resort to chemicals, which have their own problems. I am very strict about my rotations and as a result I don't have any soil borne diseases or pests.

Following a rotation allows you to make the best use of nutrients in the soil. Some crops require heavy doses of compost or FYM, while others do well on much poorer soils. If you feed heavily for hungry crops you can grow lean feeders in the same ground the following year, with no further treatment. Nitrogen fixing legumes and green manures included in your rotation will also provide nutrients, helping to maintain the fertility of your soil. Obviously some soils, by their very nature, can be short of certain minerals or trace elements and these will always need rectifying, but in general most of the nutrients that a plant needs can be found in gardens that have a good crop rotation.

To design a rotation you need to know what nutrients each type of plant requires, and which ones suffer from the same diseases. It would be no good rotating cabbages with cauliflowers for instance – they are closely related, with similar nutritional requirements and are affected by the same pests and diseases. There is a full description of each of the vegetable families at the beginning of the Vegetable A–Z section, and information on its place in the rotation is included in each vegetable chapter. For ease of reference I have included a summary of the vegetable families:

■ **Alliums or alliaceae** – onions, garlic, leeks, spring onions, asparagus (although this last plant is a perennial).

■ **Brassicas or cruciferae** – cabbages, calabrese, broccoli, cauliflowers, kales, Brussels sprouts, kohl rabi, turnips, swede, radish, rocket, cresses and many of the oriental leaves.

- **Chenopodiaceae** – beetroot, spinach, Swiss chard, perpetual spinach.
- **Cucurbitaceae or cucurbits** – pumpkins, cucumbers, marrows, courgettes, squash, melons.
- **Compositae** – lettuce, chicory, endives, salsify, globe artichokes, Jerusalem artichokes.
- **Gramineae or grasses** – sweetcorn.
- **Leguminosae or legumes** – peas, broad beans, runner beans, French and dwarf beans.
- **Solanaceae** – potatoes, tomatoes, aubergines, peppers and chillies.
- **Umbelliferae or umbellifers** – carrots, parsley, coriander, lovage, parsnips, celery, fennel, celeriac, dill etc.

It is important to find the right rotation for your needs. Consider which vegetables you want to grow and how much space you have. When I started my garden, I took an eight-year rotation from Eliot Coleman's book '*The New Organic Grower*' (see bibliography). After the first year I found that I needed to adapt the rotation to grow the vegetables for my box scheme in the right quantities, in the types of bed I have. The important thing is never to alter the basic principles behind the rotation.

Although I stick to the original rotation on paper I have substituted some crops. I have also developed new rotations in two separate gardens, to take account of the types and quantities of vegetables I need to grow. Don't worry that the rotation you choose will not always suit you, you can easily change it. However the longer the rotation you start with, the easier it is to make changes in the future.

Note that plants in the Compositae and Chenopodiaceae families don't suffer from persistent soil borne diseases and so can be planted anywhere in a rotation.

Simple rotations

The simplest rotation is one spanning four years. It is based on very simple principles that include pest and disease control, providing a leguminous crop before a nitrogen hungry crop and maintaining the fertility of the plot. It is adequate, as long as you don't find that you have a soil-borne disease that takes longer than four years to clear. The order of vegetables in the four-year rotation is:

- potatoes/tomatoes
- brassicas
- legumes/squash
- alliums/umbellifers

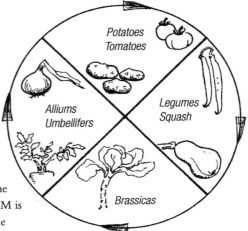

I use this rotation (*right*) in the section of my garden that has the most friable, darkest soil. I grow early potatoes, squashes and pumpkins, over-wintered brassicas and summer carrots. The beds are square, better suited to sprawling squash plants than rows of legumes. The fertility that would be added by the legumes in the rotation is provided by the pits of well-rotted FYM that I grow the squash in. When the plants are finished I cover the beds with more FYM, which provides enough fertility for the hungry brassicas as well as the following root crop. More FYM is added with the potatoes. When these have been harvested the ground is rotovated then sown with autumn lettuce, chicory and leaves. These are 'free' in a rotation because they do not suffer from soil-borne problems.

Complex rotations

The benefits of a longer rotation lie in a more balanced fertility, greater intervals between the same crop types and the occasional year devoted to green manure or a long-term mulch for perennial weed control. I use an eight-year rotation for my main garden. The beds are long and suited to growing crops in rows. I have two further gardens, with wide beds, where I use a six-year rotation. The size of the beds allows me to use my two-wheeled tractor and its attachments, and grow sprawling plants. I grow sweetcorn in these gardens, where there is space to grow it in a block for adequate pollination. Sweetcorn is wind pollinated so if the plants are spread out in long rows the likelihood of satisfactory pollination plummets, leaving you with few kernels on each cob.

The eight year rotation

The eight year rotation (*right*) also taken from Eliot Coleman, has several important factors that make it particularly useful for organic growing. It separates crops of the same family – note the four-year gap between potatoes and tomatoes, which are closely related. The leguminous peas and beans, which fix nitrogen, precede the nitrogen-hungry brassicas and tomatoes. The rotation also has space for a green manure crop at the end of each season, although I don't necessarily sow these every year.

I have adapted the eight-year rotation to suit my needs. I use it in my main garden, where I have 27 long, narrow beds. This allows for a very diverse rotation – many crops are only repeated in a bed after 27 years!

I tend not to grow sweetcorn or potatoes in this rotation because wider beds, that I have elsewhere, are far more suited to wind pollination of sweetcorn and the machinery that I use for growing potatoes. However, every now and again I will grow a particular type of potato, such as Pink Fir Apple, in these beds so that I can give them individual treatment.

I generally use the beds designated for potatoes and sweetcorn to grow lettuce, spinach and beetroot, which can fit anywhere in the rotation. I also grow these crops in some of the squash and tomato bed, as squash is grown in square beds and a lot of the tomatoes are grown under cover. I sometimes grow peppers and chillies in the tomato beds but they usually need to be covered with a mini polytunnel or cloche system of some sort.

I have learned that potatoes and squash leave a clean soil so I follow them with root crops, which benefit from a clean seedbed. Courgettes are particularly good for this because I grow them through black plastic or a thick straw mulch.

Rotation crop	Actual crop
Squash	Bush marrows and pumpkins
Potatoes	Strawberries
Sweetcorn	Long term mulch
Brassica	Kales and Brussels sprouts
Peas	Peas
Tomatoes	Tomatoes
Beans	Broad beans
Roots	Coriander and parsley
Squash	Lettuce
Potatoes	Lettuce
Sweetcorn	Lettuce
Brassica	Cabbage
Peas	Peas
Tomatoes	Swiss chard and perpetual spinach
Beans	Broad beans
Roots	Over-wintered onions
Squash	Courgettes
Potatoes	Lettuce
Sweetcorn	Beetroot
Brassica	Kohl rabi, cabbage, calabrese
Peas	Peas
Tomatoes	Peppers and chillies
Beans	French beans
Roots	Over-wintered garlic
Squash	Courgettes
Potatoes	Speciality Potatoes
Sweetcorn	Sweetcorn

You will notice three beds of lettuce in a row in the rotation – lettuce is a crop that does not suffer from soil borne diseases. It is grown in succession from June to September, and is followed by the lettuce and chicories grown after the first early potatoes in the four-year rotation. More lettuce and leaves are grown under cover in the polytunnels. The single bed of perpetual spinach and Swiss chard are supplemented by a later sowing elsewhere.

The six year rotation

As well as my main garden, I have two other areas where I grow crops that take up more space or of which I need in larger quantities. Here I grow potatoes, carrots, parsnips, brassicas, onions, garlic, leeks and shallots. One advantage of growing the carrots in one place is that you only need a single piece of mesh to protect them from carrot root fly. I also grow runner and French beans in this garden, where there is sufficient space for them and they will not shade adjacent crops. Sweetcorn grows in this garden too, in a block and with a crop of squashes and pumpkins underneath. The rotation in the six-year beds is as follows.

Rotation crop	Actual crop
Potatoes	Potatoes and tomatoes (protected under a small polytunnel)
Sweetcorn	Sweetcorn and squash
Umbellifers	Carrots, parsnips and celeriac
Brassicas	Kohl rabi, cauliflowers, cabbage, turnips, swedes
Peas and Beans	Runner beans and French beans
Alliums	Onions, leeks, shallots and garlic

Note that the brassicas follow the legumes and the potatoes follow the sweetcorn. Research has shown that sweetcorn can increase the yields of potato crops so I try to grow potatoes after sweetcorn.

Green manures and rotations

If you don't have access to copious quantities of FYM then using green manures in your rotation is a major bonus. Green manures add large quantities of organic matter to your soil, cover the soil and hold nutrients in it over the winter. Some also fix nitrogen or access minerals and trace elements deep in your soil with their extensive root systems.

If you are growing green manures in your vegetable rotation, you must bear in mind that some of them are in the same plant families as vegetable crops. For example, fodder radish and mustards are members of the brassica family, so should be included with the brassicas in the rotation. Field beans should only be grown in the legume part of the rotation.

Some green manures, like alfalfa, need a whole growing year to be effective. Alfalfa is very deep rooting, bringing up nutrients to the surface, but the roots take a year to fully develop. It is only possible to fit alfalfa into your rotation if you have a bed free for the whole year.

(See Quick Guide to Green Manure page 42).

Green Manures

G reen manures are a way of adding fertility to your garden. They are fast growing plants grown between or alongside your crops, which are then incorporated into the soil. They have a number of benefits and I have been incorporating them into my garden plan more and more.

The benefits of green manures:

- All green manures will help improve the soils structure by increasing the humus content and adding bulky matter to your soil. This will help drainage in heavy soils and water retention in light soils.
- They can provide winter soil cover, particularly useful on light soils where nutrients tend to get washed through and on soils prone to flooding and erosion.
- They discourage and out-compete weeds (although not groundsel on my soil!)
- They can be sown in spring, summer and autumn depending on use, and can provide short or long-term soil cover.
- The quick growing types can be sown in between crops to keep the soil in good condition, well covered and free of weeds.
- You can cut them down and use the bulk as a mulch to plant through. This only works if there is no chance of the green manure growing back.
- Red clover and alfalfa are deep rooting bringing up important nutrients from the subsoil for the following crops.
- Trefoil, clover and field beans fix nitrogen and can be used for this purpose in the appropriate part of your rotation.
- White clover is good for foot traffic, eg. paths.
- They can be sown under crops so that they establish in readiness for the winter while the main crop grows above them.
- Some attract beneficial insects.

Problems with green manures

■ Some green manures release compounds harmful to seed germination when they are turned in, so let them rot down for at least a month after ploughing or digging them into the soil.

■ Never let a green manure flower unless you want it to attract pollinating insects or provide ground cover for more than a season, as nitrogen will be lost to the flower and resulting seed head.

■ Some green manures fall in the same families as vegetable crops. Fodder radish and mustard are brassicas so should only be grown in that part of the rotation. Similarly field beans belong to the bean family and rye grasses are in the same family as sweetcorn.

■ Some green manures need a long season to be beneficial, so unless you have plenty of ground to spare crops such as alfalfa are difficult to incorporate in a rotation.

■ Beware of under-sowing green manures too early. One year I under-sowed my onions with trefoil in late May. The green manure almost out-competed the crop resulting in small onions that were difficult to find amongst the trefoil!

Nitrogen fixing green manures

● **Alfalfa** is a deep rooting green manure. If left for a whole season it is said that its roots can penetrate 6m. It is a tall crop so be careful where you grow it, in terms of shading other crops.

● **Lupins** are also deep rooting and tall, and they add large amounts of phosphate to the soil.

● **Winter tares** are tall with extensive root systems.

● **Red clover** is low growing but deep rooting.

● **Trefoil**, a type of clover, is extremely useful. Unusually for a clover, it will germinate as late as September. It is low growing and will suppress weeds. It is particularly useful under long-standing winter crops such as Brussels sprouts, over-wintered cauliflowers, purple sprouting broccoli and kale. Brassicas are heavy nitrogen feeders and the trefoil will compensate for this. It is easy to incorporate in the spring either by loosening around the roots and rotovating or by turning in with a spade. So far I have found it to be the most useful green manure.

Green manures that don't fix nitrogen

● **Grazing rye** will germinate late in the year, provides good cover in the winter, has a good root system and generates large amounts of green matter.

● **Buckwheat** has an extensive root system, adds lots of organic matter to the soil and attracts hoverflies if you leave it to flower.

● **Phacelia** is quick growing and the flowers attract bees.

● **Italian ryegrass** is fast growing and bulky. It germinates well in cold soils but make sure you only use the annual variety 'Westerwolds'.

● **Mustards and fodder radish** are particularly good between crops as they grow extremely quickly. They are brassicas so should only be grown in this part of the rotation.

● **Fenugreek** is also very fast growing and can grow anywhere in the rotation.

As one of my main criteria is efficiency, I tend to use green manures that can be sown, grown and incorporated with as little effort as possible. My favourites are those that can be sown broadcast and raked into a rough soil tilth, mown if necessary and dug or ploughed in quickly. They must also be able to grow without competing with my vegetable crops.

Green Manures Quick Guide

Type	Sowing dates	Nitrogen Fixer	Bulk quantity	Deep rooting	Foot traffic	Rotation	Winter hardiness	Speed of growth
Alfalfa	Apr–July	Yes		Yes			Good	
Beans (field)	Aug–Nov	Yes		Yes		Legumes	Good	
Buckwheat	Apr–Oct		Good	Yes				Quick
Clover (alsike)	Apr–Aug	Yes					Good	
Clover (white)	Apr–Aug	Yes	Good		Yes			
Clover (red)	Apr–Aug	Yes					Good	
Clover (crimson)	Apr–Aug	Yes						Quick
Fenugreek	Apr–Aug		Good					Quick
Lupins	Mar–Jun	Yes		Yes		Legumes		
Mustard	Mar–Sept		Good			Brassica		Quick
Phacelia	Mar–Sept						Good	Quick
Radish	Aug–Sept		Good	Yes		Brassica		Quick
Rye (grazing)	Aug–Oct		Good				Good	
Ryegrass	Aug–Oct						Good	
Tares (vetches)	Mar–Sept	Yes	Good			Legumes	Good	
Trefoil	Apr–Aug	Yes			Yes		Good	

Sowing, Propagation, Modules and Transplants

A s a gardener you will spend a great deal of time sowing, budding, dividing, grafting and using all the other techniques of plant propagation. You can miss out on this process entirely by buying plants from garden centres, nurseries and other suppliers, but there are three major drawbacks to doing this. Firstly, you will not see the process of growing your vegetables from start to finish, which is part of the 'holistic' philosophy of organic growing. Secondly, plants cost money and if you need a lot then you will probably have to grow your own. Thirdly, unless you buy organically certified plants, which are difficult to get hold of, it is likely that the compost they are grown in contains prohibited materials such as chemical fertilisers and sprays. The only case for bought in plants is soft fruit bushes, which you will need to get certified virus free and ideally from an organic source.

I have been sowing seeds all my life. It is something I learned from an early age, as naturally as learning to read and write. What I have mastered in the last nine years is how to use propagators, modules and transplants. I have experimented with different ways of growing plants in all sorts of containers and, inevitably, I come back to those that I find easiest for the plants I grow, my garden and me.

Sowing and Propagating Outside

Timing your sowing

Soil temperature, weather conditions and how much you want of each crop will determine the timing of your sowings. Soil temperatures need to be above 7°C for seeds to germinate. However you should make the most of dry weather to create a good seedbed and get the seed sown in readiness for the soil temperature to rise.

One common practice is to sow parsnip seed in February. They take a long time to germinate and are thought to need a long season in which to grow to their full potential. There's no way parsnip seed is going to germinate in my garden in February unless I pre-germinate it and keep the ground covered with cloches during their initial growth. Instead I sow all my parsnips in early April and they always germinate and they always grow to a good size before harvesting from October onwards.

On the other side of the coin, some seeds, such as lettuce, won't germinate in soil that is too warm. This problem can be avoided in the summer by sowing late in the afternoon and maybe even covering the rows with planks of wood to keep the ground cool.

Sowing for succession

Some vegetables, such as perpetual spinach, crop over a fairly long period and a single sowing can provide all that you need over the season. Vegetables such as carrots and broad beans crop either just once or for a short time. To have a continuous supply of such vegetables you need to sow several batches of seed, and the timings of your sowings determines whether you will have a steady supply or a huge glut.

Sowing seeds at the right time to get a continuous supply can be difficult. If you sow a crop too early it may fruit at the same time as another that you plant three weeks later, merely because the soil temperature wasn't high enough for germination or the weather turned cold the day after you sowed the seed. As the weather becomes warmer in the spring individual crops will increase their rate of growth so that even those sown two months apart will crop within a few weeks of each other. A good example of this is broad beans. A crop sown in the autumn will bear fruit in late May and early June; a crop sown in February will fruit in late June. A third crop sown in April will fruit in July. Another example is lettuce. I sow small amounts of lettuce once every two weeks from April onwards and once a month later in the year. This gives me the right succession of maturing lettuce to make up the salad bags that I sell in my boxes.

Pre-germinating seeds

It is sometimes wise to germinate or sprout seeds before they are sown. Parsley, parsnip and carrot seed are all notorious for taking an age to germinate and it is possible to pre-germinate them on moistened kitchen towel somewhere warm. They are then sown after they have germinated. I have done this and found it far too fiddly so I prefer to sow when the soil is at the right temperature and save myself a lot of work.

On the other hand, it is a good idea to pre-germinate peas, beans and sweetcorn which are susceptible to the ravages of mice. Leave the seed soaking in water for 24 hours then drain and rinse twice a day until their roots are not more than 1 or 2cm long. They can then be sown directly in a seed drill. I always sow sweetcorn in modules and with pre-germinating you can pick out those seeds that have sprouted and leave those that haven't. This makes the best use of the compost and trays you have available and saves wasting time with dud seed.

Creating seedbeds

'Tilth' is the term that describes the size of the lumps of soil in your garden. Getting the right tilth for the type of seed you want to sow is very important. A fine tilth is needed for small seeds, and the larger the seed the coarser the tilth can be.

It is a good idea to create a sterile seedbed for fine seeds such as lettuce and carrots. This will save you an awful lot of work hand weeding later in the season. A sterile seedbed is easy to create when the weather conditions are right, so it isn't always possible for early crops. All you need to do is cultivate the soil to the correct tilth and leave it for two or three weeks. This will give the latent weeds ample time to germinate. Then go over the bed with a hoe killing off the majority of them. Hoe the bed again a day or two later and you will see the ones you missed or the ones that were tenacious enough to survive. You can then sow your seed in the knowledge that most of the weeds have already been dealt with. Be careful not to cultivate the soil any deeper than the depth you hoe, or you will be bringing extra weed seeds to the surface to germinate as soon as you turn your back.

Now you have your clean seedbed you can start to sow your seed.

Sowing seeds direct

The size of a seed is a good indication of the depth and thickness they should be sown. The rule of thumb is to sow seeds at a depth that is twice their size. Remembering that getting the depth of the row or drill right is only half of the process – you must also cover the seed with the correct amount of soil to maintain that depth. Specific details for each crop are included in the A–Z sections.

Some seeds, such as celery, need light to germinate and must be sown on the surface of the compost. It is necessary to cover the surface of the compost with glass or plastic to stop it from drying out, which it will do very quickly. Germination will be very difficult if the seed is too dry.

Small seeds such as parsley, carrot and lettuce need only 1cm depth of soil in which to germinate. It is important that the soil is of a fine tilth. Sowing small seeds at the right density can be difficult, and a row-seeder can be useful (*see Machinery, Tools and Equipment, page 21*). I have learned that it is wise to sow enough seed that you get some survivors even if something eats some of them, then be ruthless when it comes to thinning them out.

Seeds such as beetroot and spinach, being slightly bigger, will benefit from a slightly deeper sowing, up to 2.5cm deep. As they tend to be clusters of seeds it is best to space them this far apart as well or you will have too many young plants competing for the same light and water.

Peas and beans should be pre-sprouted before planting so that they get away before the mice start eating them. They are usually sown at a depth of about 5cm. For these large seeds the tilth can be quite coarse. The large tubers such as potatoes and Jerusalem artichokes are usually sown, or rather planted, at 15cm or deeper.

Care of germinating seeds

If you want your seeds to germinate quickly then you must make sure the soil is at the correct temperature and it must be moist. Watering the drills before you sow the seed will provide the moisture and covering the soil before and after sowing with clear plastic will give warmth they need.

Watering small seeds once they are covered should be avoided as it may lead to the soil 'capping'. This is when the soil forms an impenetrable crust that the seedlings can't push through. It is particularly prevalent on clay soils. The exception to this rule is when you have sown pre-sprouted seeds like peas and beans which need plenty of water to keep them growing. They are also strong enough to push through a lightly capped soil.

If you want to keep the soil warm with plastic then it's a good idea to make the seed drills a bit deeper than normal. Cover the seed with the right depth of soil and the surrounding surface will be slightly higher. When the plants emerge they will have a little room between the soil and plastic in which to grow before the plastic is removed completely. This creates a microclimate for the initial growth of the plant, and provides a little shelter from the wind once the plastic is removed.

Remember that your seeds might not be the only ones that germinate, particularly if you did not prepare a sterile seedbed. Leave sufficient space between your rows of seeds to hoe between the crops without damaging them.

Thinning seeds

The process of thinning rows of seeds is really just a case of getting rid of excess plants so that those left have enough light, water and room to grow to their full potential. The only crops I regularly thin are peas and French beans. Occasionally I thin carrots and lettuce, which I sow relatively thickly to get a reasonable number of plants. Remember that if you want to replant any thinnings you must keep their roots damp and cool whilst they are waiting. Don't bother trying to transplant carrots as they have tap roots which won't take kindly to being shoved about.

Sowing in covered seedbeds

This is a method I use for brassicas and leeks as a way of saving on seed compost and providing favourable conditions for the plants involved. The seed is sown in a prepared seedbed, either outside in cold frames or in a polytunnel.

I sow the leeks like this so that they get a quick start and are a good size to plant out in late May and June. Growing leeks in trays or modules always restricts their growth due to lack of water and nutrients; a seedbed will provide the right conditions over a longer period of time.

Most of my brassicas are also sown in outside seedbeds (in the brassica part of the rotation) under mobile cold frames. This way they are never short of water or light and they are protected from pigeon damage. When the plants are big enough, usually about 15cm tall, they are dug up and pulled away from each other for planting in their permanent positions. They are quite sturdy plants and don't mind a bit of rough treatment. To get the most efficient use of space I usually plant out brassicas in a dice pattern, that is in the shape of the five on a dice, in my metre wide beds. Other crops such as onion sets and leeks do well in this pattern too.

Propagating under cover

Some crops benefit from being sown under cover, in the relatively warm environment inside a greenhouse or polytunnel. Adding insulation can further protect plants. How you do this really depends on just how many plants you are going to grow. If you need enough propagated plants to cover five acres then you may need a polytunnel dedicated to propagation, in which case insulate it. Bubble wrap can be stapled to the frames of wooden greenhouses or clipped, using Ali-plugs, to aluminium ones. In the polytunnel, drape bubble wrap or plastic sheeting over wires strung from end to end, making a double skinned tunnel. On a smaller scale, cold frames or cloches can be used inside a polytunnel. These strategies will increase the temperature significantly during the late winter and early spring, and can negate the need for heaters, thus saving on fossil fuels.

Do make sure that the extra layers of insulation are not cutting out too much light. The emerging seeds must get enough light or they will become elongated and straggly which will make it difficult for them to grow on outside.

When the plants are big enough they can be hardened off gradually to be transplanted inside or out.

The propagator

If you're not pushed for time simply sowing seeds in modules, trays or pots, covering with glass and placing somewhere warm will give adequate conditions for germination nine times out of ten. If you want to steal a little time and get early crops you can use a propagator from as early as February onwards.

The essential elements for a propagator are light, heat, water and ventilation. They are usually housed in a greenhouse or conservatory or on a windowsill with access to a mains electricity supply. This is not essential – my propagators have their own little coldframe, and propagators can use any available alternative sources of heat.

If you keep a propagator on a windowsill you need to turn the plants round two or three times a day otherwise they will lean towards the light and get leggy. Placing a white board behind them to reflect light back on to the plants should help.

It is a good idea to have your propagators near to where you work during the day so that you can open them up if they are likely to overheat. Also you will need to check the compost in the trays and pots twice a day to make sure that it doesn't dry out. My two main propagators are housed in a coldframe with an insulated floor and sides and a top light insulated with large bubble wrap. It faces south and is quite low but its real bonus is that it is by my garden gate. I see to it on the way to taking my son to school and when I go in for lunch. At the end of the day it is near enough to my house for me to see from my kitchen window so it is no bother to run out and close it.

You can buy a purpose built propagator and these are very convenient for windowsills. I have a standard sized seed tray propagator with a warming element in its base, which sits on my windowsill and cost about £10. I use it for growing the first crops I need like parsley, celery and celeriac, followed by peppers and chillies.

Large purpose-built propagators can be very expensive, anything from £40 upwards depending on their features. When I started my garden I just didn't have any money so I made my first propagator out of old bits of wood and plastic: it is still going strong. It takes five standard seed trays plus a couple of pots. I have another propagator about half the size, which takes three standard seed trays. These two, together with the one on my kitchen windowsill, are all I need for my one and a half acres. For instructions on how to build your own propagator, *page 253*.

Using a propagator

This becomes a habit after a few years, but keeping a thermometer inside each one helps at first. I aim to achieve a fairly constant 20°C. As soon as the temperature rises during the day I open the lid on the cold frame where I keep my propagators. Depending on the weather, the propagator lids can be taken right off if necessary.

You will need to keep an eye on the humidity as well. Keeping the compost moist is essential but insufficient ventilation will increase the chances of mildews and moulds. Damping off can be a problem, seen as a blackening at the base of the stem of a plant due to lack of ventilation, excess watering and cool temperatures. As the plants in the propagator are likely to be quite tender and delicate it is a good idea to use a good quality watering can which has a fine spray brass rose that doesn't drip.

Once the young plants are big enough, they can be hardened off undercover and then planted out. You are aiming for a gradual transition from perfect conditions to relatively difficult conditions. Doing this gently will keep your plants happy and prevent growth checks. One word of caution: starting plants off too early isn't good practice as you will need to halt their growth until they can go outside.

Seed compost

When you sow seeds in containers you need to get a compost mix that is right for the individual seeds you want to grow. You can buy in seed compost, but keep to ones that have been licensed by an organic body. I mix two very basic compost mixes myself, one that I use for small seeds and one for larger seeds.

The compost mix for small seeds is roughly three buckets of sieved garden compost, one of coir fibre or peat (I will use peat if it is the type that is collected from reservoir catchments) and two small handfuls each of seaweed meal, fish blood and bone meal and lime. The lime is only necessary if you are using peat, to offset the acidity.

The seed compost for bigger seeds is the same, but I add some roughly sieved compost, small stones and sieved topsoil to help bulk out the greater quantities I need.

Sowing in modules, trays, pots and soil blocks

When sowing seeds in containers, my preference is nearly always for modules made out of polystyrene. Crops such as tomatoes and peppers will take very readily in these modules and they can be transplanted to pots quite easily before they are planted out later in the season. Soil blocks (*see Machinery, Tools and Equipment*) are very practical if you need to propagate large numbers of plants. I use individual pots for crops with a large seed, such as squash, courgettes, runner beans and cucumbers.

Be aware of the environment the containers are in. You need to keep an eye on the moisture of the seed compost and be sure that the tender seedlings aren't suffering in any way.

Transplanting from containers and seedbeds

Once your plants have grown large enough for their permanent homes, and the soil and weather conditions are favourable, you can transplant them. This is simply a case of planting them out at the appropriate spacing, watering them in and giving them adequate protection. For details of specific crops refer to the A–Z sections.

If you are transplanting from a seedbed remember to keep exposed roots cool and damp, preferably covered with damp newspaper or soil, as they will dry out quickly. If you can, do your transplanting during the cooler times of the day.

Protected Croppings

I n the British climate there are certain crops that always need protection from the weather to achieve a worthwhile harvest. Typical crops that benefit from protection are peppers, tomatoes, chillies, aubergines, cucumbers, melons and basil. Other crops do well outdoors, but if you want to extend their season, harvesting them earlier or later than usual, you will need to protect them from the elements. Other crops will benefit from protection over the winter. Protected cropping comes in many shapes and guises - from full-scale polytunnels and greenhouses to simple cloche and fleece protection.

Polytunnels

Polytunnels are large stationary units that give long term protection, but do need a certain amount of care. They come in a range of sizes, in height, length and width.

If you need to purchase a polytunnel frame, the cheapest way is to look out in your area for any sheetless frames on farms, smallholdings or in back gardens. I have acquired all of my polytunnels by word of mouth and investigation. I found the last tunnel I bought by spending an afternoon knocking on peoples' doors in an area where there were large glasshouses wherever you looked. I simply asked if they had any old polytunnel hoops. Most conventional growers with greenhouses started off using polytunnels, and if they haven't already got rid of them they are usually lying in a hedge somewhere. After five enquiries I came up with someone who had started protected market gardening about 20 years ago and updated his polytunnels in the last five years to enormous glass houses. His old hoops were sitting in a hedge; I negotiated a deal that cost a sixth of the price that I would have forked out for new frames. *(Information about siting, erecting and maintaining a polytunnel is found on page 249).*

Greenhouses

Greenhouses are also very useful but on a large scale they are far more costly than polytunnels and they need constant attention. Small garden greenhouses often appear in the classified sections of local papers.

I have a small 3 x 2m greenhouse in the warmest spot in my garden and I use it for starting delicate crops in the spring. I usually try to grow something in it in the summer but it really comes into its own in the autumn for drying onions, shallots and garlic and to ripen late squashes and marrows.

Growing crops in polytunnels and greenhouses

Growing crops undercover can be much easier than growing them outdoors but the same principles should be adhered to, particularly when it comes to irrigation, rotation and ventilation.

I use a four-year rotation in my tunnels to avoid any build up of soil-borne diseases, particularly with tomatoes and cucumbers. So far I have avoided this problem in the tunnel but if I did have trouble I would graft the tomatoes and cucumbers of my choice onto disease resistant rootstocks (*see tomatoes page 174 for grafting technique*).

I pay close attention to irrigation in the tunnels. I grow several crops in each bed so I use short lengths (about 4m) of LDPE pipe with four sprinklers attached and water each crop individually. When a whole bed is used for one crop I try to use one pipe running the whole length with sprinklers attached every metre.

I make sure that I rotate my crops in the polytunnels using the ideas set out earlier (*see Rotations page 35*). However in beds where the salad leaves are grown there will often be up to three crops a year. I also catch crop salads and other crops between the taller plants such as cucumbers and indeterminate tomatoes. I am growing sweetcorn in one tunnel this year and will be experimenting with an undersown crop of either French beans or butternut squash.

Cloches

Cloche is a general term for a range of semi-permanent polytunnels or green houses. They are used to help plants get an early start, as winter protection for salads and as full season covers for delicate plants such as peppers and bush tomatoes. Cloches come in all sorts of shapes and sizes and each type is discussed later.

Coldframes

These are like a mini-greenhouse. They can be made of wood, metal, bricks etc. Wood and metal coldframes can be bought quite easily but they are quite expensive.

It's easy to make a coldframe from concrete blocks, bricks or wood. It is a good idea to get the glass first and build the frame to fit. Keep a

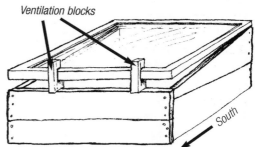

Ventilation blocks

South

look out – builders often throw out old windows and glazing companies will discard units if they don't fit the job they're working on. If you build a coldframe with bricks or blocks, be aware that gaps make attractive hiding-places for slugs.

I have four cedar coldframes with Dutch Light tops. A Dutch Light is a piece of glass that is cheaper than normal because it is only 3mm thick and a standard size. They are used extensively in greenhouses.

Low plastic tunnels

You can make long plastic cloches supported on metal hoops, like tiny polytunnels. They give a good start to early crops, and fit in well with rotations as they can be moved each season to whichever bed you want to protect. The plastic can be lifted off when necessary, for watering or weeding. I use the hoops with fleece or mesh for delicate early crops and I don't have to worry about watering as rain and dew can get through.

Glass tent and barn cloches

I use these in the same way as plastic tunnels and they do last a lot longer but are a bit of a pain to erect and take apart. A tent cloche is literally two panes of glass which lean together to form a tent. They are attached at the apex usually by simple plastic or metal clips that are available from good garden centres. Put several of these in a row and add a pane of glass to each end of the tent tunnel and you create a much warmer environment to extend cropping out of season, particularly low lying crops like lettuce.

A barn cloche is a little more complicated and much taller, therefore more useful for larger plants. A barn cloche has two vertical panes of glass as the sides of the cloche with two more panes of glass making a roof. The whole thing looks like a barn. They have a complicated wire framework to hold them together. Put end to end with a larger piece of glass at each end in the same manner as tent cloches, they provide a warm glass tunnel in which you can protect larger crops such as French beans or Sugar Loaf chicory. Unfortunately I haven't ever seen the wire framework for sale – I inherited all of mine. They are very useful and if you are ever offered them, don't turn them down. It is possible to get plastic clips for this type of cloche but I found they don't hold the glass in place so effectively.

Bale and plastic/fleece cloches

You can make a very simple cloche with straw bales and heavy-duty plastic with a gauge similar to that used on polytunnels. It will be much higher than normal cloches, suitable for growing crops such as peppers. Orientate the cloche to face south. To raise the covering a little higher you can use alcathene piping (used for outdoor plumbing jobs). Odd sections can sometimes be found at builders' yards or on skips. Cut pieces at least 60cm longer than the plastic so that they can be pushed into the ground to make a tent-like structure.

Replacing the plastic with fleece in the summer makes watering less of a bother. Later on you can put the plastic back to extend the cropping season.

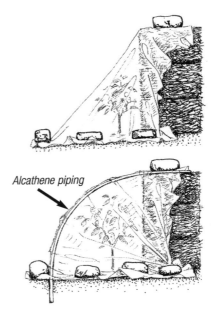

Alcathene piping

Fleece and mesh without hoops

Although not strictly a cloche these materials are often referred to as floating cloches. Fleece is spun polypropylene and mesh is nylon (*see Machinery, Tools and Equipment page 21*). Fleece is so light that it literally sits on top of the crop protecting it from both cold weather and pests, but it doesn't last terribly long. Mesh performs the same functions and is much longer lived but will not protect against spring frosts.

Simple cloches

These can be whatever you have got – old jars, plastic bottles, or purpose made bells. They can be used on individual plants such as sweetcorn, which are susceptible to the cold. I don't use them a lot because I always forget about them when it's hot and the plants get scorched. In my first year of growing I left some small pepper plants under jam jars on a grey day in April. The sun appeared not long after I left and cooked every single one to a cinder.

Old tyres are incredibly useful in all sorts of ways but as cloches they really come into their own. When I plant out members of the squash family I always put a tyre round them and cover it with a piece of glass. Panes of glass from a greenhouse are ideal – being square they leave ventilation gaps. The tyre is just high enough to keep the wind off the plant, and the tyre, being black, warms in the sun during the day and radiates heat during the night.

Fleece tents

I use these tents to provide extra protection for particularly tender plants inside my polytunnels. It is basically a square or rectangular piece of fleece that is placed around the plant with the top bunched up and tied with string to the stake. The fleece falls around the plant in thick folds and can be opened very simply if the weather is warm enough. This system has several advantages over individual glass and plastic cloches. You can water the plant without moving the covering material, it provides adequate ventilation preventing moulds and should the sun come out and overheat the polytunnel, the plants won't be burnt to a cinder.

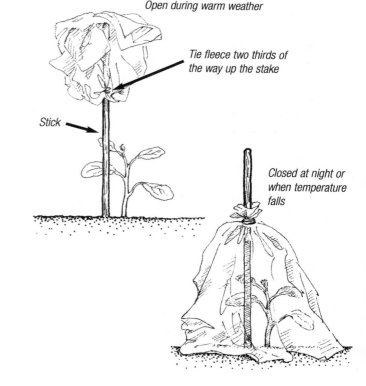

Open during warm weather

Tie fleece two thirds of the way up the stake

Stick

Closed at night or when temperature falls

Natural protected cropping, or micro climates

Although these aren't cloches as such they do provide protection in the same way. One crop is protected in the under-story of another. A good example is growing lettuce between cabbages. The cabbages are planted 45 to 60cm apart and once they begin to establish themselves you can plant lettuce that will use the space between the cabbages and be protected by them. The cabbages shade the lettuce in the summer, when high temperatures may cause the lettuces to bolt. The lettuces grow far more quickly than the cabbages and are harvested way before the cabbages provide too much shade for them to grow.

I also use runner bean structures as suntraps. I grow the beans up two long wigwams in an L shape, with the inside of the L pointing directly south. The space in the 'L' is protected and much warmer than the surrounding area. French beans enjoy a warm climate and do well grown on the inside of the L.

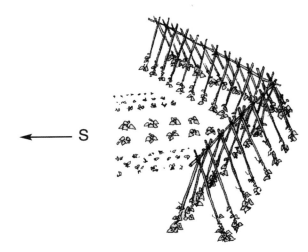

Storing Your Harvest Through the Winter

Some vegetables can stay in the ground where they grow until you want to harvest them, and will keep in peak condition through the harshest weather. Others need to be cropped when they are ready and must be stored until you want to eat them. The conditions that they require to stay fresh once they are harvested vary for different crops. For example, carrots need cool, damp conditions so that they don't dry out and onions need cool, dry conditions so that they don't rot. The other requirement for successful storage is that you must start with vegetables that are in good condition.

The weather is critical for the winter storage of vegetables. I work in Gloucestershire, where the winters are relatively mild. Gardeners to the north of this are likely to need to insulate their vegetables from the weather more carefully, with the increased likelihood of severe weather. Crops that I can store adequately in situ might need storing in a clamp or barn in Scotland. Vegetables must be protected from freezing, as if they do they will begin to rot when they thaw.

On the other hand, in a mild winter vegetables will start to rot earlier than usual. My squashes will usually store well until the spring, but last year was so mild most of them gave up the ghost by the end of February.

Crop storage - in situ

By far the easiest and most efficient way of storing many vegetables in the winter is to leave them where they have grown. There is little work involved, they don't get a chance to dry out and they are kept at roughly the right temperature (unless it gets really cold). A well-drained soil is an advantage, and a good cover of straw will help to protect them from frost.

Valuable Vegetables

Above ground

Sufrace crops that store well in situ are Brussels sprouts, cabbages, cauliflowers, chicories, claytonia, endive, kale, lamb's lettuce and oriental leaves. Brussels sprouts and kale will happily stand very severe weather, but cabbages and cauliflowers will probably need to be cut and stored in a cold shed should bad weather threaten. Cover the leafy crops with a cloche to stop them freezing if it is very cold.

Below ground

Many crops are best left in the ground until needed. These include beetroot, carrots, celeriac, celery, Jerusalem artichokes, leeks, parsnips, swedes and salsify. Carrots are best left in fairly dry ground, covered with a 15cm layer of straw. If they are outdoors cover the row with a cloche as well. The straw insulates carrots grown in polytunnels against raised temperatures should the sun come out. The roots of swedes, beetroot and celeriac can have straw drawn up around them to stop them freezing.

Parsnips, salsify and Jerusalem artichokes are beneath ground level so don't need covering. Leeks will normally stand the harshest of weather, whilst trenched celery should last well into January, and beyond if it has been grown in a polytunnel.

Barn and shed storage

This method of storage works well for garlic, onions, shallots, marrows, pumpkins and squashes. It is also good for the short-term storage of tomatoes. All these vegetables keep best in a cool and dry environment but it must be frost-free. If freezing weather is expected and your storage barn or shed isn't adequately insulated, put some heat in it for the duration of the cold snap. To find out just how cold it can get inside the shed use a max-min thermometer.

I hang my garlic, shallots and onions from the rafters in bunches of ten or so - not too closely packed as they need air to circulate around them. The squashes, pumpkins and marrows are laid out on shelves and tables, although I have so many that a lot of them end up on windowsills and in the loft of my house.

Green tomatoes can be stored in a barn or shed if they are wrapped in newspaper and placed in boxes or trays so they don't touch each other. Alternatively pull up the plant, hang it upside down and wrap each fruit in newspaper. To keep tomatoes like this the temperature should be between 14 and 17°C, so it is probably best to store them indoors, somewhere coolish, from November. They will ripen over the following few months, giving you fresh red tomatoes up to Christmas and sometimes beyond.

Storing in sand

Storing root crops in sand insulates them to a certain extent and it is easy to get at them. I use this method for beetroot and sometimes carrots. It is also useful for other root crops such as Jerusalem artichokes, celeriac, parsnips, salsify, swedes, and turnips. Only store vegetables that are sound. Remove the tops from the vegetables, preferably by twisting off. Place a layer of sand in the bottom of a sack or box, then a layer of the roots, ensuring that they don't touch each other. Fill the gaps with sand and cover with more sand. Continue adding roots surrounded by sand until the container is full, finishing with a layer of sand. Pull the roots out as and when you need them.

Clamp (underground) storage

This method of storage is usually necessary in areas where the ground freezes quite deeply on a regular basis. It provides more protection than storage in sand. As the winters are reasonably mild in Gloucestershire I do not use clamps, but if an ice age approached I probably would. It is a good way to store all root vegetables and solid cabbages.

Dig a hole in the ground, large enough to hold all of the vegetables you want to store and deep enough that they won't freeze. Line the hole with wire mesh (rabbit fencing is ideal) to stop rodents stealing your crop, then with a layer of old carpet or hessian sacks. Next fill the hole with your vegetables. Remember that you will need to access the vegetables through the winter so don't put all of your carrots at the bottom – putting them in pillars will allow you to access them all. Cover the vegetables with a layer of wire and carpet and then a layer of soil, up to 20cm thick in very cold areas. Finish with a layer of straw and a sheet of plastic to keep the whole thing dry.

When you want some vegetables simply pull the carpet and wire back to get at them. Don't open the clamp more than you need to as this can let warm air in to the vegetables, encouraging them to rot.

Old freezers and fridges

Redundant freezers and fridges make cheap and sustainable cold stores for vegetables. They are ideal as they are insulated and rodent proof, and much easier to set up and access than clamps. You can use them outside or in a packing shed to store sacks of potatoes, carrots and beetroot packed in sand, and apples wrapped in newspaper. The ideal storage temperature is 0 to 4°C, and the lid can be left ajar for ventilation when this is the external temperature. Close the lid if the weather is warmer or colder than this, but try not to keep the lid closed for long periods. One word of warning – make sure that any fridges and freezers you use are safe for children.

Drying vegetables

I do not propose to cover drying vegetables in depth. You can buy an electric food drier, which preserves peppers, tomatoes and fruits perfectly. If you can build a solar drier then you can rate yourself very highly in terms of sustainability. I don't have this sort of skill and await the arrival of a ready-made solar drier. Alternatively you can use the heat from radiators, rayburns and wood burners to dry vegetables. This rarely happens in my house because the things I like to dry are ready before I need my wood burner. If you have a rayburn you can use the warming oven as a drier. It is possible to use gas and electric ovens to dry vegetables but this seems like a waste of fuel to me.

Chillies can be dried just in the heat of the sun. Pick them when they have matured to their finished colour and leave on a sunny windowsill. They will cure, slowly, and can be left there all winter and used when needed.

Freezing vegetables

Most kitchens these days have a freezer, and many fruits and vegetables can be frozen very successfully to store for some months. Books are available that describe how best to prepare different vegetables for freezing, and it is beyond the remit of this one.

Storage guide table

	In situ	Clamps/ Fridges	Barn/ Shed	Sand	Dried
Jer. Artichokes	★★	★	-	★	-
Beetroot	★	★	-	★★	-
Brussels Sprouts	★★	-	-	-	-
Cabbages	★★	★	-	-	-
Carrots	★	★	-	★★	-
Cauliflowers	★★	★	-	-	-
Celeriac	★	★★	-	★	-
Celery	★★	★	-	-	-
Chicories	★★	-	-	★	-
Chillis	-	-	-	-	★★
Endive	★★	-	-	-	-
Garlic	-	-	★★	-	-
Kale	★★	-	-	-	-
Lamb's Lettuce	★★	-	-	-	-
Leeks	★★	★	-	-	-
Lettuce	★★	-	-	-	-
Marrows	-	-	★★	-	-
Onions	-	-	★★	-	-
Oriental Leaves	★★	-	-	-	-
Parsnips	★★	★	-	★	-
Potatoes	-	★★	-	-	-
Pumpkins	-	-	★★	-	-
Salsify	★★	★	-	★	-
Shallots	-	-	★★	-	-
Squashes	-	-	★★	-	-
Swede	★	★★	-	★	-
Tomatoes	-	-	★	-	★★
Turnips	-	★★	-	★★	-

- = not a good idea

★ = ok

★★ = best practice

Water and Irrigation

When I started my garden my life was ruled by getting cans of water to my crops. I soon realised that I needed to find a way to cut down on the time I spent watering. I introduced irrigation systems and started using mulches, as well as adding organic matter to my soil whenever I could. These changes have allowed me to spend more time on the other jobs in the garden. Whereas before I was always in a rush, I can now grow more vegetables for more customers with less effort. Using water efficiently has saved me masses of time.

Improving soil structure

Organic matter in soil acts like a sponge, so is a very important factor in water management. A sandy, stony or chalky soil drains very freely, so adding organic matter to a soil like this will help to retain water. A clay soil retains water well, but can readily become too wet for plants. Adding organic matter to this type of soil will increase the 'bulk' of the soil, improving drainage.

Mulching to conserve water

On bare soil, rain disappears very quickly. Mulching with any material you can get your hands on will keep the water in the soil, making it available to your plants for a much longer period. Using mulches to conserve water can be a bit of an art. You must remember that mulching a crop means it has all the water that it will need indefinitely. For example, garlic needs water particularly during its growing season, between April and June. If I mulch the crop in April, usually with straw, the bulbs are bigger, fatter and juicier than if I had left the ground exposed. However, if there is a long period of dry weather the crop will need extra water, so I water it with the micro irrigation system without removing the mulch.

I use a plastic mulch for tomatoes, courgettes and squashes, and need to keep a check on them while they are establishing. I make a muck sink - a hole filled with a mixture of muck and soil, which will retain water - to plant them in, but it will be a while before the roots reach down far enough to benefit from it. So in the first month or so I hand water the individual plants with a hose. On the other hand, leeks are planted though plastic and rarely need extra water. They are planted in a dibber hole that has been filled with water, and the leaves and plastic will channel any subsequent water, be it dew or rain, into the soil. If there is no rain for months on end you might need to water them.

Your mains water supply

Where your water comes from is important. Many private households still pay water rates, giving them unlimited use of mains water. This is gradually changing and it won't be so long before most houses are metered. Most agricultural and horticultural holdings already have water meters and have to pay for any water they take from the mains. This is the case with my garden, but as there are plenty of other sources of water around I very rarely use mains water. If you do have unmetered water then it is an advantage in terms of cost, but it is still environmentally sensitive to save water if you can.

Collecting water

Placing barrels around your house, sheds and greenhouses to fill with rainwater is easy, but one barrel won't catch much water. The answer is to link several storage tanks together. You can buy special plastic tubes for the job or you can create a siphon with offcuts of hose. This will transfer water from one place to another, purely by means of gravity. Once the first barrel is full of water you place a piece of hose, filled with water, at least halfway down into the first barrel and to the bottom of the second barrel. The water from the first barrel will flow into the second barrel until the levels are equal. Multiply the number of barrels and hose siphons and a downpour in the middle of summer will replenish your water supply several times over from just one roof.

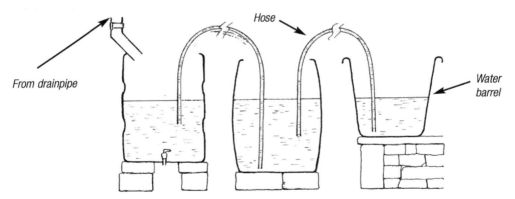

From drainpipe

Hose

Water barrel

One thing about water is that it is heavy, so it helps to have the barrels higher than the crops that you want to water. You will save yourself a lot of effort if you can use gravity to distribute the water. And the barrels don't need to be in a neat row next to the drainpipe – just lengthen the siphon hoses and you can keep barrels next to the beds that will need watering.

Water pressure

Mains water comes with pressure. The more you turn the tap, the greater the force of water that

Valuable Vegetables

comes out. If you are using water from barrels, springs, ponds etc, the pressure will be considerably lower and so extensive irrigation systems become almost useless. Whatever your water pressure, a combination of mulching, adding organic matter to the soil and using simple irrigation techniques will keep your crops adequately watered throughout the growing season.

Irrigation channels

You can dig channels from your water source, very slightly sloping downhill, to carry water to your crops. To make the lines use the method for finding the gradient in the From Field to Garden chapter, *page 13*, allowing the level to slope downhill very slightly away from the water source. These channels are particularly useful for fruit such as raspberries, which need to be irrigated during dry spells when they are forming their fruits.

Micro irrigation

All the water I use in my garden comes from springs or ponds so the water pressure is quite low. Because of this I use a micro irrigation system which requires very little pressure to operate. It is made by Hozelock, but there are others available. The system is based on 13mm diameter black LDPE pipe with sprinklers/sprayers at the top of risers (upright tubes). The risers can be screwed directly into the LDPE pipe after a small hole has been made in it and the sprayers are screwed into the risers. This means you can use different sprayers for different conditions. For example, I use mist sprayers above the cucumbers and 180° sprayers for the salad crops. There is a wide range of accessories available, making a flexible system that can be adapted to your needs.

Because of my low water pressure I need to move the pipe around my garden at intervals. I can only effectively use up to six sprayers at a time, on a 4 to 6m pipe. It can take a whole morning to water just one of my long, narrow beds. At least I can get on with something else and only have to remember to move it every so often.

I have a separate irrigation network in one of my tunnels, which allows me to water the beds separately. This is essential as I have different crops in the beds each year and they all require specific levels of watering.

Hoses, watering cans and porous pipe

During the spring and summer I often have several hoses littered about in the garden. There are five water outlets in my three gardens. To make the best use of them I need to have at least five hosepipes and sometimes a few more, to reach the furthest points in my garden.

Why don't I have longer hoses, I hear you ask. It is because any hose longer than 50m is heavy and difficult to deal with. It's much easier, and more flexible, to have shorter lengths that can be joined with hose connectors.

A watering can rose that can be connected to the end of a hose is extremely useful. I use one in my polytunnels for watering modules and trays. It is much easier than carrying a heavy watering can around. I have two watering cans but I never use them for watering. I use them to apply concoctions such as comfrey liquid to plants. I have two so that I can be using one while the other is filling from the low-pressure source. I make sure that I fill the cans with a hose as near to the plants I am watering as is possible, to avoid having to carry the cans too far.

Porous pipe is hose made out of recycled rubber that releases water slowly along its whole length. Some people swear by it. I have used this pipe but always find that there is generally not enough pressure for the water to get through. Also my water is very hard and the limescale builds up very quickly, blocking the pipe. If I could get it to work I think porous pipe would be particularly useful for crops such as runner beans that like a lot of water on a regular supply.

Weed Control

S ome people don't weed, some people weed a little, some people weed fanatically. There is a purpose to weeding and how far you take it will mirror your commitment to the quality of the vegetables you grow. If you let weeds get out of hand they will swamp your crops, shading them from the light, stealing their water and taking their food. If you let weeds seed, they will give you trouble for years and years to come. However, there is a place for weeds. Some are beneficial, such as nettles (for aphids), and I'm not averse to dandelions in grass paths in the spring to attract insects.

My philosophy on weeding is to do as much as is necessary to make my life easy and to get decent crops. In practice this involves weeding to create clean seedbeds and using mulches as much as possible. When the soil is dry enough I will hoe and if I have time I will do some hand-weeding.

Clean seedbeds

A clean seedbed is the first line of defence against weeds. It is particularly important for crops that can't be mulched until they have established, if at all. Lettuce is never mulched because of the risk of slug damage. Sweetcorn cannot be mulched until it has reached a size where the plants can survive the ravages of slugs. How to make a clean seedbed is described in the chapter Sowing, Propagation, Modules and Transplants, *page 43*.

Mulching for weed control

Various mulching techniques make up the majority of the weed control in my garden. The soil around the plants is covered with a layer of material that suppresses weed growth as well as reducing water loss from the soil. The use of mulches for each crop is described in the A–Z sections.

Common materials to use for mulching are straw, compost and grass mowings. I personally use a lot of straw. If I could get local, cheap, organic straw then I would use it, but I can only get straw from conventional systems. Chemical residues are probably leaching into my soil from it, but I feel that its advantages as a mulch far outweigh its disadvantages.

Grass mowings are useful as a mulch but only if they are taken from grass that doesn't have seeding plants in it. They are particularly useful around potato and squash plants as they provide a lot of nitrogen as they rot down. Be careful not to mulch with too thick a layer as it can get slimy.

Long-term mulches that are used for clearing ground and to control perennial weeds are described in the chapter 'From Field to Garden' *page 13*.

Hoeing

It is important to hoe between those crops that aren't mulched, such as lettuce, carrots and parsnips. How often you can hoe will depend on the weather: I only hoe when the soil is dry enough not to stick to the hoe blade. Also weed seedlings that aren't sliced in two are less likely to re-establish in dry soil.

Some crops, notably carrots, parsnips and parsley, take a long time to germinate. Once they do, it is often difficult to see them amongst weed seedlings. When I sow these seeds I cover the row with a line of sand or sow a fast-growing radish seedling every few centimetres. That way I can hoe between the rows without damaging the seedlings before they emerge.

Hoeing doesn't eliminate weeds that have established in the rows. These have to be hand weeded, although starting with a clean seedbed will reduce the problem.

Perennial weeding

I often spend a week or two in the winter digging out perennial weeds such as dandelions, docks, nettles and buttercups. It is important to deal with them during the winter – once your crops are established, or establishing, you won't be able to tackle perennial weeds without disturbing the roots of your crops. If you have a heavy soil, try and restrict perennial weeding to when the ground is dry (and the sun shining).

Flame guns

I know that biodynamic gardeners use these, and I have tried them myself. I find them incredibly unpleasant to use. I dislike the way they burn the top of the soil where organisms are battling away to incorporate organic matter into your soil for you. If you must, use them when the weeds are small and don't forget to protect the crops you are trying to benefit. There is an argument that burning clears and feeds the ground but I don't subscribe to it.

Pests and Diseases

In nature there is a balance between pests, predators, plants and agents that can cause disease. There is a great diversity: a huge variety of plants growing together, attracting predators and other wildlife while confusing and disorientating pests. In an organic garden our approach to pest and disease control is primarily preventative. We aim to mimic nature. We grow a diverse range of plants, not just fruit and vegetables but also herbs and flowers that will attract beneficial insects. By feeding the soil and following rotations we give our plants the best chance to grow strongly and withstand attack. We protect our most vulnerable plants from pests using barriers. And when we can, we help ourselves by growing varieties that are resistant to likely problems.

The opposite of such a garden is a monocrop, areas planted with a single species, which is an open invitation to pests and diseases. Once a problem has affected one plant it can spread unchecked through the crop. By its very nature such a system necessitates the use of chemical controls.

Although overall my garden is very diverse, I need to grow crops and it is not realistic for me to scatter them all around the whole garden. In practice I need to create my own mini monocrops, which make good environments for pests. If natural predators aren't adequate protection my first line of defence is a physical technique, like using mesh to keep carrot root fly off my carrots. My second line of defence will be a safe spray such as a rhubarb, elder or wormwood mixture. If this does not work and my crop is likely to fail I will resort to an organically approved pesticide such as derris. These are dangerous to the natural balance of your garden. They will kill the pests but they will also kill their predators. I don't like doing it, but I will if I believe it is necessary.

Bear in mind that the more you stretch nature's boundaries the more likely you are to fail. Avoid growth checks and stresses such as lack of nutrients, minerals, trace elements and water. Growing plants out of season is asking for trouble and not efficient in terms of time or resources. This doesn't mean that you shouldn't do it, but it will probably be more difficult than growing the plants in season.

Observation is an important part of pest and disease control. If you spend half an hour just looking at your crops every day, you will spot any problems before they become disasters. Blackfly on broad beans can be contained if you spot them early. Noticing cabbage white butterflies flying around is the first indicator that you should start checking the underside of brassica leaves for clusters of eggs.

I do not have the space to include all possible pests and diseases affecting vegetables and fruit: this chapter is an overview of the more common ones, with possible remedies. There is more detail about the pests and diseases that affect each vegetable, fruit and herb in the A–Z sections. I have included some pest and disease books in the bibliography, and some of them have very good photographs to help with identification.

Small pests

Ants feed on the honeydew produced by aphids, and they will farm aphids in order to get it. In this sense the ants are a pest, particularly on broad beans where blackfly are a problem. Ants are said to dislike urine, and may be deterred from encouraging the blackfly if a dilute urine spray is used when the plants are 60cm high or more. Ants also dislike chervil, catnip and tansy. Steep the leaves of one of these plants in a barrel of water overnight then spray the water onto affected plants. In the soil, ants can be a pest if there are a lot of them. Their burrows can disturb root crops in particular. However, the soil in the nests is very fine, and it is worth collecting it for use in compost mixtures.

Aphids are a very common problem and you are likely to need to control them. There are many different types but they all live by sucking the sap out of the shoots and leaves of plants. If left unchecked, they will destroy the plants. They secrete sticky honeydew on the plants that a black, sooty mould develops on. They also spread disease. You can spray aphids off the plants with a jet of water, being careful not to damage the plants in the process. A rhubarb, elder leaf or wormwood spray will kill aphids without causing harm to ladybirds or bees. Soft soap can also be used but it will kill caterpillars as well as the aphids.

Capsid bugs have a shield-shaped body and eat leaves, flowers and buds. They are not really a big problem and I have never tried to control them in any way.

Caterpillars are a problem on many plants. The obvious sufferer is the brassica family, where whole plants are stripped of their leaves. The same can happen to gooseberry bushes and damage is often caused to other plants. The safest method of controlling caterpillar damage is to check the underside of leaves for little clusters of eggs. If you see any, just squash them. If you miss any you will quickly notice an infected plant by its gradual defoliation. At this point you will need to pick the caterpillars off one by one and feed them to the chickens. Covering brassicas with fleece will stop butterflies laying their eggs in the first place but this takes a lot of fleece and I just don't like the look of acres of fleece stretching across my garden for a whole summer. Safe controls that will curb a bad attack of caterpillars are salt spray and soft soap.

There is a biological control, Bacillus thuringiensis, allowed under organic standards. It kills caterpillars and nothing else. It is sprayed onto the leaves and when the caterpillars eat it, they die. I have used it once, on some winter cabbages that were beginning to be eaten by caterpillars. I had a fine crop of cabbages with absolutely no sign of caterpillars. My reservations are that it is indiscriminate – it kills all caterpillars that eat the sprayed leaves. There are many types of butterfly that I want to survive in my garden. Not only are they beautiful but they are part of my gardens balance, pollinating flowers and providing food for the birds.

Chafer grubs are common in my garden. They are about 4cm long, fat and white, with black bottoms and orange heads. They are usually found curled in a C shape and really are disgusting. They feed on roots and potatoes so if you find them, feed them to the birds. If you have chickens, they will think that the grubs are heaven sent.

Cutworms look rather like chafer grubs but they have a black head and an earthy coloured body. They eat through the stems of small plants at soil level. Ground beetles eat them and hoeing will help to bring them to the surface for birds to eat. If you find a line of wilting plants, dig about in the soil for them and feed them to the chickens.

Eelworms, or nematodes, are microscopic worm-like pests that affect onions and potatoes. In onions the young plants become stunted and swollen, and are susceptible to secondary rots. There is no control so as soon as the symptoms are noticed, pull the plant up and destroy it. The best way to avoid eelworm in onions is to keep to a sound rotation. If you do get onion eelworm, grow lettuce or brassicas for a year or two to clear the ground – it can survive in other crops without obvious symptoms but these vegetables aren't carriers. Make sure you buy onion sets and seeds from reputable growers.

Potato cyst eelworm is another kettle of fish and a serious problem – see Potatoes for more information.

Flea beetles are tiny, shiny, irridescent beetles that jump when something disturbs them. They can devastate a crop by eating thousands of tiny holes in leaves, particularly members of the brassica family. Use fleece or mesh to protect seedling crops and keep plants well watered in dry conditions.

Gooseberry sawfly caterpillars are pale green with lots of black spots. They eat the leaves of gooseberry bushes from mid to late spring, virtually stripping the plants of their leaves and can also affect red and white currants. The flies lay their eggs on the underside of leaves in the centre of the plant and they hatch into the caterpillars, which do the damage. Careful inspection of the leaves in the spring, squishing any eggs you find, will help control them but as there are three cycles in any one season it might be better to spray with derris or pyrethrum.

Leather jackets are the larvae of daddy long legs, or the crane fly, and they are ugly. They have a grey body with almost no head and definitely no legs and they eat roots and stems. They tend to be grassland pests so their numbers should decrease over the years if you have converted your plot from grass to a vegetable garden. Their predators are ground beetles and birds.

Millipedes have two pairs of legs per segment of body, unlike centipedes that only have one. They come in a range of colours and can damage seedlings and tubers and sometimes strawberry fruits. I wouldn't say they were a big problem unless you find huge quantities of them.

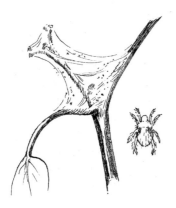

Red spider mite (RSM) is often a big problem in hot dry summers when they thrive both indoors and out. They are not visible without a magnifying glass but you can tell when you've got them because the leaves turn pale and there is a fine cobweb between the leaves and stems.

RSM affects covered crops, particularly cucumbers, mainly due to the higher temperatures, but they can also affect raspberries, strawberries and beans. Keeping indoor crops well watered, and misted if possible, seems to deter RSM. Outdoors, RSM is only usually a problem in very hot and dry summers so providing adequate water when these conditions prevail will prevent bad attacks. See cucumber problems in the A-Z for more information.

Slugs really are the most common and well-known pest in the garden. I use a range of tactics to combat them, but not beer traps. These are time consuming and I would need thousands dotted about my garden to make much difference. Inside my polytunnels, my greatest line of defence is ponds with frogs in them. I often find toads in the tunnels too. Both will keep slug populations down considerably and you can tell that they work because any significant slug damage is usually within a couple of metres of the doors, where the slugs are getting in from the outside. Another trick in tunnels is to have small planks of wood down between the rows of salad leaves. These are principally to tread on to avoid soil compaction, but if there is any slug damage on the seedlings all I need do is check underneath the planks for the culprits. Slicing slugs in half with my knife has become quite a satisfying chore.

Outside, slugs are another problem. Try to avoid creating hiding places for them such as blocks and planks around raised beds. I practise cultural techniques such as sowing susceptible crops in open expanses of dry earth. I also try to judge the weather when I sow the seed. In my experience, wet periods usually last three or four weeks, so if I can sow seed after about two weeks of wet weather the seedlings are likely to emerge through dry soil and should avoid the worst of the slugs. Admittedly this is rather hit and miss, but once the seedlings have emerged covering them with cloches will keep the surrounding soil dry and provide warm conditions which will encourage the plants and deter slugs.

A biological control for slugs (a nematode) is available and so far I have heard mixed responses to its effectiveness. It is a costly product and I have never tried it.

Snails, much like slugs, will eat almost any foliage very efficiently, and leave slime all over plants. They are much easier to see and much more pleasant to pick up than slugs. Walled gardens are particularly prone because walls provide lots of dark and moist cracks for snails to hide in. The only wild bird that is really keen on snails is the song thrush. Indian Runner ducks really love snails and slugs and don't eat vegetables. If you are tempted to keep poultry, you would do well to have a couple of these loose in your garden. Ducks do have big feet though, so you would need to protect your seed beds and young plants.

Thrips feed by sucking sap and will cause a white mottling effect on the upper side of leaves. They are usually black or pale yellow with narrow bodies 2mm long and two pairs of wings. In terms of vegetables, thrips affect onions and peas. In onions the thrips cause the leaves to discolour, leaving them less able to absorb sunlight. In peas thrips affect the pods, inhibiting seed development. They are more of a problem in hot and dry summers so adequate watering will keep them at bay. Mild infestations shouldn't cause a problem.

Weevils are black with pear shaped bodies and feed at night on leaves. The larvae are plump white grubs with no legs and an orange/brown head. They feed on roots and tubers. The larvae can be exposed during the winter with light digging, but they don't do a lot of damage really.

Wireworms are the larvae of the click beetle. They are thin, shiny, orange worms with red heads, 1–2cm long. They eat into tubers and roots, particularly potatoes, creating little black channels that are unsightly and make your crop difficult to sell. Because they are a grassland grub the best way to avoid them is not to grow roots in the first year after pasture. They can be caught by burying bits of potato in the soil for a few weeks, then digging them up and destroying them. As they don't like being disturbed a cultivated garden is not their favourite home so their numbers should reduce as the years go by.

Whitefly are a little like aphids in that they suck sap from leaves and excrete honeydew, which sooty black moulds grow on. They are often found on the bigger leaves of brassicas and if you can put up with them they tend not to be too much of a problem. Where they are a nuisance is on tomato plants. Keep the flies away by growing French marigolds around your tomatoes.

Woodlice, or chucky pegs, are known to most people. They live in the top layer of soil and eat decaying organic matter. However, they have a taste for young plants as well, particularly annual spinach and French beans grown under cover. I tend to tolerate woodlice because there's not much I can do about them. Keeping chickens in the polytunnel for a few weeks in the winter will clear up woodlice and virtually very other insect in sight.

Controlling small pests

Several approaches should be taken to controlling insect pests. Encourage as many natural predators as you can. Protect crops with physical barriers and keep an eye on your plants to spot any problems before they develop. As a last resort there are safe sprays as well as biological control – introducing a predator to a troublesome pest. General methods are described – for information specific to particular crops, see the A - Z sections.

Encouraging natural predators

The most obvious and natural way of keeping pests to a minimum is to encourage their predators into your garden. Providing good cover, habitats and food for them will entice them in and hopefully they will stay.

Anthocorid bugs eat aphids, mites, thrips, caterpillars, weevils and capsid bugs. They are particularly useful on soft fruit bushes and top fruit trees, where the bugs will eat eggs and pupae that are hiding in the cracks and crevices of the bark ready to cause trouble in the spring.

Birds will eat grubs, caterpillars, slugs, snails, aphids, aphids' eggs and pupae that over-winter in the top few centimetres of soil. Encouraging robins, tits and finches into your garden will lessen the numbers of these pests - lightly digging the ground in the winter will keep these birds happy. The song thrush, if you've got one, is invaluable as they love to eat snails. If you have no suitable hedging or trees around you, put up some nest boxes and you will encourage these birds to stay.

Centipedes are long, thin and shiny brown with segmented bodies, similar to millipedes. Each segment has one pair of legs so they are easy to identify. They eat small insects and slugs. They are found just beneath the soil surface and under old bits of wood etc. They need ground cover but they can find this adequately themselves.

Devils coach horses (or rove beetles) are really frightening looking beetles, very shiny and black and reminiscent of scorpions. Despite their looks they are good for the garden, eating root aphids, slugs, root fly larvae and many more pests. They tend to work at ground level and when you find them, they curl their back end up in just the same way as a scorpion.

Earwigs are usually seen as a pest but they have their uses in the garden, eating woolly aphids and codling moth eggs (a problem if you're growing apples and pears). They are often found in sweetcorn cobs but they are easy to knock off when harvesting. It's best to tolerate them even if you don't like them.

Ground (carabid) beetles are the shiny black beetles that scurry away and hide as soon as you uncover them. They are really good at consuming soil level pests, eating eelworms, cutworms, leather jackets, insect eggs, slugs etc. Encourage them with ground cover and don't mow your paths too often as they particularly like long grass to hide in.

Frogs and toads are really easy to keep in your garden. The current trend of building ponds in gardens can only be a good thing for frogs and toads and a bad thing for slugs. Both frogs and toads eat large numbers of slugs and are perfectly happy to stay in your garden given the right habitat. I have a pond in each of my polytunnels, which are virtually slug-free as a result. Toads only need water during the spring, to lay their eggs in, and merely providing a few slates and piles of rocks around the garden is enough to keep them happy. Frogs prefer to have a pond available all year round. Frogs and toads always return to the place they hatched to spawn so catching the adults and putting them in your pond is a waste of time. If you want them to breed in your pond you will need to get frogspawn (clumps of eggs) or toadspawn (long strings of individual jellies).

Hedgehogs are active at night, eating slugs, cutworms, woodlice, millipedes and wireworms. They can be encouraged to stay in your garden by leaving piles of logs and sticks for them to hide under during the day. Unfortunately there's not much hope of hedgehogs getting into my garden because it is surrounded by rabbit fencing. I did see one once and have no idea how it got into the garden, but I've never seen it since.

Honey and bumble bees pollinate flowers, fruits and vegetables. They are essential in keeping the garden healthy. Bumble bees are particularly useful as they will continue to fly around in the poorest of weathers when honey bees stay inside. Although they don't do much in terms of pest control, they are what makes your garden fruit. Using anything stronger than a safe insecticide is not advisable as they will kill bees as well as the pests you're trying to control.

Hoverflies look like wasps but are smaller, flatter and almost silent in flight so you shouldn't have much trouble recognising them. There are as many as 38 different varieties in this country and all of them are useful in the garden. Hoverfly larvae eat aphids, up to 600 each. Encourage the hoverflies into your garden by growing the plants they like and they are likely to reward you by laying their eggs on your plants, so there will be plenty of larvae on patrol. Any open, flat flower such as fennel, poached egg plant or convolvulus tricolor will attract them.

Hoverfly and larva

Lacewing larvae also eat aphids. Lacewings are easy to recognise, a light shade of green with very fine see-through wings. Lacewings can be encouraged into the garden with daisy type flowers including mustard and yarrow. You can encourage them to stay by putting lacewing hotels in your garden. These contain a pheromone lure that attracts the lacewings in November. Put the hotel in a shed for the winter and return it to the garden in the spring to release the lacewings.

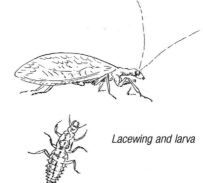

Lacewing and larva

Ladybird larva

Ladybirds and their larvae, which look like little blue dragons with bright orange spots on them, are well known as aphid eaters but they also eat thrips and mites. When they emerge in the spring they usually feast on the nettle aphid. This is one of the first aphids to appear and gives a boost to the ladybird population. The nettle aphid is specific to nettles so it's safe to encourage it in your garden, with clumps of nettles. As the season progresses the ladybirds and their larvae move on to other plants, eating aphids voraciously.

Parasitic wasps have a great Latin name, Aphidius, and they can do just as much damage as hoverfly larvae. They lay their eggs inside the eggs, larvae and pupae of other insects, where the young grow and hatch out before the host has a chance to grow up, thereby killing it. Different types of parasitic wasps kill caterpillars, whitefly and root fly larvae so they are well worth having in your garden. They can be attracted into your garden by providing umbellifer (fennel family) and compositae (daisy family) flowers, or can be introduced as a biological control.

Wolf spiders run across vegetation looking for insects to eat. They are often noticeable because the female carries a white ball full of eggs around with her. They seem to particularly like straw mulches as I see hundreds of them when I walk across straw in my garden.

Shrews eat insects, slugs, woodlice and earthworms. Never try and trap them in any way, although if you have traps for mice it is likely that you will catch a shrew occasionally.

Slow worms look like snakes but are really lizards without legs. They eat slugs, slugs and more slugs and should be left alone to get on with their job in the garden. Picking them up will often cause them to shed their tails, which can't do them any good.

Mechanical controls

Mechanical controls are basically barriers that keep insects away from your plants. You can use fleece, mesh or netting, all of which can be expensive. (*See Machinery, Tools and Equipment page 21, and in specific crops in the A-Z sections*).

Biological control

Biological control involves using insects to control insect pests. They are basically parasites or predators that are introduced to a crop that is infected with the host. Examples include Bacillus thuringiensis, a bacteria that devours caterpillars from the inside, and Phytoseiulius persimilis mites which eat red spider mite. Amongst other things, biological controls are available for aphids, vine weevils, whitefly and mealybugs. I tend not to use these controls because they are expensive. On a large scale biological controls are a much safer form of pest control than the natural pesticides and chemicals that can be used. (*See page 265 for sources and suppliers*).

Safe insect repellents and insecticides

Derris is based on rotenone, a natural extract from tropical plants. It is allowed under organic standards and will kill caterpillars, aphids, thrips, sawfly, flea beetles and mites. It has the advantage that it breaks down quickly in the soil. It is only to be used as a last resort and never routinely, as it also kills ladybirds and bees and is poisonous to fish.

Pyrethrum is made from the flowers of Chrysanthemum cinerariafolium. It acts directly on the pest and breaks down quickly. It can be used against aphids, flea beetles and small caterpillars. Like derris, pyrethrum should be used only as a last resort. It can be difficult to get hold of pyrethrum to use in an organic garden – the synergist piperonyl butoxide, which is not acceptable under organic standards, is often added to make it more effective.

Quassia is made from the chips of the tree Picrasma quassiodes. It is safer than derris and pyrethrum because it doesn't harm bees or ladybirds, but it does kill anthocorid bugs. It also kills aphids, sawfly, leaf miners and some caterpillars. You can buy it from chemists. Follow the instructions on the packet to prepare a solution to add to soft soap and spray onto the affected plants.

A rhubarb or elder leaf solution kills aphids and does not harm ladybirds or bees. Simmer 500g of rhubarb and/or elder leaves in about 2l of water, for an hour. Dilute one part to three with water and spray on the affected plants.

Soft soap is another safe solution, which kills aphids and caterpillars. Add 50g of potassium carbonate to 4l of hot water. Let it cool then spray on the affected plants.

A salt spray will curb a bad attack of caterpillars, without harming beneficial insects. Dissolve 50g of table salt in 4l of water and spray on to the plants. Never over-spray salt solution as an overly saline soil is not good for growing vegetables.

Tansy, wormwood and garlic

Tansy is a very effective insect repellent that can be grown in pots around the garden.
Wormwood is a perennial that will grow quite happily in the herb bed and can be used to make an insecticide. Boil 250g of wormwood leaves in a litre of water in an old saucepan. Used as a spray, the resulting broth will kill all sorts of aphids, but not the creatures that feast on them.
Garlic is said to repel insects of all sorts. Steep five chopped cloves in 5l of water for a night or two. Spray plants that are susceptible to aphid attack in particular and it will keep them at bay.

Unapproved chemical controls

If you are reading this book it is unlikely that you are planning to use serious chemical controls. They are dangerous and often unnecessary. Once they are in the food chain they will stay there, and one day they will kill us.

Big pests

Birds can be really useful in the garden, but they can also cause a lot of problems. For example, bullfinches are very good at eating pests that live in and around your soft fruit bushes but they will strip the buds from them in the winter. If you have problems with birds, net your crop.

Rabbits are my worst big pest problem. I keep them out with rabbit fencing around each of my three gardens. I use the standard mesh size (31mm), 1050mm high. The netting is attached to a post and wire fence to keep it upright. It is always recommended that rabbit netting be buried in the soil to stop rabbits burrowing underneath. I am lazy when it comes to this sort of work and lay the bottom 20cm along the ground facing outwards from my garden. The turf quickly grows through this to hold it down and any rabbits that come up against the fence try to dig down and meet more resistance.

Electric rabbit fencing is also available, and this is a good idea on a large scale. However, it is expensive and relies on an electric fencing unit (yet more expense) and an electricity supply. If you have mains electricity then this is handy but if you don't, you have to use two car batteries, one to run the electric fence and one on charge. Also you have to keep the grass down under the fence to stop it shorting out. I have little time for such maintenance in the summer months, and one of the advantages of my permanent fencing is that I can do any work on it in the winter.

If rabbits do manage to get through your fence, you will soon notice rabbit droppings amongst your vegetables and on your paths. You just need to go round the fence looking for holes in it, usually at about 20cm high, or holes beneath the fence. Use stones to block the holes in the ground and fill the holes in the fence with wire. Rabbits are really thick, they don't bother to burrow round the stones.

It is said that rabbits don't like tansy. I don't know if this is true but it's worth a go. If you have a rabbit problem and don't want to fence, maybe growing tansy plants around your garden, or in pots to place around where rabbits come into your garden, may encourage them go in the other direction from your vegetables.

Mice can be a problem with peas and beans. I sow these seed direct, but make sure they get growing quickly by pre-soaking them first. I have much more trouble with mice in my polytunnels in the spring. I literally have to trap them (this can be done humanely or inhumanely) before I sow any seeds that they are likely to eat. They are partial to all curcubit, bean, pea and sweetcorn seed. Last year I had to resow my curcubitae three times before I got a decent number of plants. What was most annoying was finding curcubit plants growing in other polytunnel beds where the seeds had been buried by the mice. Unfortunately they didn't take the plant labels with them so I had no idea what was what.

Moles can be a pest, burrowing along beneath a fresh crop of young seedlings and disturbing the roots. I have found this only happens when I have watered along a line of seedlings in dry weather. The water attracts worms, a real delicacy for moles, so you can't blame them really. Otherwise, I see moles as a valuable indicator in just how worm retentive my soil is, not to mention the way their tunnels help aerate my soil. The other thing to note is that moles are fiercely territorial and one acre of land will support a single mole family. So at worst you will have one or two moles to an acre.

Deer can be a real pain. They come into my garden from time to time, sometimes they do damage and sometimes they don't. Currently they are not enough of a pain to do anything about them. If I had regular damage I would consider putting up a deer fence, which would need to be a minimum of 2m high. If you can't do it yourself, get a fencing contractor in. The slight advantage to having a deer fence put up is you can attach rabbit netting to it. Also you have a perfect framework for soft fruits such as blackberries, hybrid berries, raspberries and cordon apples and pears, and whatever else you fancy.

Diseases

Ironically, it is the organic grower that is often at a loss when identifying diseases. The basis of organic growing is to create and maintain a healthy system in the first place and this tends to prevent problems from developing. I often think that I should have worked in a conventional market garden to learn to recognise pests and diseases. However this may well have put me off growing vegetables altogether so I'm glad I didn't.

There are so many possible diseases that I cannot hope to cover them in detail here. I have given an overview and suggested action for common problems. There is a fuller account of possible problems for each vegetable in the A–Z sections.

Botrytis, or grey mould, is the most common garden disease and appears as spotting on leaves which develops into a furry grey mould. It is far more common in cool and damp conditions and is often the result of inadequate ventilation in polytunnels and greenhouses, and overcrowding outdoors. Keeping a clean garden can help and any signs of this mould in polytunnels and greenhouses must be removed to prevent its spread.

Powdery and downy mildews are another common problem. Powdery mildew dusts the surface of leaves, particularly those of the cucurbitae family, usually when it is hot and the plants have not had quite enough water. Good ventilation and cutting off the affected leaves keeps it at bay. Downy mildew can get inside a plant and rot it completely. Both can be exacerbated by feeding with too much nitrogen. A potassium permanganate solution can be used to check mildews on pea plants. Add 10g to 12l of water and spray on the pea plants. For other affected plants, such as gooseberries with American mildew, dissolve 500g of washing soda in 20l of water, add 250g of soft soap and use as a spray. Plants affected with downy mildew can be sprayed with diluted milk. A copper fungicide will also keep downy mildew under control but this is a last resort and must not be used routinely.

Rusts affect many different plants, but particularly the allium family. They can be avoided by keeping plants well watered in dry spells and spacing the plants correctly to allow good ventilation. Excess nitrogen will make the leaves more susceptible to rust. It is possible to get varieties with rust resistance so if you have a particularly bad problem, always try and use these.

Sooty moulds are the black covering that grows on honeydew secreted by aphids. It is only really a problem for the plant if there is enough to block out the light, in which case the plant will gradually die. Treat the aphid problem and the sooty mould won't be a problem.

Wilts (Verticulum and Fusarium). Wilts are common in tomatoes and cucumbers grown in small gardens or in a greenhouse or polytunnel, where there is not sufficient space to follow an adequate rotation. It is also usually prevalent in conventional cropping systems where it is controlled with chemicals. The plants wilt at fruiting stage, recover overnight, then wilt again. The disease gets progressively worse until the plant dies. You can make sure that it is wilt by cutting into the stem about 60cm above the ground. If it is wilt there will be staining in the stem (brown for fusarium and grey for verticulum). If you have this in your soil then your best answer is to graft your desired variety onto a disease resistant rootstock - see the tomato section for further information.

Blight is an airborne fungus that affects potatoes and tomatoes and is prevalent in cool, wet summers. It starts as brown patches on the edges of leaves and spreads down stems, gradually killing the foliage. It then passes into the soil and affects the tubers, which go brown, rotten and very smelly. It can also get into the ground by dripping from infected leaves.
Bordeaux mixture (copper fungicide) is used in the control of blight in potatoes and tomatoes, but it is likely to be banned under organic standards fairly soon. As it is preventative rather than curative you must have some idea of how bad a season it is for blight before using it. Keeping in touch with other growers and DEFRA will give you some warning. Blight seems to nearly always start in the west of the country, spreading gradually to the drier areas of the country. Bordeaux mixture is basically copper sulphate and needs dissolving in water before being applied to the leaves of potato and tomato crops. It needs to be reapplied every two weeks for adequate protection. My strategies for containing blight are described in the potatoes section.

Seeds and Seed Saving

Seeds are the all-important germs of life that take our plants from one generation to the next. They might look like nothing much, but when you think what can grow out of them, they are amazing. We must take care of them to get the best from out garden: they need to be stored in the right conditions and they do have a best before date.

Seeds

A seed is a small capsule containing the genetic make up of the plant that it will grow into, and enough nitrogen to give it a start. Adding warmth and moisture starts the seed's wake-up mechanism, and germination begins. Most seeds have just enough nitrogen, potassium and phosphorous to get them to the baby stage. After that they need nutrition from an external source, the medium they are growing in, to develop into their mature stages. Seeds come in all sorts of shapes and sizes and their characteristics tend to reflect their plant family. For example, a carrot seed looks like a small fennel seed: they are both members of the umbelliferae family. Likewise the seeds of tomato and potato plants look the same, as do the leaves and fruits. You are never likely to grow a potato from seed as you would a tomato, though you could have fun trying.

Buying seeds

Try to select organic seeds if you can as these are best suited to grow under organic conditions. It is wise to choose disease resistant seeds, but if you have not had a problem with disease in that particular crop and you fancy trying one that doesn't claim resistance then there's no reason not to try it.

I buy most of my seeds from Tuckers growers' list. This means I can buy my seed in bulk at a reasonable price. I buy additional seeds from other catalogues depending on the variety I want and where it is available. (*See page 266 for addresses of seed companies*).

Buying all the varieties you need can add up to quite a lot of money. If you don't want to buy a lot, for whatever reason, you could try setting up a seed buying group with friends and colleagues. Members of LETS systems, Friends of the Earth, local allotment or organic groups are often interested in this sort of activity. It makes sense if you can cut your seed bill by sharing the cost with others.

Valuable Vegetables

How long do seeds keep?

If you are buying seeds for a large market garden then it's often worth bulk buying to reduce costs, even if you're not going to use all the seeds in that year. For example, the cost of bean and pea seed is quite high in individual packets but they last at least two years so you can buy them by weight and save quite a lot of money. Seeds must be stored in dry, cool conditions. If you have a big fridge then put them in the bottom in an airtight plastic container. I use an old filing cabinet in a cool part of my house. The following table gives you an idea as to how long seed will keep:

One year	onion, parsnip.
Two years	runner beans, peas, salsify, swede, sweetcorn, Swiss chard, turnip.
Three years	French beans, broccoli, cabbage, carrot, cauliflower, lettuce.
Four years	Brussels sprouts, celeriac, celery, kale, kohl rabi, leek, radish, tomato, broad bean.
Five years	squash, pumpkin, cucumber, beetroot, spinach.

Seed and tuber saving

Seeds and our genetic heritage are falling more and more into the hands of multinational biotech companies. More and more hybrids are being introduced and genes are being patented, taking plant breeding out of the hands of gardeners. Saving seed is helping to preserve the genetic variety of our heritage vegetables. It does seem wise for us to hang on to our native diverse seed bank if we can.

While I am a great believer in seed saving, I literally don't have the time or capabilities to save all my own seed. Seed saving is a huge subject and requires a lot of organisation and dedication, neither of which I have to spare. It's all very well being a jack of all trades, but not if you end up being master of none.

However, some seeds are very straightforward to save, so I do. I try and save the seeds from coriander, runner beans, garlic and shallots every year. Others, such as those of the brassica family, require far too much effort and skill for me to bother about. I have given a brief description of the seeds, bulbs and tubers I do save and how I do it. Remember that if you save the seed from an F1 or other hybrid it will probably not grow true to type next year. Don't forget to label and date any seed you save. Enthusiasts should read Back Garden Seed Saving for more details (*see bibliography*).

Broad, French and runner beans

These are easy to save. Just leave the last 2 to 3m of plants in the row and let the bean pods develop until their cases go brown and withered. Strip the plants and leave the withered pods somewhere dry and cool and then remove the seeds. If you have people helping you in your garden, remember to let them know which plants you don't want them to pick, perhaps by tying a ribbon or string to the plants. With runner beans I put a separate wigwam in a different part of the garden from the main crop and leave them to mature.

Garlic

It's not necessary to grow garlic from seed, just plant some cloves from the bulbs you grew the year before. When selecting the bulbs for replanting, make sure that you pick the biggest and least damaged, and they must be disease-free. There is no evidence to suggest that the biggest cloves produce the biggest bulbs but I have been selecting my bulbs for four years and they are definitely getting bigger and better every year. This might be because I now know how to grow a better bulb after doing it for nine years. If there is any sign of disease or virus it is better to buy in new stock and start again.

Jerusalem artichokes

Leaving a few plants untouched over the winter will provide enough tubers to dig up and replant in February or March.

Lamb's lettuce

Leave a couple of plants outside to flower in the spring. One or two plants will provide enough seed for the next years crop and more. If you leave them where they are, they will seed direct and produce lots of baby plants which can then be transplanted to a polytunnel or greenhouse to grow on to a bigger size.

Lettuce

Lettuce seed is cheap and relatively difficult to save but can be done by leaving a couple of plants to run to seed.

Peas

Pea seed is easy to save but it is time consuming. As with French beans, leave one end of the row and mark it to make sure it isn't picked. Let the pods dry as much as possible before picking, then leave on a warm windowsill until completely dry. Remove peas from the pods and store in a cool, dry place.

Rocket

If left to flower, rocket (and wild rocket) will reseed itself readily.

Peppers and chillis

These are certainly one of the easier vegetables to save seed from. Pick the ripe fruit and let them dry completely on a windowsill, then just remove the seeds. If you grow more than one variety close together they may cross-pollinate.

Salsify and scorzonera

Sowing a few seeds in your flower bed and letting the plants go to seed the following year is the easiest way to save seed. They seed themselves quite readily; the first year I grew them they continued in the same area for another three years on the edges of beds.

Shallots

It's best to save the bulb rather than the seed. Keep a proportion of the crop to replant and try to save the biggest bulbs, or clusters, and you will find you get bigger shallots every year.

Tomatoes

Saving seed from tomatoes is quite easy. Remember that hybrid varieties will not grow true from saved seed. Just take some tomato seed from the fruit and put it in a jam jar with some water for a couple of weeks. It will go mouldy, which is fine. Then pour off the excess liquid and mould, rinse the seeds and lay them out on kitchen towel on a sunny windowsill until they are completely dry. Store in an old envelope somewhere dry and cool.

Introduction

I n this section I describe how to grow all of the vegetables that I sell in my box scheme. It is also possible to grow many exotic vegetables, with perseverance and the right equipment, but I believe that this is inappropriate. As a nation we have been growing vegetable varieties that suit our soils and climate for centuries. These vegetables are well adapted for the conditions that prevail here, and I think that we should continue to develop and appreciate what we have nurtured over generations. They provide us with a wonderful range of foods, varying through the year as the seasons change.

Vegetable families

If you want to recognise vegetables and understand the way they grow, it is handy to know a little about their origins. Vegetables are classified into types, or families. Knowing which vegetables are related allows you to predict what pests and diseases they are likely to suffer from, whether they add fertility or not, and where they should be grown in your rotation. You can nearly always tell the type of family a plant belongs to by the seed it produces. Plants that appear to be exceptions to this usually do fit once we find out more. For example, potatoes are closely related to tomatoes, and the seeds are very similar although we very rarely see them because we grow potatoes from tubers.

Leguminosae

This family includes clover, peas and beans. They are all important in our diets, providing a useful source of protein. In terms of gardening, they are beneficial because they fix nitrogen in the soil, adding fertility for the following crops. Nitrogen fixing is a complicated process but it is useful to understand it. Bacteria live in nodules on the roots, and fix nitrogen from the air. The nitrogen is used to feed the bacteria as well as the plants they live in. For the garden to benefit from this process, the roots of the plants should either be left in the ground once the crop has been harvested or added to the compost heap. If you grow clover as a green manure, cut the plants and leave them on the surface or dig them in to the bed that you grew it in, for the nitrogen to benefit the next crop. In general, leguminous plants grow well in soils rich in phosphorous and potassium, but dislike acid soils. Most pea and bean seeds are big enough to be sprouted before planting which speeds up the growing process.

Cruciferae

This is the brassica family, including all the cabbage type plants - Brussels sprouts, cauliflowers, kales, calabrese, swedes, turnips, radish, kohl rabi, cabbages and broccoli. They are biennials, so they can provide us with a leafy crop for a whole year before they run to seed. The seeds are quite distinctive being pellet or ball shaped, a bit like lead shot. Some of the radish roots are particularly deep rooting which helps to penetrate soil pans and break up the subsoil. The most important disease in this family is club-root.

Solanaceae

This family includes potatoes, tomatoes, capsicum and aubergines. Potatoes and tomatoes have very similar fruits and leaves. They originate from central and south America and suffer in cold weather. A hint of frost will scorch the leaves, halting growth and fruiting. They are susceptible to pests such as eel-worm, so must be rotated in the garden. You may have heard gardeners asking smokers not to touch their tomato crops, or even smoke near them. This is because tobacco is a member of the same family and often carries viruses that will infect tomatoes. Another big problem is blight which can travel from potatoes to tomatoes and vice versa quite easily but doesn't seem to cause capsicums and aubergines any problem. Potatoes have quite a dense canopy which helps shade out weeds leaving a clean soil for the next crop. In my experience you still have to weed or mulch potatoes to achieve this, despite their canopy cover.

Umbelliferae

This family includes carrot, parsnip, celery, celeriac, parsley, lovage, fennel and dill. You can recognise these as umbellifers when they flower as they all have masses of tiny flowers splayed out a little like an umbrella. If you can leave any of these plants to flower in the garden it will be beneficial, even though the plant is effectively finished from your point of view. The flowers attract hoverflies, and hoverflies and their larvae eat vast numbers of aphids. Carrot and parsnip roots are good at penetrating deep into the soil bringing up useful nutrients from the subsoil. Also for helping to break up soil pans and improve soil structure.
A common problem with umbelliferous plants is the time it takes for the seed to germinate. In ideal conditions it can take three weeks, longer if the soil is too cold. A major pest of the umbellifer family is the carrot root fly. They lay their eggs in the soil at the top of the root. Maggots hatch out of the eggs and eat into the root. They can make it almost inedible. Carrot root fly usually feeds on the roots of cow parsley and hemlock, which are also umbellifers.

Alliaceae

This is the allium family, including onions, shallots, leeks, garlic and surprisingly, asparagus. You can recognise them by the way the leaves grow straight up from the base of the plant. The leaves aren't veined and tend to be like blades, similar to lilies. The shape of the leaves are perfect for channelling rain down the leaves and stems to the base of the plant directly to the roots – natures answer to design-er engineering. They store their energy in their root bulbs, allowing them to regrow the following year. Alliums suffer from pests and diseases such as eelworms and white rot so they must be rotated quite strictly, but if you leave some to flower in borders or pots they will help attract beneficial insects.

Chenopodiaceae

This is the beetroot, spinach and chard family. They are tolerant and hardy, easy to grow and so good for you that I have come to love them as vegetables. The seeds tend to come in little clusters, which actually contain 4 or 5 seeds each. Sow them thinly to avoid the need for thinning. They suffer from so few pests and diseases that rotating them isn't important. Even so I tend to rotate them to maintain a balance in the soil nutrients. They all have very similar leaves which contain oxalic acid and this can be dangerous in large quantites. The herb sorrel is in the same family and has large concentrations of oxalic acid, so don't eat too much of it.

Cucurbitaceae

This is the cucumber, melon, squash, pumpkin, courgette and marrow family. They all have elongated seeds, retain water in their fruits and are not tolerant of cold conditions. They tend to have trailing shoots and large leaves and are reminiscent of tropical plants, which is their origin. They must have plenty of water during the growing season and the more delicate and fleshy they are, the more prone they are to viruses and pests. Squashes and pumpkins are quite tough and grow well outdoors in this climate, whilst delicate cucumbers and melons need more heat and lusher conditions so are best grown indoors.

Compositae

This is the daisy family, which includes lettuce, artichoke, chicory, endive, salsify, scorzonera and dande-lion. The flowers give them away, all of them resembling the common garden daisy. The salad vegetables in this group tend to have a bitter taste with a milky sap and this bitterness is very good for you – it stimulates the production of bile which helps aid digestion. This family make up much of the bulk that I put in salad bags. Globe and Jerusalem artichokes tend to taste very earthy. All the members of the compositae family rarely suffer from disease, but as with all other crops, it is wise to rotate the short-lived plants if you can.

Gramineae

This is the grasses, which includes cereal crops. The only vegetable I grow in this family is sweetcorn, which really is very like grass only very tall and with large kernels.

Artichokes - Globe

Globe artichokes are seen as a great delicacy in this country. They have the same earthy flavour as Jerusalem artichokes and being a perennial plant will produce heads for three or more years before needing to be replaced. A bonus of growing globe artichokes is that the plants are very attractive.

Types and varieties

The usual variety grown is Green Globe which produces large heads. Purple Globe gives smaller heads but the plants are more hardy and as globe artichoke plants are particularly susceptible to the cold and wet this is probably the better variety to grow.

Soil, site and rotation

Globe artichokes like a well-drained soil and although you don't need a fine tilth it's a good idea to try and raise them up a bit from the surrounding ground on a slight mound. They prefer a pH of 6.5, need plenty of sun and like a sheltered site.

They are a member of the compositae family which is not affected by many pests and as it is a perennial then it does not fit into a standard rotation. However, as plants only last for three or four years you can choose a different site in the garden for new plants.

Sowing and planting

It is easy to grow new plants from the suckers you find at the base of established plants. Dig around the root in the spring to reveal the suckers and slice them off with a sharp knife. Plant them in their growing positions, 45cm apart.

If you don't have access to established plants you will need to raise plants from seed. Sow in 7.5cm pots in late winter at 18°C. When they have emerged put them somewhere warm until April or May then plant out as you would the suckers. In a good season the plants will sometimes produce heads in their first year but they usually come into production the following year.

Food, water and mulch

Adding organic matter to the soil will benefit the plants but it should be done before planting up a new bed and put on as a mulch in subsequent years. Despite liking a well-drained soil, globe artichokes do need plenty of water so it's a good idea to add a straw mulch around the plants and water well in dry weather.

Seasonal care

The most important thing to remember when you are growing globe artichokes is to protect the over-wintering base from cold and wet. In October or November, before the really hard frosts set in, cover the bases of the plants with a thin layer of straw then a square of plastic and then another mound of straw. This will stop the bases from rotting even in the harshest winter. If you're lazy, like me, just cover with a large clay pot with a hole in it.

Succession and continuity

Basically you get globe artichokes when they decide to form heads, from July to September. Globe artichokes also take up a lot of space. So, if you want to sell them you will need a large bed with 45-60cm square allocated per plant. You will only get one or two globes per plant.

Problems

The main problem is slugs so chose a dry period in the spring to plant out and don't mulch until the plants are established.

Harvest, storage and sale

It is important to harvest the heads when they are still closed because as soon as they start to open they become tough. If you harvest them when they are very young the whole head can be eaten. To cook them, steam them for 15 minutes then peel off the leaves and dip the base in butter.

I never sell globe artichokes as I only grow a few in my back garden. They need a lot of my time and space and I'm never convinced that they are worth the effort. However, I do plan to grow them on quite a large scale as I can imagine the delight on my customers faces when they find globe artichokes in their boxes.

Profit and efficiency

As I have said above, globe artichokes require a lot of time and space and I'm not convinced that they are profitable. However, they are a delicacy and they will add considerable value to vegetable boxes even if only as a one off.

Hints and tips

Don't mulch the plants until they are established.
Get new plants form basal suckers.
Purple globe artichokes are hardier than the green variety.
Protect the crowns in winter.

Artichokes - Jerusalem

The edible tuber of the Jerusalem artichoke has an incredibly earthy flavour and can be roasted, made into soup or added to stews. They are relatively easy to grow and remarkably pest free. They can be grown in the same spot year after year and, given that they can grow up to 2 metres tall, can also be useful as a windbreak.

A word of caution when eating – this plant has the nickname 'fartichoke' due to its affect on the human digestive system. For most people this is a mild symptom that is quite harmless but for some it can cause uncomfortable abdominal pain. If you've never eaten Jerusalem artichokes before try a small amount the first time round and increase as you see fit. Peeling the tubers helps to offset this problem.

Types and varieties

People are often confused by Jerusalem artichokes, mainly because they are less well known than globe artichokes. The main difference is which part of the plant you eat – in the case of the Jerusalem artichoke it is the tuber. There are a number of varieties available but by far the easiest to cook with are Fuseau. This has fewer knobbly bits than most varieties and so is easier to clean.

Soil, site and rotation

Some people grow Jerusalem artichokes simply by leaving a patch of ground which has had artichokes in it and allowing any that are left in to regrow. If you're a lazy gardener then this method will suffice, but if you're growing them for sale a little care and attention will reward you with good sized tubers and plenty of them.

I always grow my Jerusalem artichokes in the same place, to prevent them spreading across the garden and to make use of a piece of ground next to a hedge where they won't shade other plants. The ground is mucked every two years and in the intervening year I don't add anything. They like an acid soil so keep the pH below 6.5.

Sowing and planting

In March I clear the bed and dig up any remaining plants for seed tubers. I then add a layer of fairly raw muck and cover the bed with plastic – this reduces the incidence of perennial weeds and prevents any rogue tubers from regrowing. Cut a cross in the plastic every 45-60cm in a diagonal pattern (like a number five on a dice), three rows thick in a 1.5m wide bed. Plant the tubers through the plastic in a 20cm deep hole, with the shoots pointing upward. The exact depth isn't really important but the shoots should be a good 10cm beneath the surface. Water each tuber then cover the plastic with a 10cm layer of straw, leaving the area immediately over the tubers clear. This bed can then be left for the whole season until you are ready to start harvesting in late October.

Food, water and mulch

If the weather is particularly dry in August, when most of the bulking up the tubers occurs, make sure you water the bed well. Adding composted muck every two years and watering in August will give you tubers ranging from 5-25cms long. Mulch as described above.

Seasonal care

There is little to do during the growing season as weeds and moisture are taken care of with the initial mulching. When harvesting the plants, chop up the stems into lengths and add them to your compost heap so that their ends stick out of the sides of the heap. The stems, being hollow, will help introduce air into the heap.

Succession and continuity

Jerusalem artichokes don't store well, they start to dry up after a few weeks, but they can be left in the ground until you need them. They can be eaten all through the winter and make a nice change from the usual run of parsnips, swedes and leeks.

Problems

Being a member of the daisy family (compositae), Jerusalem artichokes are related to sunflowers and lettuces and consequently will suffer from the same problems, namely lettuce root aphids (Trama troglodytes). These are beige or grey aphids, 2 to 3 mm long, found on the tubers and they secrete a white powdery substance. They can make the plant wilt in dry, sunny weather. The only method of control is to rotate the crops, as the aphids will over-winter on any tubers left in the soil. I have had root aphids for two years with no effect on the size of the tubers or the vigour of the plants, but I will move the Jerusalem artichoke bed should the infestation become detrimental.

Sclerotinia is a fungus that appears as a white fluffy growth with large black sclerotia in it, usually on the stem. It is encouraged by cold and damp weather and is best controlled by burning any affected material and rotating the crop every four years. Slugs will attack the odd shoot as they emerge from the soil but Jerusalem artichokes are very strong growers and the majority of those you plant will get away quickly before the slugs really get a chance.

Harvest, storage and sale

Artichokes can be harvested from October to February/March. Dig as many as you need as they will only store in a closed paper sack for 2 to 3 weeks before going soft and wrinkly. Each plant should give between 10 and 20 tubers. As a general rule, I tend to only give my customers artichokes once or twice a year as some people really can't eat them.

Profit and efficiency

Jerusalem artichokes are worth more than most root crops and as there is little outlay in terms of seed and labour they are quite a profitable crop. You can prepare the bed they are to grow in as early as February which means they won't take up valuable spring work time.

Hints and tips

Warn your customers about the possible affect of Jerusalem artichokes on their digestive systems and suggest recipes like roasted artichokes.

Use old artichoke stems to introduce air into the compost heap.

They are a good alternative to potatoes for those who are intolerant of starch.

Asparagus

Asparagus is a vegetable that I grow only for myself. As with globe artichokes, it requires a lot of time and space. Although it is a perennial vegetable that can last up to 20 to 25 years you get very little from a large area. This makes it a speciality rather than profitable vegetable for sale. It takes 2 to 3 years to establish a bed ready for harvest so the land is effectively wasted for that time.

Types and varieties

You can grow asparagus from seed or from crowns (one year old roots). You will get a crop more quickly from crowns as you have effectively stolen a season on the seed. You can also increase the speed of cropping by buying hybrid crowns that will crop after one year.

Soil, site and rotation

Asparagus needs good drainage and a pH of 6.5 together with plenty of sun. The most important factor is to keep perennial weeds from invading the crop. When you prepare the bed make sure that you remove any perennial weeds because once the asparagus starts to develop it's difficult to dig around it's roots without causing damage.

Asparagus is a perennial crop and survives for twenty odd years; thinking in terms of rotation it might be wise to choose a new site when you are planting a new bed.

Sowing and planting

In spring sow seeds in a seed bed, thinning to 10cm apart, or in 15cm pots. The plants will be ready to move to their permanent bed, 35cm apart, the following spring.

If you have bought crowns then make sure you soak them for a couple of hours before planting. Dig a trench the width of your spade and make a small mound in the bottom. Place the crowns on the mound, spreading their roots over it. Fill in the trench with a mixture of compost and soil and water the crowns in well.

Food, water and mulch

Water in dry weather. In the autumn, after weeding, apply a layer of compost or muck and then mulch with straw.

Seasonal care

Weed the bed in the winter before feeding and mulching.

Succession and continuity

Asparagus will crop from April to May. The spears will continue to shoot up from the ground for about 4 to 6 weeks and will provide you with a very tasty vegetable when there is little else to be had. Stop cutting in June and leave some of the rootstock to grow up into ferns during the rest of the season.

This growth will provide the roots with the nourishment they need to grow fresh new spears the following year. Your bed should last for 20 to 25 years so start a new one after 10 to 15 years. It should be in full production by the time your first bed begins to slow down.

Problems

Asparagus beetles are very distinctive, mainly black with scarlet and gold spots. They can be seen on the ferns in the summer and eat the leaves and shoots. The larvae, which look like little grey grubs, are found on the plant later in the season. They also feed on the leaves, eventually destroying the plant. The easiest method of control is to dust with derris but as my asparagus bed is only 2m by 4m it doesn't take me long just to wander around and pick the beetles off and squash them. This won't destroy all the culprits because you'll always miss a couple, but it keeps the problem to a minimum.

Asparagus rust appears as orange blisters on the stems and leaves in the summer but if you keep the soil well fed and watered the plants will often grow through the problem.

Harvest, storage and sale

Asparagus plants need to establish themselves for one or two years before they are ready for harvest. It is not obvious when they are ready but they must have time to establish their rootstock before you plunder their spears. Begin harvesting the spears lightly in the second year when they are ready to cut and then more vigorously in subsequent years. Never harvest all the spears as you need to let some of them establish to produce the tall ferns which grow during the summer and replenish the root. When the spears are about 10cm above the ground and their tops are still tightly closed, cut them about an inch below the ground. If selling your asparagus tie them in small bundles, raffia will not mark the stems, and try to make them all the same length by leaving more of the root on the smaller spears.

Profit and efficiency

The only way this crop can be profitable is if your running costs are low, that is you own the land, and you can charge a good price for the crop.

Hints and tips

Remove all perennial weeds from the bed before planting your asparagus.
Reduce the time between planting and harvesting by buying hybrid crowns.
Start a new asparagus bed in time for it to be productive before your first bed begins to slow down.

Aubergines

Aubergines are a difficult crop at the best of times and it has taken me years to master them. They come in many shapes and sizes; white, green, striped, long, round, stumpy as well as the more familiar long purple varieties. I do grow them for my customers, but I love them and mostly grow them for myself.

Types and varieties

Aubergines need a long and warm season to crop to their full potential. Considering our climate and growing them to sell, I would recommend an F1 variety which should do well. Non-hybrids are fine if you just plan to grow them for your own consumption. Try Vista F1 and Long Tom.

Soil, site and rotation

Aubergines are related to tomatoes and peppers so grow them in this part of the rotation. They benefit from a long, warm season so it is a good idea to grow them under cover in the greenhouse or polytunnel.

Prepare the bed for the aubergines by working in a good dose of well rotted muck or compost, a barrow full every square metre will do. The plants will be transplanted into their final growing bed so a medium tilth will do.

Sowing and planting

I start the seed off at 18 - 21°C in a propagator, in late February. They start off in polystyrene modules and when 10cm tall I put them into 10cm pots. They stay in the propagator until they have doubled in size and are then transferred to an open propagator in March (one with the bottom heat still applied but with no top). This system dries the root ball out more quickly than in a covered propagator so it's important that they are adequately watered.

In late April to early May the plants should be ready to be transferred to the polytunnel. It really helps if you give them extra protection from the cold, in the form of a double fleece tent around each plant. Leave this in place for a week or two, unfolding it during the day when it's warm enough and remove it completely when the plants have got used to their new environment. You will need to stake each plant with a metre high stake and you can attach your fleece tent to the stake.

Food, water and mulch

I only water the plants until the first flower buds appear and then I start to feed with comfrey liquid once a week. If it is particularly dry and hot I water them between feeds.

Seasonal care

When the first tiny aubergines start to make an appearance I limit the number of flowers and side shoots that are emerging. It is often suggested that you should limit each plant to 4 fruits, but I have managed to get between 6 and 10 fruits on plants by giving them a long growing season. If you have a kind autumn the plant will continue right into October.

Succession and continuity
It is difficult to get any continuity with aubergines, they will be ready from early August to mid October.

Problems
As for peppers and chillis.

Harvest, storage and sale
Harvest the fruits when they have a good shine on them. They will store if kept cool but they tend to lose their shine. Sell as and when they become available.

Profit and efficiency
Aubergines are relatively expensive to buy in the shops and are generally much sought after. Producing fresh aubergines for you and your family or to sell will always be profitable because they are in such demand. I try to provide each of my 100 customers with aubergines twice a year and I have plans to increase this figure.

Hints and tips
Ensure a long growing season.
Grow an F1 variety to sell.

Beetroot

Such a maligned vegetable yet such a treat to eat and what a fantastic colour for a simple root vegetable. Beetroot is a great favourite of mine, not only does it taste fantastic but it is easy to grow. It has little need for rotation and the appetite of a dustbin, that is, eating up all the leftovers in the soil. Also its versatility in the kitchen leaves nothing to be desired. It can be grated raw, steamed for 20 minutes as a cooked vegetable, made into Borscht (Russian soup), baked like a potato, roasted, made into juice or pickled. If you're not sure whether you like beetroot or not try your own home grown version but be careful not to over cook it.

Types and varieties
There are plenty of varieties to be had, with round or cylindrical roots and all manner of colours; yellow, crimson, orange and white or alternately coloured rings. They all seem to be easy to grow but beetroot does have a tendency to bolt so I stick to one variety, Boltardy. Not only is it resistant to bolting but it can grow to a mammoth size without getting tough.

Soil, site and rotation

Beetroot will grow on fairly poor soil. It needs a pH of about 6.5 and good drainage. A medium tilth is okay as long as you use ordinary seed that comes as a cluster – if you use the new mono-seeded varieties you will need a finer tilth. Beetroot can be grown in most sites but will grow best in full sun. However, it is a very easy vegetable to grow and if you have a shady area then use it for beetroot because although it will take longer to grow it'll get there eventually.

As a member of the chenopodiaceae family, beetroot suffers from few diseases so can be placed anywhere in the rotation. However, I tend to grow it in unused potato or tomato beds.

Sowing and planting

Beetroot needs to be sown about 2.5cm deep in rows 30cm apart. You can grow beetroot in blocks by sowing 1 or 2 seeds per module and planting out once they have grown enough to form a root ball (about 2.5 to 5cm high).

Food, water and mulch

On my soil beetroot requires little feeding so I do not add muck or compost. It does need extra water when it is very dry but as long as you use a bolt-resistant variety it should grow well with average rainfall. As a general rule I don't mulch beetroot; they don't really seem to need it unless it's a particularly dry year.

Seasonal care

Rows of beetroot will need weeding a few times through the season. When they have grown an inch or two is a good time to hoe and hand weed around the rows where the hoe can't get to.

Succession and continuity

You need to make at least four sowings. The first sowings can be made under cover in late February or early March. You can sow outside by late March if you've warmed the soil, early April if you haven't. I follow this with more sowings in May and June. This will keep you in beetroot throughout most of the year. Those sown in June can be covered with straw when the weather turns frosty or lifted and stored inside for the winter.

If you sow beetroot at the density I have suggested it's possible to get a lot more beetroot out of a bit of ground than is usually suggested. As the beetroot reach a size a little bigger than a golf ball you can start to pull them out of the row, leaving the smaller ones more space, light and nutrients to carry on. This method saves a lot of time, space and effort as you don't need to sow beetroot every five minutes to make sure you have them at an edible size all through the season.

Problems

If the season is very dry and you neglect your beetroot they will suffer with aphids on their leaves, which stunt their growth. Keep them well watered and they won't suffer too much.
The beetroot roots sometimes get a little chomped around the top by adventurous slugs and can get

92

nibbled by rabbits and mice.

My most common problem with beetroot is the black warty growths that sometimes appear on the roots. This is caused by boron deficiency. I could treat it by adding borax or seaweed meal but the damage is so little that I'm more inclined to just keep adding compost and muck to the soil each year.

The beet leaf miner is a small white maggot that can eat the internal tissues of the leaf, making them go pale then papery. This is usually not much of a problem but if it seems to be affecting the growth, remove the affected leaves and burn them.

Harvest, storage and sale

Start harvesting when the roots are a little bigger than a golf ball. They can be harvested up to cricket ball size without losing their tenderness but they sell better when they are smaller.

When harvesting beetroot keep the leaves on to sell with the root. The leaves are a good alternative to spinach and can be eaten raw in salads (this is not generally known so tell your customers about it in newsletters) or lightly steamed and eaten with oil and vinegar. As the season progresses the leaves begin to look a bit tatty and it's better to remove them before sale. Twist, rather than cut, the tops off and you'll find they don't bleed.

You can leave beetroot in the ground until quite late in the year, sometimes all the way through, but it is best to pull a few, twist off their tops and either keep in a sack somewhere cool or bury them in sand in a bucket.

Profit and efficiency

Beetroot aren't a hugely profitable crop because their market price is often very low. During the early part of the season I charge 80p for a bunch of 4 beetroot with the leaves on but later when they are sold without their leaves the price is reduced to between 50p and 60p. This is because the flavour and tenderness of the early beet far outweighs that of the older specimens. Also the young leaves make a colourful addition to a salad and can be used as a substitute for spinach. As it is a relatively easy crop to grow with good staying power and few management problems it rates as better than average on the efficiency side.

Hints and tips

Introduce your customers to this vegetable with recipes, information and advice on cooking because many people are unaware of it's sterling qualities.

When cooking always scrub the beetroot to remove all soil. Never remove the top, bottom or any blemishes before cooking or it will bleed, reducing the colour and taste of the root. To cook beetroot as a simple vegetable, steam for about 20 - 30 minutes, depending on size, then top, tail and skin. I always cook too many so that I can eat them cold the next day or slice them into vinegar to make them last even longer in the fridge. They can also be baked, like potatoes, or grated raw as a salad vegetable.

It might also be advisable to warn your customers of the dramatic but harmless effect beetroot can have on the colour of their urine and faeces.

Brassicas

This section refers to Brussels sprouts, cabbages, calabrese, cauliflowers, kale and sprouting broccoli. Each is covered individually in the Vegetables section but this chapter describes the features that they have in common.

Types and varieties
See individual descriptions.

Soil, site and rotation
Brassicas like a firm ground, with a pH of 6.5 to 7. They can be planted without cultivating the soil. This will save time and leave the soil flora and fauna to get on with its work undisturbed by digging and rotovating. However, brassicas are heavy nitrogen feeders so, if you can, add compost or muck. To save time and energy I have started to put compost on top of the soil in February or March and then transplant brassicas through it in May and June. The covering also acts as a surface mulch, stopping weeds and reducing evaporation of water from the soil.
It is important that all brassicas are grown in the brassica part of the rotation because of club root disease, which can persist in the soil for twenty years or more. In my rotation I grow brassicas after a nitrogen fixing pea crop. For brassicas that are going to stand through the winter choose a site that isn't too exposed or too damp.

Sowing and planting
Brassicas are sown in a seed bed within a cold frame in March, in rows 15cm apart and 1cm deep. Make sure you label them because you can fit several brassica sowings in one cold frame. When they've grown to about 15 - 20cm tall, they can be transplanted to their growing position. Make a small hole deep enough to accommodate the roots and place the plant in the hole, refilling with soil as you go. They need to be about 60cm apart in a dice pattern. Tread around each plant to firm the soil, and water them in. I always save a couple of transplants of each variety as replacements for any that get eaten or don't take in their new position.

Food, water and mulch
The nitrogen left in the soil by my pea crop and the surface layer of composted muck that I add to the soil will supply nutrients for my brassicas in the uncultivated soil. It's important to keep the young plants watered during dry spells but once they've taken they should be able to survive without irrigation. In the summer sow a low growing green manure such as clover or trefoil under the crop to help provide soil cover during the winter and to out-compete annual weeds. You can sow a green manure directly on the surface of the compost mulch because by the summer much of it will have rotted down into the soil. If it hasn't rotted down enough then rough the soil up a bit with a long handled fork, taking care not to disturb the plants. If you don't have a surface mulch then broadcast the green manure seed by hand before the last hoeing of the crop. When you hoe the seed will be incorporated into the soil.

Seasonal care

Brassicas need little seasonal care other than weeding. The surface mulch of compost, if you have one, should keep most weeds down but if you have an open soil around the plants make sure it is hoed fairly regularly. During the winter I remove the yellowing leaves from the brassicas and any that have fallen to the ground and put them on the compost heap.

Succession and continuity

See individual brassica types.

Problems

Cabbage root flies lay their eggs in the soil at the base of brassica plants and when the larvae hatch they go straight into the brassica stem and begin to eat it away. The usual sign is leaves turning yellow and purple and the young plants falling over. One way of combating this problem is brassica collars, or squares made from 15cm squares of old carpet, underlay or cardboard with a slit in to the middle so they can be tucked around the individual plants. These stop the cabbage root fly from laying their eggs in the soil surrounding the brassicas. I would recommend using cardboard around the plants rather than carpet as it is drier and so inhibits slugs from sheltering under the squares at night. This method is simple and effective on a small scale but on a large scale it is both a time consuming and boring job. Instead, I cover the beds with fleece for

the first month, which stops the cabbage root fly and pigeons (another annoying pest) and gives the plants a little shelter. Once the brassicas have taken and are growing away the fleece can be removed.

Caterpillars are the main pest of brassicas that people ask me about every year. There isn't an easy solution unless you keep your brassicas under fleece during the summer, an expensive and unsightly option at this time of year. If you are only growing a few brassicas you can get away with picking the caterpillars off individually or searching out the butterfly eggs on the leaves and rubbing them off (some eggs are found as small orange clusters on the underside of leaves). On a larger scale you will need to spray with Bacillus thuringiensis, a bacterium which infests and kills caterpillars but doesn't affect any other insect or bird. In practice, Brussels sprouts and kale don't seem to be attacked as much as the other brassicas and you can get away with not spraying these varieties.

Club root is a soil borne fungus that stunts brassica plants by distorting their roots. I have never experienced it in my garden, probably because it was a field before it was a garden; it is often a problem in gardens where rotations have been ignored and once you have it you can't get rid of it. It is particularly bad on more acidic soils and where the underlying drainage is poor. Kale is far more tolerant than other brassicas, and it is possible to get some brassica crops if you start the plants off in a soil-less compost and grow them on to give them a head start. This method will produce a crop but the disease will take over eventually. Adding calcified seaweed to the planting hole seems to help as well, probably because it has lime in that will increase the alkalinity of the soil. If your brassicas always suffer from club root add a good handful of calcified seaweed when planting out the young stock and prepare yourself for a pleasant surprise! If you are growing veg to sell and you can't grow all the brassicas you need to you will either have to buy them in or tell your customers that you can't supply them with this particular crop – giving your customers information will help them to understand the difficulties of growing organic crops. The only way to eradicate club root is with chemicals!

Slugs will ravage young brassicas in the spring so I rarely plant them through plastic and certainly never through plastic with a mulch on top. I also avoid using collars to stop cabbage root fly for reasons mentioned above. The only way to avoid slug damage is to plant out during a dry spell and water individual plants as necessary – don't water the whole bed with sprinklers or sprayers as this will encourage the slugs!

Pigeons will destroy young brassica plants in the spring when there's little else for them to eat and in the winter they'll peck away the tops. In the spring I always cover newly transplanted brassicas with old fleece until the plants have taken a hold. If you notice any signs of damage in the winter, net the crop. It's noticeable that pigeons are less interested in red brassicas.

Mealy cabbage aphid only usually attacks brassicas that are stressed particularly in hot, dry weather. Keeping plants well watered, and fed if necessary, will stop these grey aphids. Hoverflies and ladybirds will help control mealy aphids. Failing that, a bad outbreak when it's particularly hot, can be dealt with by spraying with insecticidal soap.

Flea beetles are small and shiny and jump when you pass by them. They make small holes in the leaves of brassicas and can devastate young plants in very hot dry weather so make sure the young crop is well watered and covered with fleece.

Harvest, storage and sale
See individual brassica varieties.

Profit and efficiency
See individual brassica varieties.

Hints and tips
See individual brassica varieties.

Broad Beans

I used to hate broad beans when I was young and we bought them from the shops. The dry, leathery, sour taste used to make me want to throw up and if they came to the table in a white sauce I felt even worse. Now that I grow them myself I look forward to them every year because I've learnt to eat them at their best, when they are fresh and small. In my experience, any broad bean that gets bigger than a 20p piece must be cooked with a view to removing the pale green skin that covers the bean within. Of course, a broad bean smaller than a 20p piece can be eaten with the skin left on.

Types and varieties

There are two types of broad bean, one that is planted in October/November to grow over the winter and one that is planted in the spring. The over-winter variety I use is called Aquadulce Claudia and has survived every winter that I've grown it, producing broad beans two to four weeks earlier than their spring sown counterparts. They come at a time when my customers are wishing my vegetables into existence after the long winter break.

As the Aquadulce Claudia begins to peter out the spring sown variety will take over. I use a variety called Bunyard's Exhibition, which I settled on as much for its name as any thing, but it is a solid and reliable cropper that seems to follow on well from the winter variety.

Soil, site and rotation

Grow broad beans in the beans section of your rotation. The seed is large and can be sown in quite rough soil of a medium tilth. The pH of the soil should be 6.5. Choose an open site as any shade will make the plants grow toward the light and, being tall plants, this will encourage them to fall over.

Sowing and planting

I sow broad beans in a dice pattern at 20cm intervals, this gives me six rows to each bed. As they're grown in a block, they're less likely to be blown over. Sow each bean 4 to 6 cm deep and lightly rake over when you've finished. I sow the winter variety in October, and then make 2 or 3 sowings in spring, in late February, late March and late April.

Food, water and mulch

I always feed broad beans in one way or another. The winter variety gets a light dressing of composted muck once the plants are 5 to 6cm tall whilst the spring varieties have composted muck rotovated into the soil before planting.

Bean plants need weeding and will dry out, so to kill two birds with one stone I lay a straw mulch between the plants when they get to 15cm tall. The mulch will stay on the ground till the following year, keeping it weed free, moisture retentive and protecting the soil from the ravages of winter.

Seasonal care

If your site is exposed in any way it might be necessary to protect your broad bean plants from the wind. The simplest way to do this is to put wooden stakes in the corners of the beds and every 2 to 3 metres between then tie string around the outside of the whole bed at knee, waist and neck height so that the plants can't fall over. When the plants are roughly 1.5 to 1.8m tall pinch out the tops to prevent black fly (see below).

Broad beans can be subject to a problem called chocolate spot (see below) so I always dress the bed with potash (usually wood ash) during the winter.

Broad beans will take nitrogen from the air and fix it on their roots so when the beans are finished cut the stalks at soil level and sow a green manure in the bed to protect the soil over the winter. If you have used a straw mulch then just leaving the bed with the cut stalks is sufficient. This will give you a good supply of nitrogen for the following crop which should be nitrogen hungry – usually a brassica of some sort.

Succession and continuity

The autumn sowings will begin to crop at the end of May and continue into June. After this the spring sowings will take over. If you have made a sowing in February, March and April you should have a continuous crop into August. Be careful not to make sowings after the beginning of May as they often won't crop at all.

Problems

Black fly is the worst problem with broad beans. They are aphids that over-winter on blackthorn in hedgerows and appear in the spring to suck the fleshy tops of the broad beans. They multiply very quickly and spread down the plant onto the pods, sucking the sap from the plant. The black fly produce honeydew that is attractive to ants. You will often see ants running up and down the plants farming the black fly, chasing off the black fly's natural predators and even moving them to new succulent bits of your broad beans.

There are a number of ways to stop black fly. One is to pinch out the tops of the plants as soon as you see any signs of black fly or as soon as the plant is tall enough. Alternatively just squash the aphids with your fingers – a fiddly, messy and boring job on a large crop. Another method is to encourage ladybirds and hoverflies to your broad beans with an attractant plant such as limnanthes douglasii (poached egg plant). This needs to be sown in the bed during the early spring. Sowing summer savory amongst the beans seems to help too; either the ants and/or the black fly don't seem to like it. Summer savory is also a good herb to add to cooked broad beans – that's what I call companion planting. The ants can also be deterred by watering the base of the plants with a dilute solution of urine (say 5 parts water to 1 of urine). Stopping the ants reduces the amount of black fly but will probably not stop it completely.

The permitted chemical approach is to spray each plant top with a derris solution as soon as the black fly appear. It takes a second or two to unfurl the tops and inspect for black fly and you only need treat the affected plants. Make random checks every 3 or 4 days and you should get away with using the minimum amount of derris. On a bigger crop it would be far easier to spray the tops once a week with a large sprayer. However one of the major principles of organic growing is only to treat a problem if it exists and one of my major principles is to use the least amount of 'permitted' pesticides as possible if there is a problem. It would be better to spray instead with a wormwood and tansy mixture as this doesn't kill ladybirds (*see Pests and Diseases page 74*).

Chocolate spot appears as brown spots on the leaves and stems of the plant and is a fungal disease triggered by a lack of potash in the soil. If it gets bad the brown spots extend and join up going black in the process and destroying the plant. I treat the bed with wood ash during the winter but any other potash source can be used (*see Nutrients page 34*)

Harvest, storage and sale

Beans are ready to pick when the beans can be felt within the pod. To harvest a broad bean take the pod and snap it down away from the stalk. As with all vegetables the fresher the better. If you are harvesting for market and you don't have time to pick them on the same day as delivery then try to harvest in the evening before sale. The pods will stay cool overnight and will be of better quality than if they're harvested in the heat of the day.

Profit and efficiency

Broad beans are not really a difficult crop to grow (unless you get a bad attack of blackfly!) but as with all beans and peas, their drawback is in the harvesting of them which is time consuming. One redeeming feature is the winter type that can be sold for a higher price because it is so early.

Hints and tips

Never sell big broad beans – you can tell when they get too big because the bean begins to distort the pod it's growing in. You will keep your customers if you give them the sweetest, freshest, and, in the case of the broad bean, smallest vegetables.

Don't try to grow broad beans in polytunnels – they will crop but will give a much bigger harvest outside as they seem to prefer a cooler climate.

Brussels Sprouts

Sprouts are not everybody's favourite vegetable. This is probably because they were force fed them as a pale and mushy mess when they were young. Try serving them, steamed for no more more than ten minutes and you are sure to get a positive reaction. Being so hardy they are also nearly always available during the winter so it's easy to overdose on them early on. I always grow enough Brussels sprouts to keep me supplied over the winter but I don't grow many for sale purely because I hate picking them. There's no worse job than picking Brussels sprouts while the wind directs freezing rain into your face and your fingers are so cold they don't feel like they are yours anymore.

Types and varieties

I grow three varieties, an early called Early Half Tall which can be picked from September onwards, a mid season called Rampart F1 which crops from November and a late called Braveheart F1 which crops from December to March. If you're growing for sale choose the hybrids as they tend to mature all at the same time so that you don't have to hunt around each plant for the buttons that are ready. The non-hybrid types are better for growing for your own use as you get a more staggered cropping. Use the red variety Rubine if pigeons are a problem in your garden, as they tend to ignore red brassicas.

Soil, site and rotation

See brassica section.

Sowing and planting

See brassica section.

According to garden gospel, Brussels sprouts need a long growing season and should be started in January and February. I've never done this and I always get a good crop of sprouts. I start mine with all the other later cropping brassicas in April and May. Brussels sprouts need a firm soil or the sprouts will 'blow', becoming loose little cabbages instead of tight little buttons.

Food, water and mulch

See brassica section.

Seasonal care

See brassica section.

The stalks of Brussels sprouts are very hard and can take up to two years to rot down, so when the plants have finished at the end of the season pull them up and bash the stalks with a hammer before putting them on the compost heap.

Succession and continuity

If you really like Brussels sprouts you can harvest them from September to March by growing a selection of varieties (see above). I don't bother to harvest until after the first hard frost as the flavour is much sweeter after they have suffered some frosting.

Problems

See brassica section.

Harvest, storage and sale

Sprouts mature from the base of the stalk upwards so pick them from the bottom up. If you plan to sell them when it's very cold and frosty it's a good idea to harvest them either before or after the frost, as this will save your fingers from what feels like frost bite. Invest in a pair of Marigold gloves and although your fingers will still freeze they won't get so raw.

In cold weather you can store sprouts for a week or two but it is best to sell them freshly picked for the finest flavour. Don't sell them too often as not everyone likes sprouts!

If I grow Brussels sprouts just for the few people who live around me I need about 20 plants of the three different varieties listed above to keep us supplied from October to March. If I grow them for sale then I grow as many as I can. A good F1 plant will probably give you between 30 and 60 saleable sprouts, enough for 2 or 3 ordinary sized boxes (at about 500gm per box).

Profit and efficiency

I don't usually grow a lot of Brussels sprouts so I tend to buy them in for sale but they are relatively expensive. I plan to grow more and just grit my teeth when harvesting as they are a good alternative to cabbages and kale. One way to avoid picking them is to put a whole stalk in the box and let the customers do the work themselves.

Hints and tips

Wait until after the first frost before picking Brussels sprouts because they become much sweeter.
Tread the soil firmly when planting to stop the sprouts 'blowing'.
Wear Marigold gloves to harvest in cold weather.

Cabbages

Given the right varieties, cabbages can be grown all year round. And they will produce greens during the hungry gap when there is little else available.

Types and varieties

To grow cabbages all year round you need to grow spring, summer and autumn/winter varieties. Spring cabbages are usually a pointy shape and are sown in the late summer. They grow over the winter to heart up in the spring. Summer cabbages are sown early in the year, they can be pointy or round, and produce cabbages from early to mid summer. Autumn/winter cabbages are sown in the spring, heart up in autumn and stand through the winter.

There are many different varieties of each type and I use a range to produce succession, colour and texture for the veggie boxes I sell. I do not sell spring cabbages so I only grow a few for my kitchen, either Offenham or Flower of Spring. The summer cabbages I grow are Greyhound or Spitfire F1, both pointed varieties, and a ball-headed type, Stonehead F1 that stands well. For autumn and winter I grow three types; a red variety, either Red Drumhead or Hardora F1, a Savoy type, Christmas Drumhead, and an ordinary green leaved variety Tundra F1.

Soil, site and rotation

As for brassicas. Make sure the site of your winter cabbages is not in a frost pocket as they will benefit from the warmest conditions you can provide.

Sowing and planting

As for brassicas.

Summer cabbages can be grown slightly closer together, about 45cm apart, as they are quicker to crop than the later types which should be planted out at 60cm spacings. Spring cabbages need to be started in July or August and planted out in September or October – they will stand through the winter and heart up in the spring.

Food, water and mulch

As for brassicas.

Seasonal care

As for brassicas.

Succession and continuity

See types and varieties above. I don't produce my boxes during the spring so the first cabbages I sell are summer ones. These are usually ready in June and are followed by the autumn and winter cabbages as the season progresses. Savoy types are often the hardiest type and will stand outside through very severe weather, providing fresh green cabbage in the depths of winter.

Problems

As for brassicas.

Winter cabbages are harder to grow as they don't all perform so well as the earlier types. Being winter varieties you will expect them to stand for much longer than the spring and summer types. This means that any damage they might have suffered from pigeons, slugs or caterpillars will leave them vulnerable to mildews and rots for a longer period of time. If you can provide them with some sort of protection then this will help. Ensuring that caterpillar damage is kept to a minimum during the growing months will increase your yield considerably.

Harvest, storage and sale

When harvesting cabbages I always pull the stalks up and then cut the cabbage off the stalk. You can leave the stalk in the ground as it will reshoot with three or four baby cabbages. This is fine for your own use, but on a large scale these tiny cabbages never get used up. If I pull the root when I harvest then I'm not leaving the root in longer than necessary (which might encourage disease) and the bed is being cleared at the same time. The roots and stalks are given a good bashing with a hammer or the back of a hatchet or axe and put on the compost heap.

The ball headed type of summer cabbage can be harvested on the day of sale or even the day before. The pointy types flag quickly in hot weather so it's best to harvest these on the day of sale. Autumn and winter cabbages can be harvested much earlier if necessary particularly if there is frost threatening.

If the individual cabbages are very big cut them in half or even quarters for small boxes but make sure you cover the cuts by putting them in plastic bags.

I don't put cabbages in my boxes every week in the summer but I intersperse them with spinach and later in the season I alternate with calabrese, cauliflowers, kale and Brussels sprouts.

Profit and efficiency

Autumn and winter cabbages are very cheap to buy in so I grow very few of them. I concentrate on the summer cabbages, and red cabbages for the autumn, as these give a better return for my time.

Hints and tips

Keep covered during early growth to stop cabbage root fly and pigeon damage.

Calabrese

This is a really important crop to grow for sale because so many people like it, particularly kids, and families that buy boxes will stay with you if you can supply the sort of veg that kids like. It isn't the easiest of crops to grow but it can, if harvested consistently, keep cropping for weeks. There is a lot of confusion about calabrese and broccoli which are essentially the same crop – broccoli (sprouting broccoli) is the winter type and calabrese is the summer type.

Types and varieties

I use two types, an early called Corvet F1 and a later variety called Shogun F1. They both produce large central heads followed by smaller spears on the side of the plant, just as tasty and very useful as a subsequent crop. The variety Trixie F1 is more tolerant of club root than others so try it if you have club root in your soil.

Soil, site and rotation

As for brassicas.

Sowing and planting

As for brassicas.

Food, water and mulch

As for brassicas.

Seasonal care

As for brassicas.

Succession and continuity

Using early and late varieties will help extend the season but the best way to keep the plants producing is to make sure that you harvest all the spears as and when they are ready. This will encourage the plant to produce more. If you let the plant flower it will stop producing shoots and although this will inevitably happen, you can keep the plant producing for much longer by regular cutting.

Problems

See brassicas.

Harvest, storage and sale

Harvesting calabrese is quick and easy. In hot weather the cuttings begin to wilt quickly so harvest early in the morning, spray with cold water and store in a cool place until packing. If you're picking for yourself, do it just before cooking. Most people like calabrese and if you've got it you can put it in your boxes every week.

Profit and efficiency

It's worthwhile growing as much as you can as it's so popular. It's also very expensive to buy in.

Hints and tips

Harvest the spears regularly even if you're not planning to sell them, to keep the plants cropping for longer.

Carrots

Carrots are a difficult crop to grow well. They are fiddly to germinate and the whole crop can be rendered unsaleble by carrot root fly. However, they are also indispensable and I certainly couldn't run my box scheme without them. With a little care and attention it is possible to grow very good carrots and they always taste a lot sweeter than those bought from the shop.

Types and varieties

In general there are two main types, summer and winter carrots. Summer carrots are longish, thin, lightly coloured and exquisitely sweet - for carrots, that is. They are for growing and eating in the summer and have a very short shelf life. I use Early Nantes for summer use. Winter carrots tend to be fatter, darker and less sweet, but can be stored for the whole winter given the right conditions. I use Autumn King, which stores well, and Chantenay Red Cored, which matures a little earlier.

Soil, site and rotation

Carrots are grown in the root (or umbellifer) section of the rotation, preferably in an open site. The finest tilth you can achieve is best for carrots as the seed is very small. They do like a light soil, ideally with no stones or compost (unless it has been well rotted), which will make the roots fork.

Sowing and planting

It's a good idea to create a clean seed bed for carrots, to minimise weeds. Sow thinly - a dribble of seed is enough - in rows 30cm apart and 1cm deep.

Carrots take a good three weeks to germinate. When they do decide to pop up above ground level, they have delicate cotyledons that are very popular with slugs. They can be pre-germinated for better results. Try to minimise the risk of damage by sowing outdoor carrots at the end of a warm, wet period so that they germinate during the following dry spell.

Food, water and mulch

Carrots will not need food, water or mulch during the growing season. Having tap roots, they are quiet capable of searching out moisture for themselves. However, if it is very dry once they have started to grow away, a good soaking won't go amiss.

Seasonal care

Once they are 2 - 3cm high hoe, weed and thin each row and then pray for rain to resettle the remaining plants. Alternatively, thin and weed when the weather is muggy and still so that the carrot root fly are less likely to smell the delicate seedlings.

Early types can be thinned to 2.5cm apart whereas main crops are better off at 7.5cm apart. Push the soil back into the holes that are left after thinning, to stop the carrots going green on the shoulder. Finally cover the carrots with mesh or fleece to prevent carrot root fly damage (see Problems below).

Succession and continuity

The first crop I sow is in the polytunnel in early March, using Early Nantes. In mid April I sow more summer carrots, outside. I sow winter carrots outside in mid April and again in late April/early May, then in the polytunnel in August. In this way I have an almost continuous supply. The first summer carrots are ready in June and the stored winter carrots carry on until about April.

Problems

Producing a satisfactory carrot crop is quite a challenge. The first thing to watch out for is 'capping' when the soil dries and forms a hard crust on top. It tends to happen more on clay soils and stops the tiny carrot seedlings from pushing through the surface. Avoid the problem by covering the rows of seeds with sand or sieved compost. This also helps demarcate the rows, making hoeing much easier before the carrots have emerged.

When the plants first appear above the soil they are likely to be slaughtered by slugs. My defence is in numbers. I sow an area no smaller than 4 x 4 metre square, and grow a sacrificial slug food such as lettuce around the edge. I also try to surround the whole patch with slug unfriendly material. If I can sow the carrots during a wet period, with luck they might germinate in a dry period when slugs are less active.

Carrot root fly larvae is the next major problem. Carrot root flies appear in month of May and can smell a carrot at 50 paces. Once they've logged on to their target, they fly straight to it and lay their eggs in the soil around the plant. When the eggs hatch, the carrot root fly larvae emerge and burrow into the root. In bad infestations the carrots are inedible, unless you liquidise the whole crop for soupe aux carrottes avec purée d'asticots. The only practical answer is to cover the crop for most of the growing season with a physical barrier that lets in light and water but keeps out the flies. I use either mesh or fleece. Of the two, mesh is a more sustainable solution because it is far more hard wearing. I find that the flies don't get into the polytunnels so carrots grown here are safe. Another idea is to surround the crop with strong smelling cut herbs like lemon balm to disguise the carrot smell. These will need to be be topped up regularly.

If carrots aren't that important in your diet then you needn't worry too much about the flies. Scatter some seed about your plot and you might come up with a few roots which aren't too badly damaged to use. But if you have young children and/or a great fondness for carrots then it is wise to protect your crop. Advocates of companion planting claim that growing onions and even salsify amongst the crop will stop carrot root fly. I have tried this without success.

Harvest, storage and sale

To harvest carrots, pull them up and twist the tops off. Summer carrots should be sold with their tops on because they look so attractive. However, the tops will draw moisture from the root making it shrivel much faster, so I always tell my customers to pull them off when they get them home.

Winter carrots can be stored in cold, damp sand, or if they have been grown under cover, in the ground. In November, when the carrots stop growing, allow the soil around them to dry out slightly then cover the crop with straw. This protects the roots from frost and later keeps the soil cool, preventing the carrots from regrowing. The carrots can be lifted from under the straw as they are needed until late February, after which they tend to start sprouting. At this point the remaining carrots can be harvested and packed in damp sand somewhere cool, giving you carrots for a further month or two.

Summer carrots are quite expensive so I grow all my own for sale. Winter carrots, on the other hand, are very cheap to buy so I grow enough to keep my boxes going until the end of October when the price plummets and then I buy them in.

Profit and efficiency

Summer carrots are more profitable than winter carrots, and the first ones out of the tunnel are particularly so. Growing winter carrots for sale is not really an economic proposition unless you can keep them in the ground or in a cold store.

Hints and tips

Always use fleece or mesh to prevent carrot root fly damage.
Sow carrots at the end of a wet period so that they emerge in dry soil and escape slug damage.

Cauliflowers

Cauliflowers have a reputation for being very difficult to grow although in my experience they are no more difficult than any other brassica. Like cabbages they can be grown all year round, although getting cauliflowers to heart between November and February is very difficult.

Types and varieties

I tend to use a hybrid like Stella F1 for summer crops and follow with an autumn type like Snowcap. For winter varieties I use whichever varieties are available to crop in March, April and May – the seed companies tend to change them on a regular basis so there's no point me giving you variety names here.

Soil and site

Cauliflowers need a lot of feeding so it is worth cultivating cauliflower beds and adding as much composted muck as you can spare. If your soil is on the poor side, use the variety Stella F1 which is reputed not to need quite as much nitrogen as other varieties. A medium tilth is fine as, like all the other brassicas, you should use transplants.

Sowing and planting

As for brassicas.
Cauliflowers do need a lot of space so give them between 60 and 75cm in a dice pattern.

Food, water and mulch

As for brassicas.
If you don't get around to adding compost to the soil you can add nitrogen as liquid feed just before they begin to heart. Cauliflowers need water throughout their growing season so water in dry spells.

Seasonal care

As for brassicas.
Check your cauliflowers regularly as it isn't obvious when they are ready. If the curds show, take some of the bottom leaves off the plants and cover the curds to protect them from the sun, or cold, depending on the season.

Succession and continuity

The first summer cauliflowers should be ready in August, follow them with an autumn type which will head up in late October/November. The winter varieties should crop in March, April and May.

Problems

As for brassicas.
If you have club root you're unlikely to get a crop of cauliflowers at all, as they are the brassica most affected by this disease.

If your cauliflowers get brown hearts this is a sign of boron deficiency. It's difficult to tell if you've got a problem until you harvest the crop. If you do find a problem you can add seaweed meal and compost to the next cauliflower bed before planting. This should make sure it doesn't happen again.

Harvest, storage and sale

Harvest cauliflowers as you need them. You can cut them a day or two before sale but if it's hot the outer leaves will wilt and make the cauliflower look sad. Keep an eye on the crop because it's easy to forget about them and then find that they've started to bolt before you've had a chance to harvest them.

Profit and efficiency

If you have a small garden then this crop is probably not worth growing for sale because it needs so much space. My policy is to grow a summer crop before the caterpillars start, buy in cauliflowers during the autumn and grow over-winter types for my own use when I'm not selling boxes.

Hints and tips

Make sure they get plenty of nitrogen.
Don't forget about them.
Winter varieties provide food during lean months.

Celeriac

Celeriac is not a traditional British vegetable but it is growing in popularity. It is very similar in taste to celery but rather than eating the stem and leaves, you eat the swollen root. If you're selling celeriac, make sure people know what to do with it by giving them recipes.

Types and varieties

There are not a lot of varieties to choose from but try to select one that is resistant to hollowness, such as President. I usually use Giant Prague.

Soil, site and rotation

Celeriac is sown in seed trays and planted out so a fine to medium tilth is suitable. It does prefer a pH of 6.0. Unlike most of the other root vegetables, add composted muck to the plot before planting celeriac. This helps to balance the pH and makes the soil more water retentive - one of its most important requirements. Celeriac is an umbellifer so it is grown in the root section of the rotation, preferably in an open, sunny site. I have grown celeriac in polytunnels but it grows far better outside, as long as it is given plenty of water.

Sowing and planting

Celeriac should be sown in trays at about 18°C in late February or early March. Once the individual plants are big enough to handle transplant them into modules. Grow them on until spring when they should be hardened off before planting out 20–30cm apart in a dice pattern. Although you need to keep them moist, watch out for slugs at this point. Try not to let the plants dry out in the modules as they are prone to bolting.

Food, water and mulch

Celeriac requires no extra feeding but irrigation and mulching is very important. As the crop establishes, ensure that it never dries out, particularly during dry hot weather. Once the plants are a good size, safe from slugs, mulch with straw after it has rained.

Seasonal care

Hoe before you mulch the plants and periodically check that the soil is moist underneath the mulch. In late summer strip the outer leaves away from the bulb. In late autumn add more straw to cover the bulbs up to the leaves, to help keep frost off the roots.

Succession and continuity

Celeriac is ready to harvest from October. It can be left in the ground with a covering of straw. If very cold weather threatens it might be worth digging a few up before the ground gets too hard.

Problems

Hollowness can be a problem, usually caused by the plants drying out at some point. Try growing a variety that is resistant to hollowness. Slugs are a problem when the plants are small so try to plant out during a dry spell.

Harvest, storage and sale

To harvest celeriac for sale, dig up the roots and twist the tops off. Then with a large, sharp knife remove all the sticking out roots. Celeriac can be stored in damp sand for use through the winter. Alternatively, leave the plants in the soil under a layer of straw.

Many people don't know what celeriac is, let alone what to do with it, so it is worth putting a recipe sheet in the veg box too.

Profit and efficiency

Celeriac is one of the more expensive roots to buy in. It is easier to grow than celery and more worthwhile than say swedes or turnips. It does need a bit of looking after though, so it is not particularly efficient to grow.

Hints and tips

Keep moist at all times, preferably with a thick mulch.

Celery

Celery is one of my least favourite crops to grow. There's nothing worse than spending a whole season nurturing the plants only to find when you come to harvest them that the stalks are hollow! The most important thing to remember is to keep it well watered, which means keeping an eye on it all season.

Types and varieties

There are two types of celery, trench and self-blanching, or green. Trench varieties will stand through the winter with some protection. I use Solid White, or Solid Pink that has some colour in the stalks. By far the easiest to grow is the self-blanching type like Celebrity because it does not need earthing up to whiten the stems.

Soil, site and rotation

Both types of celery need a pH of 6.5, an open site and should be grown in the root, or umbellifer, part of the rotation. Self-blanching celery should be planted in a flat bed that has had composted muck added, and with a fine to medium tilth. Trenches, a spade's depth and width, should be prepared for trench celery. Line the bottom with composted muck and cover with a 3cm layer of soil. The celery is planted in the trench and will be earthed up as they grow.

Sowing and planting

Start the seeds off in early March in trays at a temperature of 18°C but don't cover them because they need light to germinate. Prick out the seedlings when they are big enough to handle and plant them out into modules. Grow them on until May then harden them off in a slug free cold frame. Plant the self-blanching type in a dice pattern, 30cm apart. Plant the trench types 30cm apart in the prepared trench. Water them in well.

Food, water and mulch

Celery is a hungry and thirsty crop. Keep an eye on the soil moisture, as dryness will cause hollow stalks. Self-blanching varieties can be mulched with straw early in the season but with trench types you will have to wait until they have been earthed up. Feed with liquid manure if you have any.

Seasonal care

Self-blanching celery can be left until autumn once it has a mulch on, but make sure it doesn't dry out.

Trench celery needs attention in August, when the blanching process starts. Pick off any suckers from the base of the plant then tie cardboard or newspaper around each plant so that the leaves stick out the top. A good alternative is to use the cardboard tubes from the middle of rolls of fabric (ask at a sewing shop). Cut them to size first and push them over the top of the plant. Then, fill the trench with soil until it reaches the top of the blanching tube. The tube will stop the celery from filling with soil. Make sure the soil slopes away from the plants so they don't rot in a puddle. You can now mulch the bed, up to the leaves. In the autumn cover the rows with cloches.

Succession and continuity

By growing both types of celery I can harvest it well into the winter. I have plans to grow it in the polytunnel too, to extend the season. Outside, self-blanching types are harvested before the first frosts. The trench celery can be covered with cloches in the autumn and harvested into December or January.

For the polytunnel I will sow trench celery in April and transplant them in July, following the French beans. The celery will then be ready the following February.

Problems

Slugs are a problem when the plants are small, so try to plant out during a dry spell.

Celery fly damages the leaves, turning them pale green then brown and shrivelled. This is first seen in late spring. Pinch out the affected leaves and destroy them.

Celery leaf spot shows as little brown spots on the leaves. If you catch it early on removing the leaves is usually enough. A bad case might need the remaining leaves to be treated with Bordeaux Mixture until harvest.

Harvest, storage and sale

Harvest the self-blanching types as soon as they're ready, and use them up before the first frost. Next, harvest the outdoor trench celery up to Christmas, then move on to the tunnel celery. To harvest, lift the plant with a fork and trim the roots off. Trim the leaves as well to tidy the plant up. If you sell self-blanching celery, remember that most people are used to eating blanched celery so tell them why it's green. Also point out how much tastier it is!

Profit and efficiency

Celery is profitable in terms of time if you use the self-blanching types. However, the blanched type is more popular and easier to crop into the winter, so it's worth growing both types.

Hints and tips

Keep well watered.
Grow some in tunnels for a winter supply.
Self-blanching varieties are the easiest to grow but won't stand hard frosts.

Chicory

Chicories come in all shapes, sizes and colours. If you want to add variety to your winter salads they must be grown. They are planted mid season so can be used to follow on from early crops and act as winter soil cover.

Types and varieties

There are plenty of varieties to choose from and I'd recommend that you try out as many as possible. I use five main varieties. Sugar Loaf is a large, self-blanching, sweeter type that stands a lot of frost. Rossa di Treviso has long pointed leaves that turn red in winter. Palla di Fuoco has round heads with red leaves and white veins. Variegata di Castelfranco has green leaves blotched with red. Grumolo Verde is a rosette-shaped plant with round green leaves. There are also forcing types such as Brussels Witloof, which you can use to produce chicons which are blanched shoots that are forced to grow in the winter in heat and darkness.

Soil, site and rotation

I grow my chicories following my early potatoes. I just need to rake the soil level after harvesting the potatoes in June, before it dries out and becomes more difficult to work. Chicory doesn't suffer from diseases and can be placed anywhere in the rotation. However, I always grow them in the same part of my rotation so the soil always gets at least a four year break.

Sowing and planting

Sow chicory after midsummer, any earlier and they will run to seed. Sow 1cm deep in rows 30cm apart. If it doesn't rain within a week, water them in the evening.

Food, water and mulch

Chicory needs no feeding, and only wants watering if it gets very dry. Mulching will only encourage slugs.

Seasonal care

Thin the plants to about 30cm apart, and keep the bed free of weeds.

To produce chicons from a forcing variety, lift the roots after the first frost. Cut off the leaves to within 2.5cm of the root and replant them close together in a pot or box of soil, pressing the soil down firmly. Five in the centre of a 20cm pot is fine. Put them somewhere dark, above 10C, and they will produce chicons throughout the winter. Remove the chicons carefully for a continued supply.

I am going to grow chicons in situ this winter, under a cloche covered with black plastic. In July I will sow the seed directly in my warmest polytunnel. In November I will cut the leaves back and cover the plants with the dark cloche. Hopefully the chicons will be ready by January, but I won't know until I've tried it.

Succession and continuity

Individual leaves can be picked from some chicories and added to salads. The ball headed Pallo di Fuoco and Sugar Loaf need to be cut whole and taken apart so that you can add individual leaves to salad bags. Most chicories will last through the season and will continue to grow if covered with cloches.

Problems

Slugs can be a problem but they would rather go for a sacrificial lettuce crop planted next door.

Harvest, storage and sale

Never put too many chicory leaves in salad bags because they are bitter (*see Salad Bags page 235*). Once the plant has run to seed the leaves become too bitter to eat.

Ball headed chicories can be sold whole, but I usually separate the leaves for use in winter salad bags. If you have time to raise chicons they can be harvested right through the winter for sale when there is little salad material available.

Profit and efficiency

Chicories, together with other winter salad leaves, keep my salad bags going well into winter. They are easy to grow and double-crop the land so they are quite profitable.

Hints and tips

Chicory does not need to be rotated so it can fit in after any early crops.
Sow after midsummer to avoid bolting.

Claytonia

This strange looking plant is also known as miner's lettuce, winter purslane or Indian lettuce. It has squarish leaves on the end of a long thin stalk, and it tastes lovely. It's a winter vegetable, slow growing but easy. It makes an attractive and nutritious addition to salads and is full of Vitamin C.

Types and varieties

There are no varieties.

Soil, site and rotation

Claytonia can be placed anywhere in the rotation, but the seed is tiny so it needs a very fine tilth.

Sowing and planting

Sow broadcast in August and rake in very lightly. Water in with a fine spray. The plants should be thinned to about 10-15cms and will benefit from protection at first. Alternatively sow in modules, planting out in September at the above spacing.

Food, water and mulch

Although there are no particular requirement for feeding or mulching this plant it is a good idea to water it regularly in it's early stages and then only during warmer weather in the winter months if it is grown under cover.

Seasonal care

Weed between the plants.

Succession and continuity

Claytonia stands all winter so there's no need for continuous sowings.

Problems

None.

Harvest, storage and sale

Harvest the leaves individually for yourself but if you're selling salads then harvest the whole plant, and add one or two plants per salad bag.

Profit and efficiency

Claytonia takes a long time to grow and you don't get much leaf for the amount of space. It is definitely worth growing for your own use and if you are selling salads in the winter it is an unusual and tasty leaf to add to salad bags.

Hints and tips

Worth growing for its flavour and nutritious content.

Courgettes

Courgettes are one of my favourite summer vegetables. They have a unique taste and can be cooked very easily. Try cooking them whole on the barbecue: eat with sausages and toasted finger rolls followed by barbecued bananas for a whole meal with no preparation and no washing up.

Types and varieties

I have had trouble in the past with Cucumber Mosaic Virus, courgettes being a member of the cucurbit family, so I always grow a resistant variety such as Patriot F1.

As well as dark green courgettes I always grow a yellow variety, Gold Rush, because they add so much colour to my boxes. Further variety can be provided by the open pollinated types, which produce light green fruits.

I also grow varieties with interestingly shaped fruit, to add interest to my boxes. The variety Tondo di Nizza produces fruit that is round rather than cylindrical. They are best picked when they are no more than 10cm in diameter, before they become spherical marrows. I also grow 'spaceships', flat, saucer shaped fruit with scalloped edges. The white variety is called a custard marrow and the yellow variety is a hybrid called Sunburst.

Soil, site and rotation

Courgettes need a good deal of water during their growing season. To reduce the need for constant watering I grow them on what I call a 'muck sink'. I dig pits every 1.2m along the row, 30cm deep and 60cm in diameter. Add a couple of spadefuls of FYM and fill in the hole, mixing the soil with the manure. Put a stick in the top of each mound so that you know where to plant the courgettes. The soil should have a pH of 6, and courgettes fall in the squash part of the rotation.

Sowing and planting

I always start courgettes off under cover, in 7.5cm pots. To grow in the polytunnel I start them in a propagator in March, or for outdoors I wait until mid April. Once the plants are beyond the two leaf stage, and after the last frosts, harden them off over a few days and then plant them out in the prepared bed. Position the plant so that the soil level from the pot is a good 1cm above the surface of the surrounding soil, to prevent stem rot (*see Cucumbers page 118*).

At this point the plants are at their most vulnerable. The move to a new environment is a shock and their roots need to find their footings in fresh soil. They can also get wind beaten and the delicate stalks will soon give up the ghost without protection. So, once planted out and watered in (gently with a fine rose if possible) protect the young plants by placing a tyre over each one. Make a lid with a square pane of glass - a piece of cloche glass is fine. This is a simple and efficient way of protecting the young plant, acting like a mini cloche. It will shelter the plants from the wind but allow ventilation, and will help protect against the cold, and possible frost. Once the plants are established, when the leaves begin to reach the outside edge of the tyre, it can be removed.

Food, water and mulch

The courgettes should need no feeding, as nutrients are provided by the manure in the 'muck sinks'. As the plants become established under the tyre cloches, make sure that they get enough water. Until the roots grow down into the 'muck sink' the plants will need watering. Mulching once the plants are established will save a lot of time later in the season. The 'muck sinks' will not hold enough water for the plants during very dry periods. A week or two after removing the tyres I spread a mulch of either straw or strawy manure across the whole bed and around each plant. As well as helping to retain moisture in the soil, this minimises the need for weeding. It also ensures that the ground is relatively clean and well fed for the following crop – usually over wintered onions.

Seasonal care

If the weather is wet the young plants in the tyre cloches are very vulnerable to slugs. Slugs may take refuge in the tyre so be sure to check regularly for the lurking menaces. Simply lift the tyre with one hand and stab any slugs with a knife. Once the courgette plants get away and the mulch is down they need little care other than the odd bit of irrigation if the weather gets very dry and hot.

Succession and continuity

Succession is difficult with courgettes, unless you can spare a little space inside for an early crop. If you do grow a crop indoors, choose a variety that doesn't spread too much. The hybrids tend to produce more compact plants than the open pollinated types. You can delay the end of the season outdoors by covering the plants with fleece, but by this time it hardly seems worth the extra effort. As the seasons change it seems more fitting to start eating the courgettes cousins, the squash family.

Problems

The worst problems I've encountered with courgettes are Cucumber Mosaic Virus (CMV) and mildew. The first sign of CMV is the leaves puckering and turning yellow. The fruits, doing the same, then become hard and inedible. There is no cure so you must pull up the affected plants and burn them. If you leave them the disease will spread. Use resistant varieties and keep the plants free of aphids, which will carry the disease from plant to plant. Mildew tends to occur when it's very dry and hot in the day following by the damp, cool nights of late summer. The leaves go white then become dry, like cracked paper. This problem can be delayed by keeping the plants well watered during dry spells. However, by the time mildew becomes established the courgette season is normally nearly over anyway. If the plants suffer from mildew early in the season, try a diluted milk or chive spray on the leaves.

Harvest, storage and sale

Harvest courgettes frequently so that none of them grow into marrows. Even if you don't need or want all the courgettes that your plants produce, harvest them before they get bigger than 25cm long, or 10cm in diameter for spaceships. When the plant is growing a marrow it will not produce new courgettes. If you are selling courgettes, harvest them as necessary, preferably in the early morning. Store them in a polystyrene box somewhere cool until you need to sell them. Do not store them like this for more than two or three days, as they will deteriorate. When they are not fresh they lose their shine and I wouldn't recommend selling them like that.

Profit and efficiency

Being tender plants, courgettes are time consuming at first. Once they get going you can give your customers courgettes every week if you have enough plants. About 25 plants are sufficient for me to give my customers courgettes every other week.

The slackest month for my box scheme is August, because everyone goes on holiday and my sales drop by about a third. As courgettes crop mainly in August it's wise not to grow too many plants or you will have a huge surplus.

Hints and tips

Grow resistant varieties.
Use muck sinks.
Give good protection early on.
Harvest regularly.

Cress

There are several types of cress that can be grown, the most well known is watercress. This is very fiddly to grow as it needs clean running water. Land cress is very similar in flavour, and much easier to grow. All types of cress are useful in salads.

Types and varieties

Watercress can be grown in very wet soil but land cress will tolerate fairly dry conditions. Another variety is Greek cress which tastes quite peppery and is an unusual addition to salads.

Soil, site and rotation

A cool and shady site is best for cress, in the brassica part of your rotation. It is worth considering growing it under brassica plants to take advantage of the shade and to keep it in the correct part of the rotation. Prepare the soil to a fine tilth.

Sowing and planting

Sow the seeds 1cm deep in rows 15cm apart.

Food, water and mulch

Keep the soil very damp. Cress tends to be low growing so mulching isn't really effective, but you could try using grass mowings as a thin mulch.

Seasonal care

Hoeing and hand weeding will be necessary during the first few months of growth.

Succession and continuity

Sow land cress every month or so during the growing season for a continuous supply. Protect the last sowing with cloches to keep it cropping over the winter. I have grown watercress in my polytunnel soil, and from one sowing I harvested from May through to February.

Problems

Growing watercress requires very clean water. If sheep are near the water source they can infest it with a snail which attaches itself to the plants. If this is ingested by humans it can cause liver fluke, which can be fatal. If you find watercress in a stream you can use it, but you must cook it – try watercress soup.

Harvest, storage and sale

Use land cress and Greek cress as a cut and come again crop to enhance salads and salad bags. It won't store so only pick as needed. I buy in watercress from the wholesalers during the winter months. This supplements the salads I sell as the watercress I grow dwindles in the colder months.

Profit and efficiency

Not profitable as such but good as a salad ingredient. I buy watercress in bunches of fifteen at a cost of about 60p each and sell them on at 85–90p each.

Hints and tips

Land cress is easier to grow but watercress will crop for longer from a single sowing, so may be worth the extra watering.

Cucumbers

Cucumbers are well worth the effort if you are selling your vegetables on a small scale. If you are growing them just for your own use, don't go overboard on the number of plants you have – one plant can produce up to 70 cucumbers in one growing season!

Types and varieties

There's a lot to be said for the hybrid varieties of cucumbers, which produce all female fruit. They produce huge quantities of long, straight, mild green fruits. Their taste, admittedly, is not as strong as the dark green, prickly ridged type, but there are a lot of them. Recently I have been growing three types of cucumber, to give my customers variety. For 'normal' cucumbers, I grow a hybrid, usually Birgit F1 from Mr Fothergills, with long, straight, bright green fruits. I also grow mini cucumbers, Delta Star is a reliable variety from the Organic Marketing Catalogue and Marketmore, an outdoor ridge type from Mr Fothergills which also has resistance to mildews. My customers get cucumbers that they're used to and are introduced to the different flavours of the non-hybrid types. Variety keeps my customers interested in the vegetables I grow whilst also giving me the opportunity to experiment. I grew a cucumber called Crystal Apple last year. The flavour was good but had tough skin and lots of pips. I didn't get any comments, which usually means that my customers didn't think too much of it. I tend to agree and so won't be growing them again.

Soil, site and rotation

I operate a four year rotation in the polytunnels, and the cucumbers get a bed to themselves. In March I work in my best compost, then I erect the cucumber framework that they will grow up.

Cucumber frames

Cucumbers need a sturdy, accessible framework to grow up. This can't be a permanent structure, because I use the beds for other crops three years out of four. To be realistic, the framework has to be quick and easy to construct. I try to get it up in March, in a wet spell when I can't work outdoors.

1. Use one upright pole per plant. They should be pushed well into the ground, a good 1.7m apart. Use the polytunnel hoops as a guide – they are usually 1.7-2m apart, and it will make attaching string easier.
2. Attach a length of string to the top of the door frame at one end of the polytunnel, for each row of cucumbers.
3. Loop the string around each of the poles in the row until you reach the far end, then attach the string to that door frame. Be sure that the string is looped, not tied, as the poles need to be able to slide along the string.
4. Attach strings to the poles at 90 degrees from the first string, between opposite polytunnel hoops.
5. Tie string diagonally from the bottom of each pole to the top of the next.

Each plant will grow up the pole and send out side shoots that can be attached to the diagonal strings. In a double row of cucumbers, this structure should provide ample support, make the best use of space and allow suitable access to the cucumbers. Humidity can be concentrated around the vegetation and there will be sufficient air movement to lessen the incidence of disease and moulds.

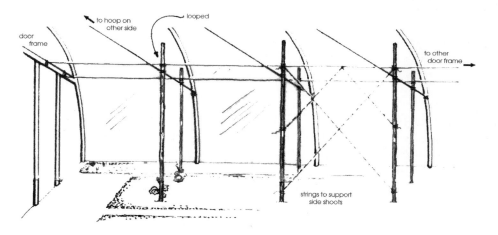

Sowing and planting

Cucumbers require a temperature of 18 - 21°C to germinate. I start mine off in early March in a propagator. They soon need a stake in the pot or they will flop over. Once they are about 30cm tall, harden them off in an open propagator which can be closed at night and which should be turned off in early April. Once they've acclimatised, and when the weather isn't too cold, put them in the polytunnel protected under fleece tents. After a day or two plant them next to the stakes in the prepared bed. Always plant cucumber plants so that the top 1cm of compost that they have grown in stands proud of the surrounding soil they are planted in to prevent stem and root rot. Water gently around the base with tepid water, to encourage the roots to grow into the surrounding soil. Protect with fleece tents again, which can be unwrapped during the day and removed completely once they start to grow away.

Food, water and mulch

One of the particularly useful features of a cucumber frame is that you can attach a system of micro sprayers on the top. Water can be sprayed in all directions to create humidity amongst the plants and to water them in as natural a way as possible. Thread LDPE pipe (13mm thin black irrigation pipe) along the length of each row tied to the top of the framework. Attach the sprayers at the recommended interval (usually every 1.5 to 2 metres). In very hot weather you need to mist the plants every 30 minutes so, if you can afford it, a timer attached to a tap is ideal. Timers which operate this frequently are often over £200 and they'll need an electric supply. If it's cold, reduce the amount of spraying to compensate for the lower rate of transpiration.

Seasonal care

During rapid growth, shoots should be trained along the poles and strings every other day. Keep a check on the side shoots as you will only be able to cope with about a third of the total produced. Allow the plants to grow as far as the strings reach, and your pathways will fill with head high cucumbers dangling from the strings. Three or four times during the season cut out any excess or weak-looking foliage. This will increase ventilation and discourage rots, particularly powdery mildew. Later in the season remove much more of the growth to make the plants more open and light.

Succession and continuity

I usually get a cucumber or two by the middle to end of May and they get into full swing by the end of June. If the weather is good they will continue to crop heavily into October. The first cold snap in the tunnel will finish off any remaining fruits.

Problems

Red Spider Mite (RSM) are a common problem during very dry, hot weather. The mites are very small and you will probably need a hand lens to see them. They over-winter in polytunnels and glass houses, becoming active in June. The first sign of trouble is the leaves turning a dull green, then yellow. Severely affected leaves are covered with a fine webbing, a bit like a spiders web. To avoid the problem, mist the plants regularly, particularly during very dry, hot weather. I also grow coriander beneath the plants. I have no proof that it keeps RSM away, but it seems to help. If your plants become severely affected then an application of derris should kill off most of the mites and can be repeated after a week or two if necessary. The biological control for RSM is Phytoseiulius persimilis - these look very similar to and require the same conditions as the mites, which they eat. In practise I find that by the time you've identified the problem, ordered and received the control, the weather's changed and it's not warm enough to release the critters. It is a very expensive and arbitrary way of trying to control a pest, unless, of course, you have three acres of cucumbers under cover.

Powdery mildew is a white, powdery fungal growth on the leaves. It weakens the plant by effectively blocking light from the leaves. Although it is a fungus, powdery mildew is encouraged by dry soils and a lack of adequate ventilation around the plants. To control this mildew, cut off all the infected leaves, repeating as necessary. It is said that watered-down milk will stop the fungus.

Cucumber Mosaic Virus (CMV) causes a yellow mosaic patterning on the leaves, causing stunted and distorted growth. The fruits become hard and inedible and the plant dies early. The virus is usually transmitted by sap-feeding creatures such as aphids, so it's important to check for aphids early on. Squash them by hand if you find them, or spray with an insecticidal soap. The only method of control that seems to work is to use CMV resistant varieties. Affected plants should be burnt to prevent the virus spreading.

Foot and root rots can occur quickly and lead to other fungal problems such as fusarium and verticullum wilts. To avoid foot and root rot, plant out so that the soil level in the pot is 1cm higher than the surrounding soil level, and water around the raised soil. Sow the seed in clean pots and use sterile compost. Keeping to a rotation system should avoid problems with the soil. However, if you do have problems, you can graft your desired variety of cucumber onto a resistant rootstock (*see Tomatoes for grafting techniques, page 176-7*).

Harvest, storage and sale

All my produce is sold as fresh as possible. Cucumbers need harvesting regularly and when I pick them I must take into account that I only sell my boxes for three days mid-week. I harvest cucumbers on a Sunday or Monday morning, before they warm up in the sun, and store them in a polystyrene box in a dark, cool shed. They are packed for sale on Tuesday, with more harvested that morning. On Wednesday and Thursday I sell the ones picked fresh on those days. On Thursday, I often cut much smaller cucumbers than I would on other days, as I will not pick again until Sunday when I do not want to find a forest of giants. If any of the cucumbers are badly marked or too big then we eat them – always save your best looking produce for your customers and treat yourself when you have excess.

Profit and efficiency

In 1999 I sold over 750 cucumbers, which had grown on just 10 plants in a 1.5 x 7m bed. The cash I took on this crop was over £500. Looked at in terms of materials, this was enough to buy and cover the 20 metre polytunnel in which they were housed.

Hints and tips

Keep the plants growing without any dips in temperature.
Keep well misted and ventilated.
Pick regularly.

Endive

Endive is similar to chicory in terms of flavour and seasonal availability. The green leaves are bitter but blanching the whole plant will make more of the plant edible.

Endive is wonderful for salad bags because it adds volume. I am not trying to cheat customers but a tightly packed salad bag will soon turn into a slimy mess and a few frilly blanched endive leaves help keep the bag open.

Types and varieties
There are two types, frisee (frizzy leaves) or scarole (plain or flat leaved). I grow two types of frizzy endive: Endivia Riccia Pancalieri because it's got such a spectacular name and has pink tinged midribs, and Wallone, which self blanches and is good for an autumn crop. The two scarole types I grow are Jeti for its size and En Cornet de Bordeaux for its hardiness.

Soil, site and rotation
As for chicories.
A shady spot is fine as spring sowings can bolt if it gets too hot in the summer or sow early crops under cover. Endive can also be grown for autumn and winter salads so it can be sown in the bed after the new potatoes have been harvested along with the chicories. Being a member of the lettuce family, it's place in the rotation is not important.

Sowing and planting
Sow 1cm deep in rows 30cm apart, from spring onwards.

Food, water and mulch
The only attention that endive needs in this department is watering, but only if it gets very dry.

Seasonal care
The plants can be thinned to 20-30cm apart and kept weeded. Once the plants are almost fully grown you can blanch the whole plant by covering it with a large pot turned upside down (make sure the holes in the bottom of the pot are blocked). Try to do this when the plants are quite dry. Blanching takes about three weeks and will produce whitish, yellow leaves. Being quite lazy I don't bother to thin the plants and their compactness in the row means that they are almost self blanching on the inside. This method makes quite attractive leaves which have a white bottom, yellow middle and green top.

Succession and continuity
Endive can be available all year. Any left outside in the autumn can be covered with cloches to extend the season right into the winter. Also make some sowings in tunnels during late summer.

Problems
Slugs.

Harvest, storage and sale
You can pick individual leaves from most types of endive and although the dark green leaves can be quite bitter, one or two in salad bags is fine. Like all salad leaves, they wilt at the first opportunity, so try to pick during the coolest part of the day and keep cool before delivery.

Profit and efficiency
Endive, together with chicories and other winter salad leaves, keep my salad bags going well into winter. They are easy to grow and double-crop the land so they are quite profitable. They can also be grown throughout the season and provide a useful early crop when grown under cover, sowing as early as February.

Hints and tips
Blanching makes the plants less bitter.
Use frisee types to open out salad bags.

Fennel

Bulb fennel is a difficult vegetable to grow because it won't stand for long once the bulbs are ready. It's main aim seems to be to bolt. It is a lovely vegetable to eat, though, and when I put it in the boxes people always like it. Once it has bolted the leaves can be used in salads so not all is lost.

Types and varieties
Fennel isn't widely grown for its bulbs in this country, and there aren't many varieties available. The main thing to look for is bolt resistance, so chose Argo or Selma.

Soil, site and rotation
Fennel needs a fine tilth and a pH of 6.5. I never add compost to the soil. Choose an open site in the root (or umbellifer) part of the rotation.

Sowing and planting
Fennel bolts at any opportunity. Always sow direct, avoiding growth checks, which encourage bolting. Sow 1cm deep in rows 30cm apart, from late April onwards. The fine leaves are susceptible to slugs, so sow a seed every 5cm and thin the surviving plants to 30cm. You can eat the thinnings.

Food, water and mulch

If it's not raining, try to water fennel every day. Once they are big enough, mulch heavily with grass mowings, straw or compost.

Seasonal care

Until you mulch the plants, keep the beds weed-free and well watered. According to garden lore, earthing up the bulbs keeps them sweet and tender. I've never earthed mine up and they're always sweet and tender anyway.

Succession and continuity

For a regular supply make several sowings through the season, from May to July. An early sowing in the polytunnel will provide an early crop and sowings made later in the year in the polytunnel will stand well into the winter.

Problems

Slugs will have the young plants so try to sow at the end of a wet spell. With luck the seedlings will be relatively safe for the first few weeks of their lives.

Aphids can attack fennel, particularly if it's very hot or dry. If you sow later in the season, when the predator populations have built up, it shouldn't be a problem.

Harvest, storage and sale

Once one of the crop has started to bulb keep a very close eye on them. The plants need to be harvested as soon as they've bulbed up, before they run to seed. Fennel won't store for longer than a week unless it is kept very cool. However, a winter polytunnel crop can be kept in the ground for quite a while because the cooler temperatures will stop them bolting.

Profit and efficiency

Fennel is difficult to grow because it doesn't stand well. Sometimes it is ready when you've got surpluses elsewhere. It is popular though and if you can grow it for sale your customers will appreciate it. Generally I try to grow enough to give each customer a bulb or two a year, and if I don't have enough then I will buy them in.

Hints and tips

Always sow direct and keep well watered as fennel doesn't like its growth checked.
Don't leave fennel to stand as it bolts readily.

Flowers

Flowers are nice to grow for your own pleasure and to put in boxes for sale. Although I don't grow flowers either for my boxes or for sale it can be worth offering boxes with or without flowers to generate extra income. Growing them can really make a difference to your garden. I also grow flowers for pest control, to attract pollinator and predator insects and to put in salads. However, as this is a vegetable book I won't go into too much detail about flowers.

Types and varieties

Flowers for sale – this is up to you but cut flowers come in all sorts of shapes and sizes. There is also great variety in difficulty of growing. A selection that is easy to grow is cornflowers, sweet peas, chrysanthemums, dahlias, anemones, ox eye daisies, marigolds, calendulas and asters.

Flowers to eat – the edible flowers I use in salad bags are nasturtiums, heartsease pansies, borage, chive, rocket and elderflower. Others can be used including lavender, marjoram, chamomile, pot marigold, rosemary, chicory, sage and hyssop.

Flowers to control pests – in terms of pest control I use flowers to attract predators such as hoverflies, ladybirds and parasitic wasps into my garden. I grow poached egg plant, lovage, fennel, dill, yarrow, chamomile and mint. I grow French marigolds or tagetes around tomato, pepper and aubergine plants in the polytunnels, as their smell is a deterrent to whitefly. Nasturtiums are dual purpose – they are edible and attract black fly away from vegetables. Coriander helps to repel red spider mite and tansy is a general pest deterrent.

Flowers to attract beneficial insects – all flowers will attract pollinating insects, but blue flowers are particularly good, including borage, chicory, hyssop, lavender, rosemary, and thyme.

Flowers and aesthetics – for general aesthetics I let poppies grow wherever they seed themselves, and any other flowers that make it past the hoe.

Soil, site and rotation

Generally speaking, flowers do well on poor soils. They are designed to produce flowers rather than fruits.

Sowing and planting

I tend just to broadcast flower seed around the garden. If you want to grow them for sale, harvesting will be easier if you grow them in beds. Growing nasturtiums in the tunnels will give you flowers for salad bags early and late in the season.

Harvest, storage and sale

Harvest flowers the day you intend to sell them. If you need to pick them earlier, tie the bunches with rubber bands and place in a bucket of water to keep them fresh. For salad bags, pick individual blossoms and place on the top of the salad. This way they will be prominent and will not get crushed.

Profit and efficiency

Flowers are only profitable if you offer them for sale. This might be in addition to vegetables in the boxes, at a roadside stall or at farmers' markets. It's wise to give people a choice with flowers as not everyone wants them.

French Beans

When I started growing French beans I had real trouble with them. This was more due to inexperience than anything. I still think they're a picky crop that can easily fall foul of birds, slugs, woodlice and the cold. However, my customers frequently asked me to put French beans in the boxes if I could, so I kept trying. Now I find that they come thick and fast, but only if they get the warmth they require at the right time.

Types and varieties

The are several types of French bean to grow; climbing, dwarf, flat, round, filet, yellow, purple, green, striped and spotted varieties to eat fresh and others for drying. I grow drying beans for my own use and for the boxes I grow purple, green, dwarf, flat, round and filet beans. This year I have also grown a yellow variety which added variety in the vegetable boxes. I tend not to grow climbing French beans because putting the framework up is so time consuming and the dwarf varieties don't shade the plants behind them.

The purple and green varieties I grow are Purple Teepee and Cropper Teepee, so called because the plants form a wigwam shape that aids harvesting. Filet beans are the small pencil shaped beans which are favoured by chefs, and I have done well with Ferrari although most seem to perform well. There aren't many yellow types but I use Sungold.

Soil, site and rotation

French beans need as much warmth as possible though so a sunny, sheltered site is ideal. They are quite tough little plants and will push through a medium tilth. The soil pH should be 6.5 and the ground needs a dressing of composted muck which should be dug or rotovated in a month or two before sowing. Place in the bean section of the rotation.

Sowing and planting

Before sowing French beans I soak them in cool water and sprout them for a few days. This gives them a head start on any mice that are about. Sow the sprouted seed in a 15cm wide trench at a depth of 5 –

6cm about 5cm apart. Although this seems like a lot you will get a certain amount of slug damage and this sowing density allows for some loss. You should be able to fit two rows to a bed. Make sure you water the beans in as soon as you've planted them as they have already started to grow in the sprouting process and they will stop growing if they are put into a dry soil.

Food, water and mulch

French beans don't need any extra feeding but they will benefit from watering during dry spells. It might be worthwhile putting a straw mulch down between the rows and if you can around the plants too (lawn mowings are easier around the plants). Wait until the plants are well established before you mulch as a spell of wet weather will encourage slugs.

Seasonal care

If the slugs don't do it for you, thin the plants so that there are no more than one or two every 15 - 20cm in the row. You will need to weed the rows and hoe between them once or twice if you haven't mulched them.

Succession and continuity

Being very frost tender but of a high value it's a good idea to grow French beans under cover at either end of the season. If sown in early April it is possible to get a crop in a polytunnel as early as June given adequate protection. You can sow the first batch outside in the middle of April, protecting the plants as soon as they appear. Two sowings can be made in May, another in June and the last one, in the polytunnel, in July.

Problems

If you start French beans before the weather is warm enough for them they will grow very slowly, leaving them susceptible to slugs, birds and other pests such as black fly. Once they appear above the ground it must be warm and dry enough for them to grow away quickly to escape the slugs and birds. Protecting them with plastic or glass cloches will definitely help but I use a length of fleece. This avoids having to remove cloches for watering and tends to be less fiddly and is therefore more efficient. When I start French beans off in the polytunnel my biggest problem is woodlice which devour the new shoots at the first opportunity. I have yet to find a solution to this problem but I do have one polytunnel that is relatively woodlice free and use that for my French bean crops. One idea I have is to put some chickens in the tunnel over winter to eat up the woodlice. However, chickens also like frogs (to eat) so this idea is on hold.

Harvest, storage and sale

Harvesting French beans is very time consuming so it's worthwhile using the varieties with coloured pods which stand out against the leaves, making harvesting that bit easier and quicker. I use brown paper bags to sell them in, even though my customers can't see them in the boxes, but this is the best way to keep them. If you are selling at a market stall, have the different colours displayed and then weigh them out into the bags.

Profit and efficiency

French beans are quite easy to grow but very time consuming to harvest so in terms of profit I'd judge them as about average. However, it seems that most of my customers would quite happily have them every week, probably because they are always a big favourite with kids.

Hints and tips

Use different colours for variety and ease of harvest.
Soak and sprout the beans for a few days before sowing to give them a head start.

Garlic

Geoff Hamilton used to say that garlic was one of the easiest vegetables to grow. It is. The difficult bit is to grow the big, fat, juicy cloves that we all like to use for cooking.

Types and varieties

There are new varieties forever arriving in the catalogues but I stick to my favourites because I save my own bulbs for replanting. I grow two varieties: Germidour and Christo. Germidour is a purple-skinned summer type with big bulbs. It is planted in October or November and has a shelf life until the following New Year, although I have found that it will store longer. Christo is a winter variety, smaller and with white skin. You can plant it in the autumn but I always wait until February, and it whets my appetite for the mad rush ahead.

Soil, site and rotation

I never add muck or compost to my soil when I plant garlic. It does need some fertility so if you have poor soil it might be wise to dig some in. What is most important is warmth and water in the growing season. A fine tilth is not necessary as you will be planting cloves and not seed. Place in the root (or allium) section of the rotation.

Sowing and planting

Garlic is grown from the cloves, the segments that make up the bulb. Push a clove into the soil until the top is sitting just below the surface. To get a big bulb you need to plant the cloves at least 20cm apart. Sow in a dice pattern to maximise the space, but if you plant in rows it is easier to hoe. Lightly rake over the soil to cover the bulbs and then leave them alone.

Food, water and mulch

For garlic to grow well the soil should be kept moist from April to June. Sometime in late March, after a period of heavy rain, I weed the bed then place a layer of straw around the plants. As well as keeping the bed moist and weed-free, the mulch will be a nice dry layer for the garlic to dry on when it is lifted. I leave the mulch in place over the winter as ground cover.

Seasonal care

Keep an eye on the soil under the mulch. Garlic will only grow big and fat with plenty of room and moisture. Irrigate during very dry spells.

Succession and continuity

I start eating garlic before it's officially ready because it is so delicious. If you grow enough of it there's no reason why you can't sell it as immature (or fresh) garlic. Once the bulb has finished swelling in June (both summer and winter varieties) it will start to dry off; you can eat it from this point onward. Both varieties are ready to lift to cure usually in July. The summer variety is used until Christmas, the winter variety is then used until I stop selling. Remember to save some cloves for planting, of all the varieties you grow.

From March to June wild garlic or ramsons are available in carpets through most broad-leafed woodlands in Britain. Use wild garlic raw as cooking destroys its flavour.

Problems

The worst disease problem that I have encountered is rust. If you keep the plants well watered from April to June they should be able to grow through it. However, being an allium they will suffer from white rot if you have it in your soil (see onions).

Harvest, storage and sale

It is best to harvest the bulbs in late July or early August, at the beginning of a dry spell of weather. Put a fork under each one and lift the bulb. Rub the soil from the roots and lay on top of the straw with the root end toward the sun. Leave them like this for as long as possible. If it's likely to rain move them under cover to finish drying, somewhere light and airy. I use an empty, dry bed in the polytunnel but greenhouse staging with shading (to prevent the bulbs from cooking) will do.
Make sure the bulbs are completely dry or they will rot. You can then hang them somewhere cool and dry with plenty of ventilation.

I rarely have enough garlic; it is a very popular vegetable with my customers. I put it in the boxes every two weeks. Unfortunately, being small and light it never really helps with the general presentation of the boxes. If I have any left over at the end of the year, I sell it loose to my customers.

Profit and efficiency

Being an easy vegetable to grow, garlic is profitable. I price each bulb at 60p, so a bed of 500 plants works out at £300. I usually grow about 1000 to 1500 individual bulbs.

Hints and tips

Try to make sure that your customers are aware of the garlic. It might help to mention in a newsletter that every other week their box looks a bit smaller because they've got a garlic bulb instead of a football-sized cabbage. Also point out that it's very difficult to buy bulbs with decent sized cloves; this is one of their perks as a box customer.
You can add value to garlic by plaiting it and selling the strings separately to customers.

Kale

I like growing kale because it's hardy, easy to grow and it seems to be coming back into fashion. It is often referred to as cattle food but in fact it is highly nutritious, varied, and if cooked properly it provides a welcome change to cabbage. It doesn't have to be eaten only in winter either, I sometimes start selling it in August. This means it has time to regrow for the winter and I get two or three pickings off one plant.

Types and varieties
I use three types of kale. Hungry Gap, or Ragged Jack as it's known in the Forest of Dean, has green/purple leaves which can be cooked or used raw in salads and comes into its own in May. Nero di Toscano is a tall, plume shaped plant with very dark green blistered leaves and the best taste of all, and can be harvested from August onwards. Pentland Brig is the frilly, or curly, type that now has a red cousin, Redbor, but these are hybrids.

Soil, site and rotation
As for brassicas.

Sowing and planting
As for brassicas.

Food, water and mulch
As for brassicas.

Seasonal care
As for brassicas.

Succession and continuity
Kale can be harvested as soon as it's ready and it's worth picking it from August onwards, giving it a chance to regrow for the winter months. Leaving the plants to shoot in the spring gives tasty spears similar to sprouting broccoli. Hungry Gap is the best kale for spring because it doesn't bolt as readily as other kales and will provide brassica greens when there is little else available.

Problems
As for brassicas.
Kale is quite tolerant of club root and is probably the best brassica to try for anyone who has this disease in their soil. Caterpillars don't seem that keen on it either.

Harvest, storage and sale

Use the most attractive leaves for sale and tie in bunches with a rubber band. This is easiest with the Nero di Toscano type. With Pentland Brig it is easiest to remove the whole top although this means there's no regrowth for later in the season.

Profit and efficiency

Kale is very cheap to buy in but being such an easy crop to grow I always grow plenty.

Hints and tips

Harvest as early as August to get two or more cuts from the plants.
If you are selling kale then it's worth putting recipes in your boxes.

Kohl Rabi

Kohl rabi is certainly not the most popular of vegetables, as it reminds people of turnips. However, it does attract a lot of interest, and given a little encouragement, people soon warm to it. For the vegetable grower, it is interesting because the stem swells into a bulb out of which the leaves grow. Very odd, and very edible.

Types and varieties

Green and purple varieties of kohl rabi are available. The seed companies seem to change them every few years. The latest attempt to encourage people to buy the seed has been to call them Green and Purple Delicacy.

Soil, site and rotation

A medium tilth is good enough for transplants from a seedbed. If sowing direct then aim for a fine tilth. A pH over 6.5 and an open site help. Place in the brassica section of the rotation.

Sowing and planting

Kohl rabi can be sown direct, 2 seeds every 15cm, 1cm deep in rows 30cm apart. Thin to one plant every 30cm. Alternatively sow in a seed bed like other brassicas. If sown early in modules, kohl rabi can crop as quickly as turnips.

Food, water and mulch

As for brassicas.

Seasonal care

As for brassicas.

Succession and continuity

Make two sowings, one in early March and one in early May. A third, later sowing will provide a root crop to store in sand for winter use. As there are plenty of other brassicas available in the winter I usually don't bother with this last sowing.

Problems

As for brassicas. However, as kohl rabi grows very fast and doesn't have huge leaves, the caterpillars don't seem to do much damage.

Harvest, storage and sale

Being almost a root, Kohl Rabi will stand for a while, but the longer you leave them the bigger and tougher they grow. They are at their best when they're just a little bigger than a golf ball. Don't let them get bigger than a tennis ball.

To harvest pull the whole plant up and slice the lower stem off a little way into the base of the bulb as it is very tough below this point. They look good if you leave the leaves on but in hot weather they wilt quickly; slice them off level with the top of the bulb. In cool weather kohl rabi will store for a few weeks.

Don't try to sell them too often, once or twice a year is usually enough in my box scheme. The purple ones lend colour in the spring when the boxes can look very green.

Profit and efficiency

Being similar to turnips it's difficult to charge a lot for kohl rabi. They do make a nice change in the boxes, so they are valuable for this reason alone.

Hints and tips

Tell your customers what they are and give cooking instructions - grated raw in salads and stir-fried are my usual suggestions.

Lamb's Lettuce or Corn Salad

This is a small lettuce-type plant, with leaves shaped like lambs' tongues. It has a distinctive perfumed flavour and is rich in Vitamin C, giving variety and nutrition to the winter salad bowl.

Types and varieties

There are several types but I always grow the variety called Large Leaved, for obvious reasons.

Soil, site and rotation

Sow the seed in a fine tilth, anywhere in the rotation. Alternatively, grow in modules ready for planting out under cover as space becomes available. It does grow much better under cover, with much larger leaves.

Sowing and planting

Sow 1cm deep in rows 15cm apart, outside in August. Transplant the seedlings into the polytunnel in September. Leave some of the seedlings outside to run to seed the following year. Alternatively sow in modules in August to transplant in September.

Food, water and mulch

Lamb's lettuce grows like a weed and needs little attention. Watering during the early stages of its growth may be necessary. As the weather cools down, watering should be kept to a minimum to prevent moulds.

Seasonal care

Weed if necessary. Crops grown outside can be protected with cloches. Their leaves will be smaller but they will still crop well and survive very cold weather.

Succession and continuity

The plants transplanted into the tunnel in September will be ready to pick in November. This crop can be followed by some plants grown outside.

Problems

Moulds will occur if there isn't adequate ventilation from September onwards and if the plants are over watered during cold wet weather. Slugs don't seem to like Lamb's Lettuce so maybe it shouldn't be called Lettuce at all.

Harvest, storage and sale

Lambs lettuces' only drawback is it's size so make sure you grow the Large Leaved variety. Once the plants are big enough pick the individual leaves for your own consumption but if you want to sell it in salad bags crop the whole plant as it's not worth fiddling with individual leaves on this scale.

Profit and efficiency

Not a hugely profitable crop but it adds interest and flavour to winter salad crops.

Hints and tips

Use the variety called Large Leaved.

Leeks

Leeks are an important winter vegetable. They are quite easy to grow and need little maintenance. There are a number of ways to grow leeks and I perfected a technique in the first couple of years of growing, more by luck than design.

Types and varieties

I grow two types of leek. Lyon is an old variety with thick stems that can be dug in the autumn. Musselburgh, another old variety, will mature fairly early but it will stand through very cold weather, until April.

Soil, site and rotation

Leeks need a soil with a pH of 6.5 and like a lot of fertility. However, I never add compost before a leek crop. They usually follow a courgette or squash crop: the soil will have been heavily mucked for that. If you have a light soil you may need to add some compost before the leeks as well.

Choose a well-drained and breezy site. One year I grew my leeks in a patch of garden that becomes a spring in the winter. I had to dig them very early, but at least they came up clean!

You will need a fairly fine tilth to plant your leeklets in. They should be planted in the root (allium) section of the rotation.

Sowing and planting

Sow the seed under cover in late March, at a temperature of 15°C if possible, in rows 20cm apart and about 1cm deep. I do this in a polytunnel bed. By mid May I have hundreds of leek plants, leeklets,

about as thick as my little finger. When they get to this size they are ready to be planted out. Plant them about 20cm apart in a dibber hole 20 - 25cm deep. Push the roots down the hole and fill with water. This will settle the roots in. You don't need to refill the hole with earth, this space will be filled by the plant.

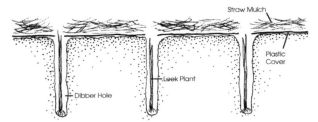

Food, water and mulch

If you can cover the bed with a plastic mulch you will cut down on weeding and watering. Lay out and secure the plastic before transplanting the leeks. Then make holes to plant the leeks through. The plastic will direct any rainfall directly down the dibber hole to the roots. Also, the straight veined leaves of the leeks channel any rainfall directly down to the roots. A layer of straw over the plastic will help to keep the roots cool and moist. If you can't use a plastic mulch, use straw alone and you won't need to water them unless the summer is particularly dry.

Seasonal care

None.

Succession and continuity

Use the earlier variety first. I usually start pulling leeks once the weather starts to feel wintery. They can crop for six months and if I start too early I will get sick of them. They will crop into April before they start to bolt.

Problems

Rust can be a problem with leeks. Planting the leeklets at adequate spacing to provide good ventilation and keeping the plants well watered in the summer should limit any problem. The plants are more vulnerable if the soil is too rich in nitrogen. You can buy varieties that are resistant to rust. Your customers will not be aware of the rust as you will remove a lot of the leaves before you sell the leeks.

Being an allium, leeks can suffer from similar problems to onions. I have never experienced these, and other than rust leeks are fairly trouble free.

Harvest, storage and sale

Dig up leeks as you need them. They can be dug the day before they are needed and they keep a nice glossy shine on their shanks. You can store them for a few days but they don't look as nice: useful, though, if you need them when the ground is likely to freeze. To harvest, dig up each leek, cut the roots off then the tops and peel away the outer layer. This method keeps them clean, ready for sale.

Give box customers leeks every two weeks, 2 or 3 in each box if they are big enough.

Leeklets can also be sold, if you have too many. Leave them in the soil until you are ready for them and sell them as gourmet vegetables, either in the boxes or to restaurants.

Profit and efficiency

Leeks are quite profitable in the winter as they suffer from so few problems and are easy to harvest.

Hints and tips

Starting leeks off under cover gives them a head start.

Leeks rarely require any extra water unless there is no rain for months on end.

Lettuce

Lettuce is the basis of spring and summer salads. It's easy to grow and there are a huge number of varieties, colours, shapes and sizes. With a little imagination it can be combined with other salad leaves, herbs and flowers to create salads for your table or salad bags for sale which are far more interesting and tasty than anything you could hope to find in a supermarket *(see Salad Bags page 235)*. I do sell the occasional whole lettuce, but 95% of the lettuce I grow goes into salad bags.

Types and varieties

Butterhead is the standard type of lettuce. Crisphead lettuces are the iceberg types. Loose leaf lettuces have very little heart to them and can often be harvested by picking the biggest leaves and letting the smaller ones grow on. Cos lettuces are upright and very crunchy. There are also winter varieties.

There are numerous varieties of each type and there is such a large choice that I'm always experimenting. I do have some varieties that I stick with because they have characteristics that are ideally suited to salad bag production.

In the butterhead category I use Marvel of Four Seasons, because it performs well in cold conditions and has a nice reddish tinge to the leaves. I use Buttercrunch for its green leaves and because it can withstand hot weather. Tom Thumb is a quick growing dwarf butterhead which can be used whole in a salad bag. If you have a surplus it can be sold as a whole lettuce in the boxes.

Generally speaking the iceberg types of lettuce are difficult to grow so I stick with the reliable Webb's Wonderful.

In the cos department, I grow Bath Cos for its huge size and taste, Little Gem for its crunchiness, and Little Leprechaun for its very red leaves.

By far the best of the loose leaf lettuces are Green Salad Bowl and Red Salad Bowl. They are very easy to pick and just keep growing. Lollo Rossa is nice with its frilly leaves, as is Catalogna for its oakleaf shape.

I find that the winter varieties don't perform very well, so I tend not to grow them.

Soil, site and rotation

Lettuces need easily available nutrients, so use your best compost. Cover the ground with a good layer and rotovate it in until you have a good fine tilth.

Lettuce needs an open site but will suffer from very hot sun. Try to grow your lettuces near to where you will pack your salad bags. There is nothing worse than having to wander all over the garden looking for different types of lettuce.

Lettuce belongs to the compositae family, which has few pests and diseases. It does not need to follow a rotation scheme so I tend to fit it in to vacant beds. These are often long, narrow beds that ought to have sweetcorn in but are the wrong shape for the sweetcorn to pollinate successfully.

Sowing and planting

The trick with lettuce is to sow little and often. To get the earliest crop, sow in modules in early February at 15 - 18°C. Once they're 5 - 7.5cm tall, plant them out under cover, preferably in a polytunnel, or outside under cloches. The spacing will depend on the size of the lettuce - Little Gem and Tom Thumb can be 15cm apart but Webb's Wonderful and Salad Bowl need a good 30 - 40cm between them. From mid March you can sow directly into beds under cover. Always sow the seed thinly, 0.5 - 1cm deep. Sowing lettuce in mid summer is always awkward because the seed won't germinate in soil temperatures that are more than 20°C. Sowings in the height of summer must be made in the late afternoon and given a cold shower. Even shading the rows with planks of wood will help. If you get a cooler period, take advantage of it and sow the lettuce then rather than waiting for a month's gap in order to keep your succession going. It is better to have some lettuce coming early than not having any at all.

Food, water and mulch

I never mulch lettuce as mulches only encourage slugs. Water is important though, water them regularly or they will bolt very quickly. Try to water them in the very early morning so they have a chance to take up the water before it evaporates. Watering late in the day provides a nice damp soil for slugs to slime over ready for their nightly feasting.

Seasonal care

When your rows of lettuce are getting crowded, water them well and thin to 15 – 30cm apart. Use the thinnings in salads or, if you're careful, as transplants. Any subsequent overcrowding can be dealt with by harvesting every other plant.

Succession and continuity

Make sowings every two weeks through the season but don't sow more than you need. I sow 3 rows of 3 metres of lettuce every two weeks, giving me more than enough for 100 salad bags a week well into October.

Remember that the different types will mature at different times – Tom Thumb can be ready in as little as six weeks whereas Webb's Wonderful will take a good 12 weeks to mature. Transplanting your thinnings will help with continuity, as they will take a little longer to mature because of the shock of being moved.

I tend not to grow winter lettuces, but extend the season by growing varieties such as Marvel of Four Seasons under cover.

Problems

Mmmmm . . . slugs. Impossible to eliminate but a range of techniques should keep them at bay. Never plant your lettuce close to walls, sleepers or other wooden or stone structures. Try to plant in open ground and prepare to lose some of your crop around the edges. Don't mulch lettuces. Water early in the day so that the surface dries and is less easy for slugs, which appear at night, to move over. Sow lettuce at the beginning of a dry period; hopefully when they emerge there will be less slug activity than there might be.

I always have some slugs on my lettuces, they can't be avoided, but because I tend to grow lettuces for leaf rather than head production, they aren't really such a big problem. When the lettuce leaf is picked it's easy to flick any slugs off. As leaf lettuce is fairly open the slugs tend not to hang around in them as long as they do in heading lettuce, which by their very structure provide a slug friendly habitat, dark, damp and full of food.

Aphids will have a go at your lettuces but a healthy plant with an adequate supply of food and water will not be severely affected.

Lettuce root aphids can affect lettuces in dry seasons. The symptoms are smaller, unproductive plants which, when pulled, have clusters of aphids around the roots. Keeping the plants well watered prevents the aphids but in the event of a bad attack, implement a four year rotation for your lettuces.

Downy mildew may be a problem in damp and humid conditions. It starts as a yellowing of the leaves, followed by a fuzzy greyish growth and leading to rots. Make sure you provide good ventilation by not overcrowding the plants and by keeping weeds down.

Harvest, storage and sale

With loose leaf varieties, pick individual leaves off from the base. For butterhead and cos types, pull the whole plant up and cut the base off, removing the outer untidy leaves at the same time. You will need to treat each lettuce according to how you want to sell it. They can be sold whole but they are unlikely to be slug free and look good. The cos types are usually the best in terms of appearance and quality. If you pick lettuce for salad bags you get to remove any critters and damaged or slimy leaves before you pack them. (*See Salad Bags page 235 for packing techniques*).

Lettuces really don't store very well, they need to be eaten or sold the day they are picked. If you can get up early enough, pick lettuce in the very early morning. They will stay fresh longer than if they are picked when it's hot.

Profit and efficiency

It is easy to grow lettuce but difficult to grow good quality lettuces. In the summer they won't be worth more than 40p -50p each. Lettuces are most profitable as a main ingredient in salad bags.

Hints and tips

Grow successionally but don't sow too many in one go or you will be inundated!
Winter lettuce are difficult to grow on a commercial scale – use other leaves instead.
Do not try to germinate in hot conditions.
Keep well watered in dry conditions.

Marrows and Pumpkins

It's easy to let a few marrows grow on your courgette plants, but I prefer to grow marrow varieties in their own right as the fruits have lovely striped skins. Marrows can be stuffed with a variety of imaginative fillings and cooked properly are absolutely delicious. Another way of cooking marrow is to coat it in ground cumin and coriander and then roast in very hot oil. Small cubes of marrow can be added to vegetable bhajis, the culinary possibilities are endless.

Pumpkins are a great crop for kids. They are delicious in pies and soups or roasted, and they are compulsory for lanterns. I always grow a lot of pumpkins – I need 50 or so to sell in the boxes and the same again for Halloween. They are grown in the same way.

Types and varieties

I like to grow Long Green Trailing marrow for its yellow stripes. I also grow Tiger Cross, a hybrid with resistance to Cucumber Mosaic Virus, to guarantee a crop.

I usually grow three types of pumpkin. The smallest are called Golden Nugget and grow on a bush plant like courgettes. The next size up is the Halloween size, I usually use Tom Fox or Jack O'Lantern. They can also be sliced to put in boxes. I also grow a variety called Mammoth, for putting in boxes. I save the biggest one for a Guess the Weight of the Pumpkin competition for Open Days.

Soil, site and rotation
As for courgettes.

Sowing and planting
As for courgettes.

Food, water and mulch
As for courgettes.

Seasonal care
As for courgettes.

Succession and continuity
Marrows and pumpkins mature at the end of the summer. They will store through the winter, often until March or April.

Problems
As with courgettes.

Harvest, storage and sale
There is usually a light frost at the start of the autumn and this is enough to kill off the leaves of the cucurbit plants. This will reveal the marrows and pumpkins, which should be harvested at this point. Store somewhere cool but not damp and they will keep well into the winter. A window sill or under a bed is ok if you don't have anywhere else.

The average marrow is between 30 and 60cm long, far too big for my customers. I cut them into thirds or halves depending on their size and cover the exposed flesh with plastic. I only put them in the boxes once or twice in the season as they aren't the most popular of vegetables. Including recipe suggestions does help. Pumpkins can be sliced into wedges and put in plastic bags before being put in the boxes. I put about 1kg slices of pumpkin into medium sized boxes

I offer my customers Halloween pumpkins at roughly the same price as non-organic pumpkins - people are less willing to pay organic prices for something they're not necessarily going to eat.

Profit and efficiency
Although they aren't very profitable, marrows provide a change in the boxes during the autumn and winter. As they don't require much care during the growing season and are easily stored, they are a valuable crop. Pumpkin slices can be added more often as they are more popular. The Halloween pumpkins are always a good extra earner and provide your customers with something a little bit extra.

Hints and tips
Don't put them in your boxes too often, and suggest recipes.
Don't give customers slices of pumpkin around Halloween time!

Onions

The most amazing thing about onions is that they are the only vegetable in the world that can make you cry. They are quite easy to grow, and combined with spring onions and shallots, can last you all year. However, I don't grow all the onions I sell. I would need far more land than I have. Also, onions are cheap to buy in the winter, so I grow only enough to see me through until the price drops.

Types and varieties

To have a supply of onions for most of the year you need to grow two types – a monocrop and an over-winter type. You can either grow them from seed or from sets (small onion bulbs which grow into big onion bulbs). Growing from seed is much cheaper than from sets but it takes a long time and is less reliable than using sets.

For the monocrop I use Turbo sets, which are a globe shape, rather than flat. The main reason that I use these is that round onions are easier to slice than flat ones. It is nice to grow a few red onions to add to the boxes as well, although they do have a tendency to bolt. I use Red Baron sets. For over-wintering onions I use Senshyu Yellow and Radar sets.

Soil, site and rotation

As with leeks, you need a fertile soil of a fine to medium tilth with a pH of 6.5. An open site is preferable. Grow in the root (allium) section of the rotation.

Sowing and planting

If you are using seed, start the onions in late January or early February. Sow them in seed trays, or in modules with 4 seeds to each block. Plant out in April, 15 – 20cm apart for single plants or 30 – 40cm apart if growing in a block.

Sets should be planted in late March. They can be grown in a dice pattern, about 20-30cm apart, or in rows, which are easier to hoe. Push them gently into the soil, with the tops covered, and lightly rake the soil over. If you want to grow red onions then it is best to delay planting sets until well into April. They have a tendency to bolt, which is less likely if they are planted later.

Over-wintering onion sets should be planted in September or October in the south. In the north it is best to grow them under cover.

Food, water and mulch

You will need to weed and water the plants until they have started to grow away, when you can mulch the bed with straw. The onions will need no more attention until harvest, but water them if it is particularly dry.

Seasonal care

Hoe between the rows before applying a mulch. If one of the plants sends up a flower head, pinch it out. When the stems begin to fall over in late July or early August, the bulbs are nearly ready. You can push all the stems over at this point so that the bulbs all ripen at the same rate.

Succession and continuity

The over winter varieties of onions will be ready at the end of May or beginning of June. The monocrop will start in late July and will store well for use until March or April the following year. The gap until the over winter varieties are ready again the following season is filled by stored shallots, which can be supplemented with spring onions.

Problems

Onions can suffer from onion fly, onion eelworm, white rot, neck rot, storage rot and downy mildew. Onion fly makes the plant yellow and die prematurely. When the bulb is uncovered there will be white maggots in it. The female onion fly is attracted by the smell of onions when they are thinned. Onion sets don't need to be thinned, so the problem is rare with sets.

Eelworms are tiny. They get inside the bulb and distort its shape. It is a soil borne problem and a rotation of at least four years will prevent it from recurring.

It is said that crows and sparrows pick out onion sets when they are planted, but this only really happens if you don't plant them deeply enough; they should be buried so that the tops don't show. The birds peck them because they are looking for nesting material and the tops of onion sets look like bits of straw.

White rot shows as a mouldy white growth at the base of onions. Small, black sclerotia or black pustules will develop in this mould and drop into the soil where they can last more than seven years. If you find affected plants be sure that you burn them and don't grow onions in that spot for another eight years. This is where an eight year rotation comes into its own (*see page 37*).

Neck rot is a disease that makes the necks of onions become grey and mouldy. It can be caused by over feeding, and make sure you stick to your rotation.

The bulbs can rot in storage if they aren't completely ripe or dry – check them regularly and take out any that show signs of rot.

Onion downy mildew is a feature of very wet weather. The stems start to rot and if it spreads to the bulb you've lost your onion. It's best to chop the affected stem off completely and try to dry the onion as it is. Sell these onions quickly as they are not likely to store for long, and warn your customers that they need using quickly.

Harvest, storage and sale

Start to sell the over-wintered onions at the beginning of June, even if they have green stems. They will not store well and should be used up before the monocrop. If you run short you can start using the monocrop from late July, when it begins to ripen.

To harvest the monocrop to store, you need to cure the bulbs slowly and thoroughly. This is best done in the sun. When the stems start to fall over, loosen each bulb at the base with a fork. The roots are exposed to the air and begin to dry out. After a week, lift the bulbs and lay them on the straw mulch.

Ideally they want to dry out in the sun. Even if it's tipping it down the straw will help to stop them rotting, but try to get them under cover if it is continually wet. A spare greenhouse or polytunnel bed is ideal but not often available. An alternative to straw is to lay them on a raised bed of chicken wire. Good air circulation aids the drying process. When the bulbs are dry, tie them in bunches of between 6 and 10 and hang in a frost free barn. If they have dried well you can remove the stalks completely and store them in nets. I try to give everyone some type of onion every week. This is nearly always possible with spring onions, shallots and both types of onion. In the winter, a box for four will have between 3 or 5 onions a week, depending on their size.

Profit and efficiency
Onions aren't very profitable because they can be bought wholesale very cheaply and sets are expensive. However, they are easy to grow, requiring little attention during the growing season.

Hints and tips
Make sure they are thoroughly dry before storing or they will rot.
Red varieties are always worth growing because they are popular with customers.

Oriental Salad Leaves

Oriental salad leaves are useful in summer salads, but they really come into their own in the winter. Being particularly hardy they are an essential winter salad ingredient. They are mainly brassicas, which must be taken into account in your rotation, but as they are quick growing they tend to avoid clubroot.

Types and varieties
I grow several varieties, ranging from mild to extremely hot and spicy. Mizuna has spiky leaves and a mild flavour, similar to Mibuna which has long, thin blade-shaped leaves. Komatsuna has a mild, cabbage flavour. The large spoon-shaped leaves of Pak Choi have a mild flavour and a wide crunchy stem. Chinese cabbages have crinkly heads that provide lots of mild salad leaves. Shungiku has a sharp, chrysanthemum flavour. Red and green mustards have large hot leaves and mustard Green in the Snow is very hot and spicy.

Soil, site and rotation
Most types are quick growing so they don't need a particularly fertile soil. Sow the seed into a finely tilled soil. They should be grown in the brassica part of the rotation in an open site. In practice I grow most of these leaves under cover for winter salad bags.

Sowing and planting
Oriental leaves are best grown after midsummer, as they are prone to bolting. All are sown in drills 10cm deep and 20 to 30cm apart. One seed every 10cm is adequate to grow a thick row of leaves.

Food, water and mulch

Keep well watered while they are growing, but don't water during cold or damp weather.

Seasonal care

If you sow the seed thinly none of the rows will need thinning, with the exception of pak choi and Chinese cabbage. These will produce big plants and should be thinned to at least 20cm apart.

Succession and continuity

The plants will continue to grow through the winter at quite low temperatures but as soon as the weather begins to warm, the plants start to run to seed. At this point their flavour becomes very hot so, beware.

Problems

They are likely to bolt if sown before midsummer. If there is a particularly hot late summer the plants might suffer from flea beetle but this is rare.

Harvest, storage and sale

You can start to pick individual leaves when the plants are still fairly small. If the whole plant is cut then regrowth is negligible. As the leaves are mostly picked in the autumn and winter they will keep fresh for longer than summer leaves, but I still recommend picking salads on the day of sale.

Profit and efficiency

Being quick and easy to grow, they are as profitable as lettuce in the salad bags and really are worth growing for sale.

Hints and tips

Give people some information about these leaves. Once customers have identified and tried them they don't look back.

Don't sow before midsummer as they bolt.

Parsnips

As a roast vegetable, parsnips can't be beaten. They're not too difficult to grow either. Unfortunately some people really don't like them.

Types and varieties

In the past I have always grown Tender and True, because it is reputed to have the best flavour. The roots are large, often going down a good metre. This helps to break up soil pans and introduce air and drainage channels. It is described as canker resistant but I find that it does still suffer from the problem, so this year I will be growing the variety Avonresister as well and, as its name implies, this should be more resistant to canker.

Soil, site and rotation

It's usually recommended that you incorporate plenty of compost into the soil prior to sowing parsnips. I have never done this and my parsnips always reach a good size. A warm soil is needed to encourage parsnips to germinate and they should be grown in the root (umbellifer) section of the rotation. The seeds are quite big so the tilth does not need to be very fine as with other umbellifers such as carrots and parsley.

Sowing and planting

It is usually recommended that parsnips are sown as early as February, so they can be harvested early. I never do this: parsnips won't germinate in a cold soil and they are best left in the ground until after the first hard frosts when their flavour becomes much sweeter. I sow them at the beginning of April. Sow three seeds every nine inches.

They are slow to germinate, particularly at low temperatures, so be patient – they usually appear after about three weeks. They can be pre-germinated for better results. I mark the lines of parsnips with sand or sow a radish seed every few centimetres. These will emerge quickly to show where the parsnip line is so that it is possible to hoe before they appear above the ground. The radishes can be weeded out easily once the parsnips have emerged.

Food water and mulch

I never water parsnips as their taproots are designed to search for water deep in the soil. The roots can crack if it gets very dry. I've never experienced this on my heavy soil, although it may be wise to mulch on light, dry soils.

Seasonal care

Parsnips do take a long time to germinate and can disappear amongst seedling weeds, so hoe carefully between the lines. As the seedlings appear they should be hoed twice and then hand weeded. Once parsnips are established there's so much leaf that weeds don't really have a chance.

Succession and continuity

Parsnips don't store for long once they have been dug up, as they dry out quite quickly, so dig them as you need them. They are best eaten after the first hard frost, which make the roots sweeten up, and before the weather warms up in March. If they start growing again they don't taste so good because all the sugars in the root are used up growing new leaves.

Problems

Parsnips are rarely troublesome. Carrot root fly can affect parsnips, but I've yet to see this. If you grow carrots the fly are likely to go to them in preference to the parsnips.

Canker is a disease that marks the shoulders of parsnips with a soft, orange-brown scar. This can be cut off, but selling parsnips with chunks missing doesn't look good. I tend to save those parsnips that haven't been too badly affected, if at all, for sale and eat the damaged ones myself. Alternatively, grow a resistant variety. There are now F1 varieties available that have increased resistance. I prefer to stick to older varieties, as they tend to have a better flavour.

Harvest, storage and sale

It is easy to damage parsnips with a garden fork, so use a spade to dig them up. Dig down the side of the row, at least a spade's depth, to reveal the sides of the parsnips. Pull the parsnips sideways into the trench and then, if they're not too big, pull them out. The roots of the variety Tender and True often reach down 1 metre or more. It is difficult to pull the root out when it goes down that deep, so I slice the root off about 30cm down. The root that is left in the soil will rot, allowing air to penetrate the soil.

Parsnips do not store very well, so it is best to leave them in the ground until they're needed. However, if they have a covering of damp soil they can be kept in a paper sack for a few weeks.

Profit and efficiency

Parsnips are relatively expensive root vegetables to buy in during the winter, so it's a good idea to grow as many as you can.

Hints and tips

Contrary to many recommendations, sow in April rather than February.
Always dig with a spade to avoid damaging the roots.

Peas

(including mange-tout and snap pod peas)

It doesn't seem possible, because peas are so popular, but there were two weeks last summer when I was swamped with peas. My customers love fresh peas (so much better than the frozen ones) but even they couldn't keep up with them. It wasn't a complete disaster: I had enough dried and frozen peas to use in soups and stews all winter and I saved a lot of them for seed.

Types and varieties

There are two main types of podding pea, round seeded and wrinkled seeded. The round type are winter hardy and will produce an early crop. They are not as sweet as the wrinkle seeded type, because they contain more starch. Varieties are few and far between, but Feltham First, Meteor and Pilot all crop well.

The wrinkled seeded varieties are far more popular. I usually use Greenshaft or Hurst Greenshaft, both of which are very sweet. Very tall varieties, which can reach 1.5 to 2m in height, are less common now, but the Heritage Seed Library at Garden Organic (*see Useful Organisations page 265*) has a good selection.

Petit-pois are very small and sweet.

Mange-tout and snap pod peas are eaten pod and all. Oregon Sugar Pod is a good variety of mange-tout and Sugar Snap and Sugar Rae are good snap pod varieties. I don't grow these for sale as I don't like to think of my customers taking a bite of pea moth grubs by mistake. With podding peas you can see the grub before you eat it. Mange-tout are very popular but they are fiddly to pick and don't amount to much in weight, nor when you see them in a box.

Soil, site and rotation
The soil of a pea bed should have a medium tilth with a pH of 6.5. It's best to work in a light dressing of composted muck before sowing. Grow in the pea section of your rotation. Peas like a bit of sun to get them ripening, so choose a sunny spot.

Sowing and planting
Before sowing peas, I soak and sprout them for a few days. This gives them a head start on any mice that are about. When pre-sprouting peas and beans ensure they are soaked in cool water and left to sprout somewhere not too hot, like a kitchen. I have soaked seeds in water and then tried to sprout them in a hot polytunnel and they just dissolved into rank smelling mush because they had started to cook. Sow in a 15cm wide trench at a depth of 5 – 6cm, about 5cm apart. You should be able to fit two drills to a metre wide bed.

Food, water and mulch
Once you have started a plant by sprouting it you must keep it growing, so water as soon as you have raked the soil over. Once the peas are 5cm high, mulch with straw. This will give them a little shelter early on, and prevent weeds and evaporation. If you have a particularly dry spell it's a good idea to water them, even if they are mulched. Be careful to avoid over-watering, though, which will make them less sweet.

Seasonal care
Once the straw mulch is down, you need to erect some sort of framework for the pea plants to climb up. This can be netting, wires or sticks. With short varieties, between 75 and 90cm tall, it is best to use pea sticks. These are the twiggy tops of the hazel poles that have been used for the runner bean supports. Cut them to about 1.2m, remove the lowest branches and push the sticks into the ground, making a hedge along both the rows. If you lean them in slightly and lay their flat sides along the rows, you won't keep bumping into them as you walk past. For the taller varieties, make a tall frame and attach netting to it for the peas to climb up.

Succession and continuity
It is possible to have peas cropping from the end of May until the middle of September.

Round seeded peas are hardy and can be sown outdoors in autumn, but a hard winter will probably kill them off. It is usually best to start them off in February, under cover to be safe. Grow them either outside under cloches or in the polytunnel in short lengths of guttering. To transplant peas sown in guttering, make a trench and slide the peas with the soil straight in. Bear in mind that they may need protection after moving outdoors.

I make my first sowing in early March, in the polytunnel. I use one of the sweeter wrinkle seeded varieties for this sowing. Start the maincrop (also wrinkle seeded) off outside at the end of March or beginning of April. These peas should be ready to harvest at the end of June. Make three more sowings, in late April, mid May and early June, for a continuous crop until the middle of September. Sowings made later than this will often succumb to mildew and fail to produce a worthwhile crop. I don't usually grow round seeded varieties because I haven't had much success with them and they're not as sweet as the wrinkle seeded types but they're worth another try to see if I can get another crop earlier in the season.

Problems

Generally speaking, mice, pea moth and mildew are the worst problems to affect pea plants. Pea and bean weevils are a minor problem.

Pre-sprouting the peas before planting will help to beat mice. In a polytunnel you can set traps (humane or otherwise), baited with cheese or soaked peas, to protect your crop at first.

Pea moths lay their eggs on pea plants when they are in flower. The eggs hatch into grubs that feed on the peas developing in the pods. I have never had a serious problem with these grubs – only about 1 in 30 pods is affected and luckily my customers seem to be able to cope with this level of infestation. Unfortunately you can't know how bad the problem is until you shell the peas.

Mildew will affect the pea plant in cool, damp conditions when the plant's roots become over dry. This can happen on summer mornings when there is dew on the ground but you haven't had time to provide good irrigation. The foliage and pods go grey and sticky and your hands smell of fish when you pick the pods. Mildew often sets in around August time when most of the peas have been harvested. Pea and bean weevils usually cause little damage, just nibbling away at the edge of the leaves. Healthy plants should grow through the problem but you can use derris if there is serious damage to young seedlings.

Harvest, storage and sale

For shelling peas, pick the pods while the peas are still small and before the pods get too fat. The peas will taste so sweet that they are nicer raw than cooked. The only way to really tell if they're ready is to open a pod and try one. They don't store well so pick as late as you can before eating or selling.

You will have no trouble selling peas as they are as popular as strawberries. Mange-tout are also popular but snap pod peas need some information with them because they are less well known.

Profit and efficiency

Mange-tout are worth growing for your own consumption but I find that they never produce a worthwhile crop to sell. In a veg box, 500g of peas looks twice as much as 125g of mange-tout, no matter that they are of the same monetary value.

Podding peas, on the other hand, are a huge success. They might be awkward and time consuming to pick but customer satisfaction makes them a rewarding crop to grow. If profitability were measured in terms of satisfaction peas would win hands down every time.

Hints and tips

Pre-sprout in cool water and leave to sprout somewhere not too hot.

Never try and sell peas that are too old. Once they get too big and old the sugar in them turns to starch and they won't be worth eating.

Peppers and Chillies

Peppers and chillies are probably one of my favourite crops to grow, because there is such a tremendous variety in colour, size, shape and heat. Given the right conditions they will crop heavily. Culturally they are very similar to aubergines, but they are slightly hardier and much easier to grow.

Types and varieties

I choose pepper and chillies to grow with the same thought in mind as when I choose tomatoes. People like colour and variety.

For a standard green block pepper I grow Bell Boy F1. It is a reliable and heavy cropper. I'm also growing yellow and orange varieties this year. I am growing an early variety called Redskin F1, outside under cloches.

Long peppers ripen from a lime green through to a deep red. I grow Hungarian Wax and Hot Banana.

I grow three varieties of chillies every year, and others as the mood takes me. Serrano has short, fat, dark green type chillies. Thai Hot Dragon produces small, very hot red fruits. The chillies on Firecracker are small and very hot in variable colours.

Soil, site and rotation

It is best to use transplants rather than direct sowing for peppers so a medium tilth is fine. Prepare the site by digging in composted muck, or half-fill a trench with composted muck then refill with soil.

Peppers and chillies do best under cover. I usually grow then in the tunnels but they will grow outside in the south, particularly if you provide shelter, such as cloches. Last year I grew peppers outside, interspersed with bush tomatoes, under high plastic cloches. This doubled the amount of produce from the space, and the peppers shaded the tomatoes from too much hot sun.

Peppers are related to tomatoes and aubergines so keep them in that part of the rotation.

Sowing and planting

I start the seed off in polystyrene modules in a propagator at 18–21°C, in late February. When they are 7.5–10cm tall I transfer them to 7.5cm pots, still in the propagator. When they have grown a little taller I move them to a sunny windowsill or warm greenhouse. They are usually ready to be planted in the tunnel or greenhouse in late April or early May.

Pepper plants need to be about 60–75cm apart. Chilli plants tend to be smaller so can be slightly closer together. Each plant will need a 1m stake. They will also benefit from the extra protection of a double fleece tent for the first couple of weeks. Unfold it during the day if it's warm enough, and remove it completely when the plants have settled in.

Food, water and mulch

I water the plants almost every day until the first flower buds appear. After this I start to feed with comfrey liquid once a week and also water every other day in between feeds. Outdoor crops should be mulched with straw to prevent evaporation from the soil. If you are growing your tomatoes underneath the peppers, the mulch will also help to keep the tomatoes off the soil.

Seasonal care

The branches of pepper plants (not chillies) will need support because as the fruits develop the weight of the crop can pull the branches off the main trunk. I simply tie string round each plant a couple of times during the season. Alternatively stake each end of the bed and run strings along each side of the row. This doesn't stop the inner branches from snapping off. It's worth noting that the branches of the long pepper varieties tend not to get so heavy but some can get quite tall so make sure you put in good sized stakes to tie them to.

If growing peppers outdoors under cloches, pay attention to ventilation: you will need to open the cloches up nearly every day during the summer.

Succession and continuity

The first peppers, from the tunnel, are ready in mid July. The outdoor ones tend to crop from early August onwards. If you want red peppers, just leave them for another few weeks and they will ripen up.

The chillies start about the same time and again, wait a few weeks and they will go red. In a good season they will continue right through October.

Problems

When very young, peppers sometimes suffer from green aphids. Make sure you inspect them, particularly after transplanting. If aphids are a problem then spray with soft soap.

Red spider mite can also affect pepper plants. Damp down paths to help create humidity.

Slugs will chomp away on plants when they are young so if you're planting outside, try to do it during a dry spell or protect them with large clear plastic bottles with their bottoms cut off.

Blossom end rot may be a problem if the plants haven't been watered regularly.

Harvest, storage and sale
When you pull a pepper, the whole branch can easily snap off. Use both hands when harvesting and try to pull the fruits back against the curve of their stem. Peppers store well for a few days in a cool environment.

My customers like colourful peppers, and they nearly always like chillies, no matter how hot. I usually put a selection in the boxes, one large green block pepper with maybe a long yellow pepper and two or three little, red devils.

Profit and efficiency
There's no doubt that peppers and chillies are profitable. They need little attention during the growing season and they are quick and easy to harvest.

Hints and tips
Try lots of different colours and shapes to impress your customers.
Keep well watered and fed.

Perpetual Spinach and Swiss Chard

Annual spinach is quite an awkward plant to grow, but luckily there are two wonderful alternatives. Swiss chard and perpetual spinach are two of my favourite crops. They are tenacious, easy to grow and have a long season. They rarely bolt, and will continue cropping well into autumn, and into the winter given some cover. If I could give my customers spinach every week, my life would be a lot easier!

Types and varieties
There is only one type of perpetual spinach. It is sometimes called spinach beet or leaf beet. It is inaccurately named: it isn't perpetual, it is biennial, going to seed in its second year.
There are three types of Swiss chard (why it's called Swiss rather than Austrian or German chard is beyond me). The green type is just called Swiss chard, or silver or sea kale. Rhubarb or ruby chard has red stems and leaf veins and rainbow chard has stems of all different colours. These coloured varieties have a greater tendency to bolt, but they add a lot of interest to the boxes. Young leaves brighten up salad bags.

Soil, site and rotation

As with annual spinach, the plants require little nutrition and only a medium tilth. They are related to beetroot and can be grown anywhere. I tend to keep them together with the beetroot.

Sowing and planting

Sow the seed in April, when the soil has warmed. Sow thickly, that is one seed every 1.5-2.5cm, 2.5cm deep, in rows 30cm apart. I get three rows to a bed and sow between 30 and 60 metres each year.

Food, water and mulch

The plants require no feeding. I water the rows if it gets really dry and I have mulched in the past with little damage from slugs. Rhubarb and rainbow chards require more water then the green plants and benefit from mulching, to inhibit bolting. When harvesting the spinach, any blemished or old leaves can be left on the surface between the rows and these will act as a mulch.

Seasonal care

You will need to hoe and probably hand weed once or twice. After this the canopy should be thick enough to suppress weeds.

Succession and continuity

The great thing about chards and perpetual spinach is that you can get three crops in one season. In May I start cutting at one end of the row. By the time I've reached the other end, in July, I can start at the beginning again. I go along the row three times. If I cover the row with cloches after the third cut, in September, I will get another cut in November if the weather's kind. For an earlier harvest, sow under cloches in March. I also sow in August in an empty bed in the polytunnel, which provides leaves up to Christmas for the boxes, and beyond for my own consumption.

Problems

I've yet to find any problems associated with chard and perpetual spinach. Being two of my favourites, I'm loath to say anything against them. But getting rid of the roots the next season can be a hindrance. I usually follow them with peas so I plough or dig in last years crop in early March, then rotovate in early spring. This process usually chops the roots up enough to prevent the spinach from regrowing and any bits that do regenerate can be hooked out by hand.

Harvest, storage and sale

To harvest chards and perpetual spinach you need only a sharp knife and some rubber bands. Before the crop is well established, I pick individual leaves. Bundle them into bunches as big as you can hold, wrap an elastic band twice round the bunch and cut across the bottom of the stalks to make them neat. When the crop is established, you can harvest the rows by grabbing a handful and cutting the plants at the base. Remove any yellow, old or blemished leaves and push any very long ones down, then tie with an elastic band. If the bunch looks a bit small, add a few more leaves.

The leaves will not keep fresh for long so pick in the early morning in the summer. Spray with cold water until they can be delivered.

Most of my customers are happy to get spinach every two weeks. I include Swiss chard in the boxes as an alternative to perpetual spinach, and every now and then I put in some rhubarb or rainbow chard instead. I also use the young leaves in salad bags, where the coloured varieties add interest.

Profit and efficiency

I can pick twenty bunches of spinach in half and hour and at 75p – 90p a bunch that's £15 – £18. That's not a bad rate for a crop that is so easy to maintain. And if you consider that you can get up to four pickings in one season off the same piece of ground, the efficiency of the crop begins to soar above other more time consuming and troublesome crops.

Hints and tips

Sow thickly.

Rhubarb and rainbow chard have a tendency to bolt so more attention should be paid to keeping them well watered and mulched.

Give customers information about the nutritious qualities of the crop. In my experience it's adults that really enjoy spinach whilst children tend to be fussy over it. Suggest recipes that include spinach, such as currys and quiches.

Potatoes

"It's like digging up gold nuggets", people often say when they dig up their first potatoes. "This is quite hard work" comes at the end of the first row. By the end of the plot, "they need to invent a machine to do this".

To supply my 100 customers with potatoes for half a year I have to grow, or buy in, around 3400kg. Until this year I have been growing between 500 and 600kg a season, which were all dug by hand. This year I have bought myself some machinery to make the job easier, and I will be growing nearly 1500kg of potatoes.

The potato is probably the least profitable vegetable you can grow, so I grow the most expensive type – the early. A 25kg sack of earlies can cost more than £17, while a sack of maincrop potatoes can cost as little as £7 by the end of the year.

Having said all that, potatoes are extremely satisfying to grow. The plants grow from tubers, called seed potatoes, rather than seed. The potatoes you eat are called 'wares'. They are related to tomatoes and there are a huge number of varieties to chose from.

Types and varieties

Good organic practice is to use seed potatoes that are certified as disease-free. They have been grown in conditions where there are no potato diseases, usually very high up or in Scotland. There are a wide variety of organic seed potatoes available now. If you're really pushed for cash you can use your own saved tubers, as long as your crop hasn't suffered from any disease. There are three main types of potato to grow, earlies, second earlies and maincrop. I have chosen all of the varieties that I use for their resistance to blight and their general good performance. Early potatoes are the tastiest. They produce tubers quickly and are particularly tasty but don't store well. I use Premiere and Swift.

Second earlies produce tubers quickly and are easy to store. However, the flavour begins to deteriorate once they have been dug up. I currently use the varieties Marfona and Estima.

Maincrop potatoes grow for a longer period than the earlies, producing bigger tubers. They are lifted in the autumn to use through the winter. Remarka and Sante are very good for organic growing, or Romano if you want to grow a red potato. I have also had a lot of success with Robinta, another red skinned potato.

There are also late maincrop varieties. These produce waxy, well–flavoured potatoes, which make good salad potatoes late in the season. I grow Pink Fir Apple every year, because my customers like them. They will store well until May but remember to keep some back for your own use in early spring.

Soil, site and rotation

Unlike most vegetables, potatoes do best in an acidic soil. This means that you can plant them straight into composted muck, which is always on the acid side. I prepare the plot by spreading composted muck, digging or ploughing it in, then rotovating. The soil doesn't need to be very finely prepared. Potatoes have their own place in my rotation, and do well in a sunny site.

Chitting

Prepare your seed potatoes for planting by chitting them. This is the process of getting them to sprout. It is most important to chit early potatoes, but second early and maincrop potatoes will also benefit. The potatoes have a head start when they are planted and will grow more quickly through the year, allowing them to be harvested earlier.

Buy your seed potatoes as soon as you can and arrange them in trays somewhere light but cool (about 10°C is perfect). Notice that the tubers have eyes, where the sprouts will grow. Position the potatoes so that most of the eyes are at the top. If there are a lot of eyes the tubers can be cut in half, but both halves should have at least three eyes. Place them in the trays cut side down, on newspaper to absorb any moisture. When the sprouts are short and green, the tubers are ready for planting.

Sowing and planting

Start your early potatoes in the first half of March, second earlies at the beginning of April and wait until the end of April to plant your maincrop.

It is traditional to plant potatoes in trenches. First, dig a long trench and fill the bottom with compost. Position the seed potatoes in the bottom then refill the trench with soil. Ridge up the soil over the plants as they emerge.

I find digging lots of trenches rather laborious and I prefer to use a simpler method. Prepare the soil by digging in composted muck , and rotovate. Use string to mark the line of your row, then make holes with a trowel and plant your chitted seed potatoes 15cm deep. Earlies should be 30cm apart with 60cm between the rows, and the maincrop should have 45cm between tubers and 75cm between rows. Fill each hole with a mix of composted muck and soil.

On particularly weedy ground, potatoes can be grown through a mulch of plastic or cardboard. Prepare the ground as above and make holes through the mulch to plant the tubers.

Food, water and mulch

Assuming that you added compost or muck to the soil before you started, the potatoes will have enough food. Once the plants have emerged and been earthed up (see below), mulch with a thick layer of straw. This will prevent evaporation of water from the soil as well as letting rain through, and no additional watering should be necessary. The mulch will also stop weeds growing, and protect any uncovered tubers from light, which would turn them green and inedible.

If you are growing your potatoes through a layer of plastic, remember that rain water will not reach them. Water through the planting holes and cover the plastic with a mulch such as straw.

Seasonal care

As the plants emerge, use a mattock (a useful, long handed tool with what appears to be the blade of a spade bent at a right angle to the handle) or hoe to drag soil up to cover them. This is called earthing up, and will protect the plants from frost. Cover the whole bed with a thick layer of straw, and keep an eye on the weather forecast. If there is likely to be a frost, cover all the plants with fleece as frost will kill the shoots and it will take time for them to regrow. I have found that it is almost impossible to get a crop of early potatoes by the middle of June without using fleece. If you delay planting your main-crop till the end of April you will probably miss the frosts altogether on that crop.

Growing potatoes with machinery

Machinery is the key to growing large numbers of potatoes. This year I have bought a potato lifter, which digs the potatoes out of the ground, and an adjustable ridger, which pushes the earth up on either side of the rows. Both of them attach to my two-wheeled tractor.

Prepare the ground by ploughing in composted muck then rotovating. Put the chitted potatoes on the ground, in straight rows. Go along between the rows with a ridger, to cover the potatoes. You may have to ridge up the plants again after a couple of weeks. Covering the bed with straw will keep heavy soils in good condition (important when it comes to harvesting), and retain moisture in lighter soils.

When it is time to harvest, remove the straw and potato haulms (foliage and stems). Go along the rows with the potato lifter, which will pick up the potatoes for you. If the soil is not friable (which it should be if you covered it with straw), the potato lifter will not work as it will throw up lumps of soil with the potatoes.

Succession and continuity

If you have space to spare in a polytunnel, you can get a very early crop of early potatoes. Prepare the bed, plant chitted seed potatoes at the same time as your outdoor crop - early to mid March. If it gets very cold, protect them with a layer of fleece. This indoor crop will be ready by the middle to end of May. Your first earlies outside, planted at the same time, will start to crop in June, followed by your second earlies in July. The maincrop will be ready to harvest in August or September.

Problems

The main problems to affect potatoes are blight, slugs and mice. Wireworms, cyst eelworms, blackleg, scab, spraing and gangrene can also be troublesome, but are uncommon if adequate precautions are taken.

Blight can be catastrophic – it was the cause of the Irish potato famine in the nineteenth century. The tubers turn black, then rot with a disgusting and distinctive, sweet smell. It is caused by a fungus that spreads in warm wet weather – be on the look out in these conditions. The first signs are brown patches on the leaves, spreading into the stems and becoming black. Once it has started to spread it can reach the tubers quite quickly.

I do several things in an attempt to beat blight. Firstly, I grow resistant varieties. I chit all my seed potatoes so that they get a quick start and will bulk up more quickly, before blight becomes a problem. Mulching is a good idea as it stops the blight spores getting into the soil from the leaves which, once wet with rain, will drip the spores onto, and into, the soil. A large proportion of the potatoes I grow are earlies, which are harvested before the blight starts. I follow them with second earlies, which bulk up more quickly than the maincrop and are harvested sooner. If the maincrop is almost ready when blight strikes, it's possible to prevent the blight from getting to the tubers by removing the haulms at ground level. I always harvest the maincrop as early as I can, in August if possible, before the ground gets really wet. The yields may be slightly down but the tubers will last longer. All of these techniques go some way to helping but if the weather is very favourable to blight, nothing can stop it. When it is a particularly bad year, I just have to buy in more potatoes, which will be expensive because all the other growers of potatoes will have been affected by the problem as well.

Slugs and mice are particularly troublesome if you are growing potatoes under a plastic or cardboard mulch. Using this method I have lost as much as 40% of my crop to nibbling pests, whereas under straw the loss is as little as 5 – 10%. If you do harvest early, there is the added advantage of less slug damage.

Scab is a cosmetic problem – the skin looks, literally, like it has scabs on it. The usual cause is that the soil is not acid enough. Be sure to add plenty of muck before planting, and grow resistant varieties. Wireworms are a feature of grassland. If you try to grow potatoes in newly ploughed pasture, you are likely to lose a lot of your crop to this pest. It is a shiny orange worm, 10 – 15mm long and 1mm across with a segmented body. It makes holes in root vegetables, particularly noticeable in potatoes. To avoid the problem, do not grow potatoes immediately after grass. On a small scale you can attempt to remove the wireworms. Skewer pieces of potato on sticks, and bury them with the skewer sticks showing. Pull them up at regular intervals and remove the wireworms. This is an extremely time consuming tactic on a large area.

Potato cyst eelworms are too small to see but they can kill the plants off early, stopping the tubers from growing to any size. There are two types, golden cyst eelworm and white cyst eelworm, and they can affect tomatoes as well as potatoes. Potato plants affected by cyst eelworms die from mid to late summer so they will only produce small tubers. The plant leaves turn a pale yellow then dry up from the bottom of the plant upwards. If you dig up a plant you will see the white, yellow or brown spherical cysts up to 1mm in diameter attached to the roots. These cysts are the female eelworms and carry hundreds of eggs each.

If you suspect eelworm, dig up as much of the plant as you can and destroy it. Potato eelworms don't respond to short rotations but if you start with a long rotation, the likelihood of getting them is reduced. There are quite a few resistant potato varieties including Accent, Nadine, Pentland Javelin, Rocket in the early varieties and Cara, Kingston and Maris Piper for the main crops. Cromwell and Sante are said to show some resistance to both types of eelworm. This is one pest which is chronic in potatoes and amply justifies buying certified potato seed tubers to ensure that you don't import the problem.

Spraing is a disease that causes brown, and sometimes red, lesions in the tuber and can only be controlled with resistant varieties. I have yet to experience this disease and it is not common.

Blackleg is a bacterial disease. It causes the leg, or stem, of the plant to rot. It is carried in diseased tubers so to avoid it use certified seed potatoes.

Gangrene is caused by a fungus, which makes the tubers rot in storage. Only store potatoes that are not damaged, and make sure they are dry when you put them in the sacks.

Harvest, storage and sale

Early potatoes are ready when they start to flower. Dig the potatoes up with a fork and leave them to dry on the soil. As earlies are sold quite quickly it doesn't really hurt to put them into sacks almost as soon as you've dug them. If you are growing potatoes just for yourself you can increase your crop by just taking the biggest potatoes. Push your hands into the soil and feel for the biggest tubers, leaving the smaller ones to keep growing. Earlies are very valuable and I limit the amount I give to medium box customers to about 1kg, and small box customers to about 500gm, a week.

Second earlies will be stored for longer so you need to make sure that they are dry. Use any damaged tubers yourself, as soon as possible. Once the second earlies are ready I give my customers more potatoes each week.

The maincrop flowers later, will be stored for months and must be sound and dry. Leave them on the soil to dry. Keep them in the dark, somewhere dry and frost-free. If you are storing them in sacks, make sure the sacks have three layers. It is vital to keep the potatoes in the dark as exposure to light will make them go green and then they become poisonous.

Profit and efficiency

Growing potatoes in an awful lot of hard work and they are not profitable because you can buy them so cheaply. But growing your own is extremely satisfying. It makes me very happy when my customers can tell the difference between the ones I've grown and the ones I've bought in (even though they're all organic).

Earlies cost the most to buy and fetch the most cash, so grow them before any other type.

Hints and tips

Don't grow too many if you intend to dig them all by hand. And if you do, get a potato digging party together and reward them with a big lunch and all your surplus vegetables.

Grow earlies for your boxes and only grow maincrop if you have the machinery.

Growing potatoes in containers

It is possible to grow potatoes in containers such as barrels and tyre stacks. Basically you start at the bottom with a layer of composted muck and plant three tubers to one barrel/tyre stack (fill the inside of the tyres with scrunched up newspaper and wet it thoroughly). Cover with soil and compost and as the potato shoots appear keep earthing them up until you've reached the top. They need a lot of water so don't neglect them. Leave them to grow out of the top and you will find that they have produced tubers all the way down to the bottom. The advantage of this method is good utilisation of space and there's no digging required. The downside is you must water them frequently and you need an awful lot of containers (tyres don't appeal to me because they're covered in road poisons). In reality you are making space available but probably using as much growing medium as you would on the level. The main advantage is to those with small gardens where space is at a premium and for this reason alone it is a very useful technique.

Radish

This is the easiest of all crops to grow. They are quick to germinate and grow, colourful and crunchy. If children show an interest in growing vegetables, you will do well to start them off with radishes.

Types and varieties

There are several types of radish. Spring and summer radishes are usually red and can be either round or long. You can also get white varieties now. I grow a variety called French Breakfast because they are big and easy to clean.

Winter radishes are much larger, and tend to be very spicy. As well as eating them raw they can be used in cooking, particularly stir-fries. I usually grow a mouli type: white, between 2.5 and 7.5cm in diameter and very long (I've grown some that reached 60cm). It's delicious. There are other types of winter radish, with red or black skin and beautiful white, or sometimes pink, centres.

Another type of radish is grown for its pods – Munchen Bier and Rats Tail. The plant grows very tall and the pods are eaten raw (as a snack with beer in Germany), or stir-fried.

Soil, site and rotation

Radishes will grow anywhere but the richer the soil the better the crop. The tilth needs to be fairly fine. They will grow in shade but do best out in the open. They are good for inter-cropping, but they are brassicas so be careful where you grow them in your rotation.

Sowing and planting

Sow at a depth of 1cm in rows 15cm apart, one seed every centimetre.

Food, water and mulch

Radishes grow so quickly that they don't need feeding or mulching. If they are grown under cover or it gets very dry, they will need watering.

Seasonal care

Thin if necessary, that is, if you've sown the seed too thickly. If there are too many plants they will not fatten up.

Succession and continuity

For an early crop, make the first sowing under cover. However, don't start them too early or you'll have a huge crop of radish and nothing to go with them. Repeat sowings every two weeks if you want radishes all summer. I usually only grow two or three crops a year, because they are easy to forget about in the madness of summer.

Problems

The worst problem is flea beetle, which makes holes in the leaves. They are particularly bad in hot dry periods. The easiest solution is to cover the plants with fleece or mesh.

In the polytunnel, you may get the odd hole around the top of the roots. Woodlice are the culprits.

Harvest, storage and sale

Keep an eye on radishes as they grow, because they will become hard and woody if left too long. To harvest them, thin the best specimens out of the rows. With spring and summer radishes, make bunches of between 10 and 20. Being so much bigger, you only need to put one or two winter radishes in each box.

You can leave winter radishes in the ground or store them in damp sand. Although they are not very frost tolerant, I often leave spare mouli in the ground, as an aerator. When the roots rot after being frozen they leave a long, deep hole for air to get into the soil.

Profit and efficiency

Radishes are cheap to buy in the shops so they are not very profitable. I charge 35-40p a bunch, which doesn't seem a lot of money. But £35 for 100 bunches, from a small patch of ground that is used for only 6 weeks of the year, seems more reasonable. And radishes fill a gap in the spring before much else is ready.

Hints and tips

You need to give your customers some idea of what winter radishes are and how to eat them because most of them will never have seen one before.

Runner Beans

People always look forward to runner beans but they tend to come a bit later than a lot of the other veg. In the countryside there are often signs outside houses on the roadside advertising runner or stick beans for sale. This gives them an image of being easy to grow and abundant, unlike peas and French beans which are rarely seen for sale in this way. This is a misconception and they are actually quite difficult.

Types and varieties

There are plenty of varieties to chose from but as the seeds are easy to save I grow the same variety each year, Scarlet Emperor. If you like colour in your garden try the variety Painted Lady that has red and white blossoms. There are also dwarf varieties which don't need any support, saving a lot of time in the spring, but they don't crop as heavily. Another downside is that being close to the ground they're more difficult to pick and the beans get splattered with mud when it rains.

Soil, site and rotation

Runner beans benefit from preparing the site well. Dig a trench and line the bottom with a good layer of well composted muck. Refill the trench with soil and the beans will start off surrounded by soil but their roots will grow down into moist rich compost. A medium tilth over the trench is fine for planting the beans. Once they get going they need a lot of water and nutrients. I get the potato ridger out to dig the trench as it's much quicker than doing it by hand.

Be careful where you grow your runner beans as they will shade the ground to the north side. I usually grow four rows about 6 or 7 metres long on the edge of the vegetable area. If they are on the north edge of the garden I put the framework in an L shape to create a sun trap that I grow other beans and peas in.

Traditionally runners are grown up a long, tent shaped sructure which can use up a lot of poles. If you run out, you can tie long poles along the central axis and along the bottom then use strings to replace the poles.

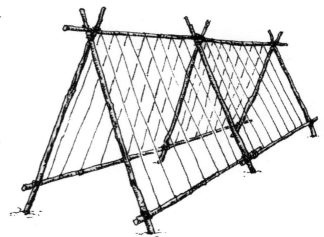

You can also grow them up wigwams. Take 6 to 8 canes and put them in a circle then tie them all together at about head height.

I have always used hazel poles which have been cut to length in the winter. Hazel poles are far more environmentally friendly than imported bamboo canes. If you don't have a source of hazel poles, use bamboo canes to begin with but plant a couple of hazel trees at the edge of your plot. These will grow hazel poles for you to use by the time your bamboo canes begin to rot. Hazel poles are more difficult to put in the ground than bamboo canes because they tend to be thicker. To get round this problem I first make a hole with a steel pole and hammer.

As you might expect, runner beans go in the beans section of the rotation.

Sowing and planting

To sow direct, wait until late April or early May and sow two seeds at the base of each pole about 2.5 – 5cm deep. I never do this because if there's a late frost it will kill them off and if it's wet slugs eat the shoots and either way you'll have to start again.

Although I need about 250 plants I always start them off in pots under cover, in mid April. I sow one bean to every 7.5cm pot and resow those that don't germinate.
You can pre-sprout them so you know which have germinated before you sow them.

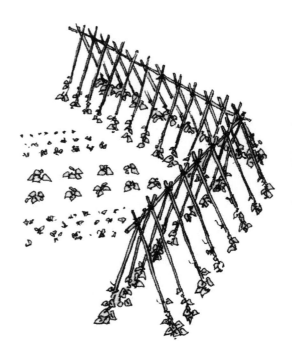

When they start to run, that is, the shoots begin to grow away from the cotyledons, start to harden them off outside. Growing so many in pots I can't carry them in and out of the polytunnel every day so I put them all outside and cover them with a double layer of fleece which I remove completely for a few days just before planting them out.

I transplant them into the prepared soil at the base of the poles where, after 4 or 5 days, they begin to grow away.

Make sure you water them in well but don't water them again in the early stages or they'll get slugged.

Food, water and mulch

Once the runner beans are a good metre up the poles or strings it's safe to put a straw mulch around the whole lot. During dry spells check under the mulch regularly to make sure the soil hasn't dried out and irrigate heavily if necessary. Their food comes from the composted muck put in the trenches.

Seasonal care

Sometimes the beans have trouble climbing the poles or strings so you might need to give them some help in the first few weeks. They will only climb in one direction, anti clockwise. Many growers pinch out the tips of the plants when they reach the top of the poles to encourage more side shoots to grow. I've never done this purely because I always forget but I never seem to lack beans.

Succession and continuity

Although you can grow runner beans for an early harvest in the polytunnel there's usually enough other produce around when they would crop so I don't bother. Once runner beans start to crop you need to pick them hard and try not to miss any as once a plant starts to produce seed it will stop producing fresh new pods. In a good year you should get runners from the end of July to the end of September.

Problems

Slugs are a major problem so if you are sowing direct, sow 2 or 3 seeds per station. Don't mulch the plants until they have started to grow well up the poles or strings.
Black fly can affect runners but by the time they arrive the ladybird population is so great that the black fly never really gets a chance.

If the flowers drop off or don't set beans the usual cause is dryness at the roots - keep a close eye on the moisture in the soil below the mulch.

Harvest, storage and sale

Runners are, like most veg, best fresh. Pick them as soon as they begin to thicken out - up to about 1.5cm but before they become too big. You can tell if they are too big if a knife won't slide easily through it. Alternatively try biting and chewing it, if it's tough it is too big!
I don't weigh runner beans for sale in the boxes as I just share out the crop between the boxes. This means customers often get a real deal on beans, getting maybe 1kg for the price of 500g and this is where they benefit and box schemes come into their own. I would much rather my customers got any surplus than putting it on the compost heap and sometimes I sell extra bags of beans at drop off points as well. Don't overdo it though, giving customers too many beans of one type every week will soon get them complaining. On the other hand, if there are not enough to go round I put runner beans in some boxes and another type of bean or pea in the others.

Profit and efficiency

Most of the time spent on runner beans is preparing the ground and framework for them to grow up. Picking can be quiet arduous too but it's nice to walk along a shady avenue of runner bean plants when it's really hot and the bees are humming all around you. If you save your own seed, runner beans will bring in a good profit.

Hints and tips

In a mild winter it's possible for the roots of runner beans to survive and regrow in the spring. This saves you growing new plants and erecting a new framework. There are a couple of problems with this method. Firstly although runner beans aren't susceptible to soil borne disease they will be taking the place of another type of vegetable in your rotation. Secondly, if they start growing early in the spring and you get a late frost you might lose your whole crop and have to start it off in pots later than you intended. If you aren't growing them for sale it might be a risk worth taking.

Salsify and Scorzonera

I do not grow salsify and scorzonera for my customers. The thin roots are not well known and my customers would require a lot of information and persuasion to readily embrace them in their boxes. The flavour is akin to oysters and they are often called the Vegetable Oyster. The difference between the two is that salsify has cream skin and scorzonera has black skin. As well as the roots, the young leaves can be used in spring salads. I find their main attraction is the purple flowers, which add interest to the garden and attract beneficial insects of one sort or another. They set seed easily and spread themselves around. Both types are supposed to repel carrot root fly.

Types and varieties

There is not much choice really, Mammoth Island for salsify and Maxima for scorzonera.

Soil, site and rotation

As for carrots. I grow them in the root section of the rotation, although you can get away with planting them anywhere as they are a member of the compositae family. Scorzonera is particularly deep rooting: if you need to break up soil pans you could sow this.

Sowing and planting

Sow direct in a fine tilth about 2.5cm deep in rows 30cm apart. Thin the plants to about 15cm.

Food, water and mulch

Salsify and scorzonera won't need extra feeding and are likely to fork in the same way as carrots and parsnips if manure is used. Watering and mulching isn't necessary, but a light mulch will help keep weeds down.

Seasonal care

Hoe between the rows. In the late autumn cover the roots with straw to protect them over the winter.

In spring they will sprout, to give young salad leaves. Like chicory, it is possible to force the roots during the early spring.

Succession and continuity

Salsify and scorzonera are ready to dig in the autumn and can be stored for use through the winter.

Problems

Generally pest free.

Harvest, storage and sale

Dig the roots in the autumn and store in sand for use through the winter. The roots tend to snap so harvest them carefully. Use the young spring leaves in salads.

Profit and efficiency

These vegetables can be profitable if they're sold as gourmet vegetables. Your best bet is to sell them to restaurants where they'll be appreciated.

Hints and tips

Grow for the flowers and salad leaves as much as for the roots.

Spinach - Annual

The flavour of annual spinach is reputed to be much finer than perpetual spinach or chard. I grow it as an early crop for my own use and as a late crop for salads bags. I don't grow it as my main spinach crop because it has a strong tendency to bolt. Early in the season it is a delicacy, but as summer approaches the perpetual spinach always seems to taste just as good. I grow perpetual spinach for the majority of my crop. It does not need successive sowings and is less likely to bolt.

Types and varieties

Any variety that is resistant to bolting is worth a try. I've grown Medania and Viking which both performed well but there are plenty of others to try. It might be that really effective resistance to bolting will only be achieved with the new hybrid varieties, but I'm loath to buy hybrid spinach seed.
New Zealand spinach will withstand long hot spells without bolting, but you need to let people know what it is when you sell it because it doesn't look like ordinary spinach.

Soil, site and rotation

Annual spinach will grow on fairly poor soil - it will even grow on gravel if you let it. A medium tilth is sufficient for planting. It benefits from a shady site in the summer months, to discourage bolting. Like beetroot it is not prone to diseases, so you can get away with planting it anywhere in your rotation. I grow the early crop in the polytunnels and the late crop in the beds the lettuces were in, once the ground becomes available in July.

Sowing and planting

I nearly always sow direct into the polytunnel bed once the soil has warmed sufficiently. My late crop goes directly into the bed outside. Sow the seeds 2.5 cm deep in rows 20 - 25 cm apart. You can start plants off in a propagator at 18°C for an early crop but they do tend to bolt very readily after transplanting.

Food, water and mulch

I never add any compost to the soil for annual spinach - it doesn't need it. Regular watering is important to prevent bolting, but do not mulch or the slugs will take the opportunity to feast on your tender young leaves.

Seasonal care

As well as watering, keep the bed free of weeds.

Succession and continuity

I grow an early crop of annual spinach under cover, for myself and my early customers. During the summer, when annual spinach is likely to bolt, I don't have the time to look after it. This is the main season for selling spinach, and I rely on perpetual spinach and Swiss chard. I sow a late crop of annual spinach in July, when the early lettuce beds have been cleared, and use this for autumn salad bags.

Problems

The main problems for annual spinach are heat and lack of moisture. I have found woodlice positively partying on the young plants in polytunnels in the spring. If you have this problem, cover the plants with plastic bottles until they are established.

Harvest, storage and sale

Annual spinach is fiddly to pick and the leaves need to be harvested into bags. This is another reason for concentrating on perpetual spinach and Swiss chard as they are far easier to handle. Individual leaves of annual spinach should be picked in the spring. In the winter I harvest whole plants (all the leaves) once they have bolted. The taste is sharper and is very good in salad bags. The dark green leaves compliment the lighter greens of chicories which tend to come into season at the same time.

Don't attempt to store spinach. Within a day of harvest it has wilted and looks very sad. Try spraying it with cold water to keep it fresh in the bags.

Profit and efficiency

Annual spinach isn't very profitable. You need to make frequent sowings and it's time consuming to harvest. However, it is useful in the overall scheme of gardening, for early and late salad crops.

Hints and tips

Prone to bolting in hot, dry weather so use for early and late crops.

Spring Onions

Spring onions are great to grow for veggie boxes. They are early, as early as May if grown under cover, and can be grown in bunches. They can also be overwintered to produce a crop outside in April.

Types and varieties

I only grow one variety at the moment, which is White Lisbon. It is reliable and will tolerate quite cold weather. It's cousin, White Lisbon Winter Hardy, will stand through the winter ready for use in the spring. I intend to grow a variety called Red Beard, which has pinkish outer skins, and the Japanese type Ishikura, which doesn't bulb up. I have grown these before and they perform well. Red Beard certainly provides interest in the boxes.

Soil, site and rotation

Spring onions get by in a medium tilth. They need a fertile soil but I don't add any compost. Choose an open site in the root (allium) section of the rotation. It is worth devoting some polytunnel space to them to get an early crop.

Sowing and planting

I only sow spring onions in rows if I'm growing them for myself. For sale I nearly always grow them in polystyrene modules, sowing about 12 seeds per 4cm block. When they are between 2.5 and 5cm tall the individual blocks are planted out, in a dice pattern about 30cm apart. They grow into bunches of spring onions, ready to be harvested whole.

For growing under cover I start the bunches in a propagator in late February. Subsequent sowings can be made until July. I sow two trays (60 units) once every two weeks. For those grown over winter, plant out in August or September.

Food, water and mulch

The only attention spring onions get is watering. If they get too dry they have a tendency to form bulbs and when they do this they can be almost too strong to eat. I will mulch plants grown outdoors with a thin layer of grass mowings or straw, to keep moisture in the soil.

Seasonal care

Hoe and hand weed if necessary and ensure adequate irrigation.

Succession and continuity

Spring onions fill the gap between last years stored onions and this years fresh over-wintered onions. If you grow an over-wintered spring onion it will become available as early as April, or even March if it's given some protection. If you can grow some under cover you can crop spring onions from April right through to December.

Problems

As they crop so quickly, spring onions don't really suffer from any major problems. Be sure to plant the bunches far enough apart for adequate ventilation, or the stems may begin to rot and the lack of light can make their stems lose their green vibrancy.

Harvest, storage and sale

Harvesting spring onions for sale couldn't be easier when they are grown in blocks. Simply lift each block with a fork and knock the soil off the roots. Tie with an elastic band and chop the tops off so that each bunch is about 30cm tall. The job is even easier if you watered the crop 24 hours before digging them: the soil will just drop off the roots. Watering nearer harvest may make the soil sticky.

Profit and efficiency

At 75p a bunch, one 60 cell module of spring onions will bring in about £45. Their worth lies in the early crop when little else is ready. They also help by eking out the supplies of maincrop onions for the less plentiful times of the year.

Hints and tips

Grow in blocks. Keep an eye on irrigation to prevent bulbs forming.

Sprouting Broccoli

This is just the best vegetable for growing between January and April. The tender young shoots are absolutely delicious and although I only grow them for myself they are definitely worthwhile.

Types and varieties

Generally there are two types, Purple or White Sprouting. White Sprouting is supposed to be tastier but I find the colour of Purple Sprouting very satisfying. For succession, the variety Rudolph will be ready in January, Red Arrow or Early White will start in February then Late Purple Sprouting will be ready in April.

Soil, site and rotation
As for brassicas.

Sowing and planting
As for brassicas although it's wise to sow the seeds in seed beds in May and plant out in July.

Food, water and mulch
As for brassicas.

Seasonal care
As for brassicas.

Succession and continuity
See types and varieties above.

Problems
As for brassicas.
Particularly during cold weather pigeons really like sprouting broccoli so throw a bit of netting over the plants to discourage them.

Harvest, storage and sale
To harvest sprouting broccoli, literally snap or cut off the shoots. Being a winter vegetable it will store for a while in cool weather. I do not sell it as it is not cropping while I am selling my boxes.

Profit and efficiency
If you sell vegetables at this time of year then it certainly is profitable because it is one of the few green vegetables, other than cabbage, available at this time of the year.

Hints and tips
Grow a range of varieties for continuity and interest.

Squash

When I started selling vegetables, ten years ago, squash were relatively unknown in this country and I had to explain to my customers what they were. Those of my customers who have been with me for some time are always delighted when the squash season starts. Newer customers, who have only recently become box devotees, are doubtful at first. How can something that looks like an asteroid taste remotely nice? But after a few weeks they are positively brimming with enthusiasm at their new find. Squash come in a wide range of shapes, sizes and colours, and provide a great deal of interest and variety in my boxes.

Types and varieties

There are so many types and varieties that I can't possibly list them all but I can give you an idea of my favourites. Have a go with them or try any others that take your fancy. Butternuts are very popular. They are bell shaped with pale orange skin and orange flesh. The sweet, nutty flavour improves in storage. However, they do need a longer season than most squashes, so grow them in the warmest part of your garden.

Acorn squash tend to be dark green with orange flesh, and are acorn shaped.

Early Acorn and Table Ace are prolific growers and have been popular with my customers.

Vegetable Spaghetti is like a rounded rugby ball, very pale green. The fibrous flesh is like spaghetti when it is cooked. It's easy to grow and prolific and my customers seem to like it too.

Little Gem and Rolet are dark green and round, the size of a cricket ball. Baked and stuffed, they're the ideal size for a single portion.

Pompeon and Sweet Mama are like dark green flattened balls, with dense yellow flesh.

Uchiki Kuri is bright orange and tear drop shaped with very orange flesh. It is beautiful, but difficult to grow. It stores particularly well.

Sweet Dumpling is pale green with dark green stripes – very attractive and, like Little Gem, just right for a single portion.

Turks Turban is worth growing just because it looks so fantastic. The fruit is shaped like a turban.

My favourite this year was a large, round, grey squash with bright orange flesh called Crown Prince. It looked great when it was cut into portions in the boxes. The flavour isn't quite so sweet as some of the squashes, and it grew well with little attention.

Soil, site and rotation

They belong to the cucurbit family so treat as for courgettes but position the muck sinks further apart. As squash plants have a trailing habit, grow them in a block. If you grow them on narrow beds you'll find them creeping across the neighbouring beds, choking the crops. I grow squash under sweetcorn: they don't compete with the sweetcorn but shade the ground, reducing water loss and weeds. I grow them like this even when space is not limited, as both need to grow in a block and it seems a waste not to combine them.

Sowing and planting

As for courgettes, but with wider spacing.

Food, water and mulch

As for courgettes.

Seasonal care

As for courgettes.

Succession and continuity

Squash mature at the end of the season, usually around September to October although some can mature earlier. They can be stored in a frost free place and will usually keep all the way through to the following May in some cases. In terms of succession, they can be available from August and September all through the winter to April and May.

Problems

As for courgettes.

Harvest, storage and sale

As for marrows but I make sure that everyone gets a good range of varieties. It's worth noting that squashes come in all sorts of shapes and sizes. How much you put in a box depends on the squash and the size of box. You just need to judge the right amount of squash for the right amount of people for one meal. To ring the changes I give my customers a bit of marrow one week, squash the next, a piece of pumpkin after that and no cucurbits the following week. I include suggestions for cooking the squashes in newsletters.

Profit and efficiency

As for marrows, but squashes tend to be much more popular than marrows so it's worth growing more of them.

Hints and tips

Grow lots of Butternuts, Acorns and Spaghettis as they seem to be popular. Grow under sweetcorn. Give new customers recipes for squash

Swedes

Even organic swedes are cheap to buy, so I don't usually grow them to sell. I always grow some for my own use in the winter, though. Swedes are generally thought of as a root crop, but in fact they are brassicas.

Types and varieties
Look for a variety that is resistant to clubroot, particularly if this is a problem in your soil. The variety Marian is said to be clubroot resistant.

Soil, site and rotation
Grow swedes in well-drained soil. For most brassicas I add compost to the bed before planting. I do not bother for swedes, as they are a root rather than leaf crop. The seeds are sown direct so prepare the bed to a fine tilth. Grow in the brassica part of your rotation.

Sowing and planting
Sow in April, 1cm deep in rows 30cm apart.

Food, water and mulch
Swedes rarely need any attention. While they are young, the plants may need watering in dry weather. Mulching will help.

Seasonal care
Swedes need to be thinned to about 30cm apart for the roots to grow to a decent size. Hoe between rows and hand weed if necessary.

Succession and continuity
Swedes are ready from October onwards and can be harvested as they are needed. Once they have been dug, they can be stored for use through the winter.

Problems
The only pests that really affect swedes are flea beetles and grey mealy aphids. If you keep the plants well watered during their early growth and in very hot, dry weather they should be able to grow through these problems.

Clubroot can be a problem so try to grow a resistant variety.

Swedes can suffer from soft rot. This is a bacterial disease, common on poorly drained soil and when rotations are neglected. The roots become mushy, and very smelly. Grow in well-drained soil, and stick to your rotation.

Valuable Vegetables

If the centres of the roots are brownish-grey and begin to rot, your soil is deficient in boron.

Harvest, storage and sale

To harvest swedes, simply pull them up. Chop off the tops and the roots, cutting part of the flesh away. Swedes can be left in the ground until they are needed, but cover the beds with straw before the first hard frost. They do keep better if they are harvested and stored in damp sand in a frost-free shed (*see Carrots page 104*).

Although swedes are a useful crop, I don't put them in the boxes more than once every two or three weeks. I alternate them with other root vegetables, such as celeriac, beetroot and parsnips.

Profit and efficiency

Swedes are easy to grow, but they are not profitable on a small scale. They are very cheap to buy from wholesalers and I consider it to be one of the crops I can afford not to grow for sale. Every few years, though, I am unable to resist the urge to sow swedes when a bit of brassica land is free.

Hints and tips

Remember that they are brassicas, not roots.
Grow for your own consumption – buy them in to sell.

Sweetcorn

Non-hybrid varieties of sweetcorn are fast becoming difficult to find. Commercial growers and gardeners alike have turned to the super sweet hybrid varieties that are now widely available. I have a feeling that this is more to do with growers trying to buy time than with real taste. Once picked, the sugars in sweetcorn begin to turn to starch, so the cobs lose their sweetness. If there is more sugar to start with, it will take longer for it all to turn to starch, so growers imagine they have longer to get the cobs to the customers before they are worthless. However, if you grow both types and eat them fresh there is little difference in terms of taste. It is the time that elapses between picking and eating which determines the taste of the vegetable.

From the point of view of the small-scale gardener, the super sweet varieties are widely available and sound very appealing. Most gardens don't have the space to grow both types, with the recommended eight metre separation between varieties. Any closer and they will cross-pollinate, watering down the sweetness of the super sweet variety with the relatively normal taste of the non-hybrid. But super sweet varieties are approximately 25% more expensive than normal varieties and the germination rate is very poor. The seed merchants really have us in their pockets – you can't save your own seed from the hybrids. I can see Garden Organic's Heritage Seed Library catalogue becoming buoyant with old sweetcorn varieties soon.

Despite all this, sweetcorn is well worth growing. It is really delicious.

My little boy has never liked cooked vegetables very much and he is more than happy to eat sweetcorn raw straight off the cob.

If you want to sell sweetcorn, grow your own. Don't buy it in, as even the best organic sweetcorn from the wholesalers will taste like cardboard after a few days. You must grow enough to put it in your boxes at least a couple of times. If your customers really like sweetcorn and you buy more outside the box scheme they will be disappointed at how badly it compares with yours. However, sweetcorn is not an easy crop to grow in this country. You really have to work hard to make sure it has a long enough season to ripen up.

Types and varieties

Probably the only two non-hybrid varieties of sweetcorn left at the time of writing are Kelvedon Glory and Golden Bantam. Of the hybrids, you can only choose the one that has the best write up, as the varieties seem to change every other year! I recommend that you avoid the super sweet varieties – in my experience the germination rate for this type is extremely poor, ranging from 10 - 25%. The F1 varieties which are not titled super sweet are far more reliable, and really are sweet if eaten as fresh as possible.

Soil, site and rotation

I always start sweetcorn off in modules and transplant them, so the soil need only be of a medium tilth. Sweetcorn does like a rich soil with a pH of about 6.5 and it must have sun. Avoid exposed sites and frost pockets if you can.

Sweetcorn is a member of the Gramineae, or grass family, so isn't closely related to other vegetable crops. I always grow sweetcorn in the bed with my squash plants, so invariably it falls in the squash part of my rotation.

Sowing and planting

Sweetcorn is notoriously bad at germinating. Always soak and sprout the seed, and only sow the ones which have germinated. This saves on compost if sown in modules and space if sown direct.

If you are growing sweetcorn in a polytunnel or in the Channel Isles, you can sow direct. Allow 45-60cm between plants and sow two kernels per station, 2.5cm deep. If you have pre-sprouted them just sow one kernel.

For growing outdoors, sow the sprouted corns undercover in mid April. Plant them 1.5cm deep in modules with 5 x 5cm cells. When the plants are between 15 and 30cm tall, plant out 45 – 60cm apart. Plant them quite deep and earth up the stems a bit, which will help them to establish roots and stabilise them.

Sweetcorn is wind pollinated, so should be grown in a block. If you grow them in long beds the pollination rate is much reduced, resulting in less well-formed cobs.

I use the space beneath the sweetcorn to grow another crop, namely trailing squash or pumpkin. The squash shade the ground, reducing water loss and weed competition, and has plenty of space for its long trailing shoots. It doesn't seem to suffer from the shade cast by the sweetcorn.

Food, water and mulch

Water the plants in well. If the weather is dry, water them again. Hoe between the plants as necessary. Once they are growing away, mulch with a fairly thick layer of straw. If you have any spare, put a layer of comfrey leaves under the straw mulch. Don't mulch until the plants are established, as it will encourage slugs, which will quickly shred the leaves of the plants. If you have any spare, give the plants a feed of comfrey liquid once or twice, preferably just as they flower. Sweetcorn are partial to potash so you can add comfrey leaves to the planting hole, as a mulch and as a liquid feed.

Seasonal care

Plants that are sown direct should be covered with fleece as soon as they emerge. This will protect them from late frosts for the first few weeks of their life. Transplanted corn should be protected with fleece if frosts are likely, or you may lose the lot and it will be too late in the season to start again. There is little more to do as the corn grows. For indoor plants, give them a gentle shake every few days once they are flowering, to ensure adequate pollination.

Succession and continuity

Sweetcorn needs a very long season to ripen, so it's difficult to achieve any continuity unless you can grow it indoors and out. An indoor crop may be ready by the beginning of August and outdoor sweetcorn is seldom ready before the beginning of September.

Problems

Mice are partial to sweetcorn seed. Sprout your seed to give them a head start and set a few traps when you sow them. Slugs are also keen to eat your sweetcorn, so don't mulch until the plants have taken and are growing away well. Birds will sometimes damage cobs, particularly if they are left too long on the plant and the outer casings begin to expose the kernels. It's difficult to do much about this, apart from harvesting before the kernels become visible.

Sweetcorn can suffer from smut. The individual corns become grey, swollen and distorted, eventually erupting and spreading powdery spores to neighbouring plants and the soil. The only way to control it is to remove and destroy the affected plants. Avoid growing sweetcorn on the same ground more than once every five years.

Harvest, storage and sale

Sweetcorn is ready to harvest when the tassels at the top of the cobs go dark brown. Try one to make sure. Take a cob and pull it down, away from the stem of the plant. Shred the leaves off and take a bite, you should be able to taste if it is ready. The corns should be a pale yellow, although this varies between varieties.

Don't try to store the cobs, but pick on the same day as delivery. They don't take long to harvest. Put as many cobs in each box as the number of people the box is designed for.

Profit and efficiency

Sweetcorn takes up a lot of space and time early in the year but you can charge a good price per cob. It is normal to get two cobs per plant but occasionally only one forms. By growing squash plants amongst the corn you are increasing the profitability of the ground used.

Hints and tips

Don't grow the super sweet varieties because they have very poor germination rates.
Grow trailing squash or pumpkin underneath.
Recommend that your customers eat the cobs the day they get them, and suggest that they try them raw.

Tomatoes

Everyone loves tomatoes. You really do have to grow them. They are almost an obsession with the English. Most people who have ever wanted to grow vegetables will have dabbled with a grow-bag and three sad tomato plants at one time or another.

Types and varieties

There are so many varieties of tomatoes that I hardly know where to begin. There are probably hundreds of varieties, in a range of colours and sizes of fruit, currently on offer in the catalogues. Some are suitable for growing outdoors and others do best under cover, or indoors. There are two main types: cordon or indeterminate varieties that grow upright with support and bush that have lower, more rambling plants.

Start by growing about six varieties, some indoors and some out – and keep trying new varieties until you have hit upon the best. I grow two outdoor types, Red Alert, a bush tomato with fruits that ripen very early, and Tornado F1, also a bush with bigger fruit, but it is a hybrid.
Indoors I grow an orange sweet cherry tomato called Sungold, something with medium-sized fruit and a beefsteak type (often Big Boy, which is reliable). These two are cordon or indeterminate varieties.
I do try out different varieties but I find it is best not to grow too many at once. I usually try one new variety each year, to produce something my customers won't have seen before.

Soil, site and rotation

As long as the soil that they are to grow in is relatively fertile, tomatoes should do well. The site needs to be sunny and the tomatoes have their own section in the rotation.

I plant my tomatoes on top of a pit of composted muck, as a precaution against dry spells and a shortage of time during the spring and summer. At each planting site, dig a hole down to the subsoil, about 1m across. Add three or four spadefuls of composted muck then return some soil and mix it up a bit. Fill the hole with the rest of the soil and mark the centre with a stick. This is important if you want to cover the ground with a black plastic mulch.

Sowing and planting

Sow the seed in modules, in mid March for indoor varieties and a couple of weeks later for outdoor ones. Leave them in a propagator at 18-21°C until the plants are about 10cm tall. If you can, keep them in an open propagator for a few days before moving them to a sunny windowsill. After a week or so pot them on into 10cm pots. In early April they should be moved to a polytunnel or greenhouse, to harden off before planting out in early May. Protect the plants with a layer of fleece when you plant them out, and put another layer on if it threatens to get colder than -2°C. Make sure you water them in but once they have begun to establish they will need less watering. Indoor tomatoes also benefit from a fleece tent until the weather is warm enough for them to cope without it. They can be planted out indoors as early as April. Cordon tomatoes need to be staked when they are planted out. Tie the growing plant to the stake regularly.

Food, water and mulch

It's important that while the fruits develop the plants receive the right amount of water at the right time. You cannot control this for outdoor plants but they seem to cope with fluctuations more readily than indoor plants. A whole range of problems can arise if indoor tomato plants don't get enough water as the fruit are developing: the flowers can drop off, the skins of the fruit split or the plant can suffer from blossom end rot or blight. I follow different watering regimes depending upon the stage of the plant. While the plants are growing I water them every other day. I reduce this to once a week when the first fruits begin to develop and once they have started to ripen up I do not water them at all. I direct the water at the base of the plants to prevent any fungus from spreading in the foliage. Once you have stopped watering weekly comfrey feeds will give them enough liquid to see them through.

During the fruiting period, tomatoes need to be well supplied with potash. As soon as the first fruits begin to develop, feed each plant with diluted comfrey liquid or a seaweed feed. Very roughly I water the plants every week with one watering can full of comfrey liquid which has been diluted 30:1. Many tomato experts recommend that you do this twice a week but I never have enough, of the feed or time. My plants do quite well with a weekly application but beware skipping it altogether as you are more than likely to get uneven ripening and blossom end rot.

Once bush tomatoes become established they are very difficult to weed, so mulch the plants before they get too big. My preference is for straw because it lets rainfall through and keeps the fruit off the soil as well as stopping weeds. If there are a lot of perennial weeds in the plot I will mulch with black plastic. If you do this you must make more effort with your watering.

Seasonal care

Cordon tomatoes need to be tied on to their stakes as they grow, and any side shoots should be removed. Side shoots grow between the leaf branches and the main stem of the plant. If you don't remove them from a cordon, you end up with an uncontrollable mass of growth and probably a smaller harvest. However, it is possible to train some of these side shoots for further production, if you have the room.

Surplus side shoots of 30cm or more can be planted in the ground and watered in, to increase your stock. They will look a bit sad for a few days but nine times out of ten the plant will take and start to grow as an ordinary tomato plant. The drawback of this practise is that it will delay the fruiting time by up to a month. This is acceptable if you're growing for yourself but if you need the fruit to put in your boxes, you need the fruit as soon as possible.

Tomatoes are self-fertile but they need to have a bit of movement for pollination to succeed. When the indoor plants first start to flower I tap each stake to shake the plants gently as I walk through the tunnels in the morning. This is enough for each flower to set its fruit. Outdoor tomatoes don't need shaking.

Succession and continuity

Get your indoor cherry tomatoes off to an early start for the longest possible season. They should start to produce fruit in June. This will be followed in July by the medium-sized fruit from indoors and the early outdoor variety, Red Alert. By August I'm usually awash with tomatoes, which continues until the end of September and sometimes into October. Outdoor tomatoes are stopped by the first frost.

Problems

Birds will peck at outdoor tomatoes but any type of cover will prevent this.
If blight affects your potato crop it is likely to find its way to your tomato crop. Keeping the leaves dry will help reduce its effect.

Whitefly can affect indoor crops. Growing Tagetes (French Marigolds) in tunnels will prevent this as their smell seems to deter them.

Blossom end rot is caused by irregular feeding and watering: make sure that you don't let it become a problem.

Grafting

Tomatoes do suffer soil borne diseases such as verticulum and fusarium wilts, but a sound rotation should prevent this problem. However, the disease can build up, particularly in green house and polytunnel soils that have been over-used. An organic solution is to graft your plants on to a resistant rootstock. These are varieties that have been bred with resistance to soil borne diseases, at the expense of edible fruits. You must grow seedlings of your desired variety as well as an equal number of the resistant rootstock strain (seeds available from Marshalls and Unwins). It is wise to grow at least 50% more than you need: the grafts don't always take and it is very easy to damage them.

1. When the plants are big enough to handle pot one of each together in the same pot, as close as possible. Do not forget to label the plants with a piece of coloured wool. (Diagram A)

2. When the plants are about 20cm tall, remove the seed leaves. Using a razor blade, make a downward slit into the stem of the rootstock and an upward slit in the variety, about 5cm up the stems. Try to cut into the middle of the stems, and try not to go right through. (Diagram B)

3. Splice them together by sliding the variety cut into the rootstock cut, and join with clear sticky tape. (Diagram C)

4. Cover the joined plants with a clear plastic bag to keep the humidity high. The graft should have taken after a week to 10 days.

5. Cut the rootstock variety off above the union and the variety below. (Diagram D)
You can now grow your desired tomato plants on a rootstock that will protect them from any soil borne diseases.

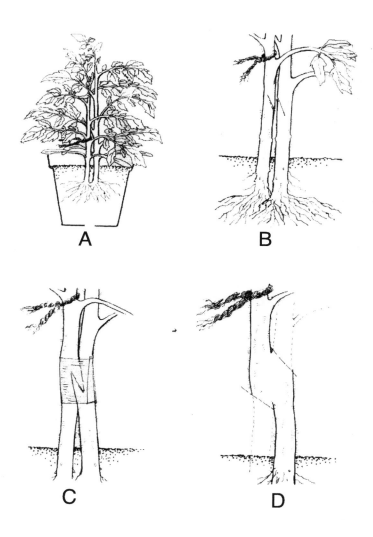

A   B

C   D

Harvest, storage and sale

Harvesting tomatoes is quite easy. Tomatoes grown under cover will be ready for sale from some time in June until well into October. I usually grow enough outdoors to last until the end of September. Any I have left beyond this point I store on the window bench of my shed: here they get a lot of warmth and light but no frost. If you have a glut of tomatoes it's a good idea to pick some before they are quite ready, to ripen somewhere free from pests and rain.

People tend to like tomatoes all year round so putting them in your box every week in season will never hurt.

Profit and efficiency

Each outdoor tomato plant will give you between 2.5 and 5kg of tomatoes in a season. I grew 25 out-door plants last season and sold a bag (roughly 750gms) of tomatoes for 75p. This works out at £187.50. Not a lot for all the work, starting them off in cells, potting on, planting out, feeding, protect-ing against blight, the cost of the fleece etc etc. The indoor tomatoes are similarly inefficient. It's really much more profitable to grow something like lettuce or garlic! But then you can't make tomato sauce to go on your pasta with a lettuce. I grow them because they are what people want. If you're having trouble getting the kids to eat vegetables, they will always eat the sweet cherry tomatoes that I put in the boxes.

Hints and tips

Use bush varieties for outdoors because they take less work.
Feed tomatoes once a week with comfrey or seaweed liquid once the fruit has set.
Use resistant roostock if you have a build up of disease in your soil.
Give customers a range of tomatoes each week.
Surplus tomatoes can be turned into sauce or chutney.

Turnips

Being a quick-cropper, turnips can easily be sown and harvested within three months. They are often eaten when they have got too big, and they are tough and taste of cabbages. If they are harvested when they are small, turnips are absolutely delicious. Even so, they are not the most popular of vegetables so I only grow two crops - a spring crop for its earliness and an autumn crop to use up vacant ground.

Types and varieties

The spring crop I grow is called Snowball. This root is almost pure white. It can be ready to harvest as early as late May, and will be one of the first vegetables I sell in my boxes.

For an autumn crop I grow Purple Top Milan. It really does have a beautiful purple top. Use Golden Ball or Norfolk Purple Top for storing.

Soil, site and rotation

Turnips are not a hungry crop, being fast growing and a root, so I never add compost. To sow direct prepare the soil to a fine tilth, or for transplanting from modules a medium tilth is sufficient. Turnips are brassicas so always put them in that part of the rotation.

Sowing and planting

For direct sowing, sow in rows 30cm apart and 1cm deep. Try to sow a seed every 2.5–5cm, to avoid thinning. For a really early crop, sow the seed undercover, in modules, three or four seeds per cell. Harden off before planting out, with about 30cm between blocks.

Food, water and mulch

Turnips are so quick to grow that feeding and mulching aren't necessary. If you are growing a succession of crops through the summer, pay attention to watering.

Seasonal care

Thinning is only necessary if you've sown too many seed. Turnips will clump together a little like beetroot and as long as the seed hasn't been sown too thickly, the largest turnips can be harvested whilst the smaller ones can be left to grow on for harvesting later. If transplanted from modules they will grow in a clump in the same way. Hoe between the rows but don't worry too much about hand weeding – the crop should be up before it becomes necessary.

Succession and continuity

Turnips can be sown outdoors from March until late August so its possible to have fresh turnips right through the summer. Starting some in modules early on in March will provide a crop as early as late May. At the end of the season, any surplus can be stored for winter use.

Problems

As for swedes

Harvest, storage and sale

Harvest turnips before they get big and tough, no bigger than a tennis ball. Turnips grow very quickly so be careful they don't become too big and tough to sell. Late crops of Purple Top Milan can be left in the ground until the first hard frosts, sometimes as late as December, without deteriorating.
To store turnips, twist the tops off and put them in damp sand in a frost-free shed (*see Carrots page 104*). If you plan to do this use a variety suitable for storing.

My customers usually only get turnips twice a year. As they are not universally popular I try to suggest recipes, such as adding small sticks of turnip to salads. Sell the smallest and sweetest turnips and those customers that were not keen on them in the first place can soon be won round.

Profit and efficiency

I wouldn't describe turnips as profitable, but they are useful in the first boxes of the season when there are few other crops available to sell. The purple-topped varieties add colour to the boxes in the autumn and winter.

Hints and tips

Keep an eye on their size as they will quickly get too big to be enjoyable.
Never sell turnips that have grown too big.

Herbs

Introduction

Growing herbs in an organic garden adds to the diversity and range of plants present. They are also important by virtue of the roles that some of them play: many of them attract beneficial insects whilst others can be used to repel unwanted pests.

The culinary uses of herbs are myriad. They are used for flavourings and the list that can be added to salads is endless. Some herbs I add to the veg boxes as a bunch or even a bag, but my main use is to add them to salad bags. Collectively they are invaluable for this, although individually they are negligible in terms of the profitability of the garden.

There are numerous herbs that you could grow, and I have included in this book those that I grow regularly in my garden. I have probably covered all of the ones you are likely to grow. Some of the herbs included are perennial and do not require much description. Those that require more attention have a fuller text.

Basil

I know that a lot of growers think otherwise, but I think that basil is one of the easier herbs to grow. All it needs is a little warmth and protection. It is treated as an annual in this country because it is susceptible to cold and frost. In the height of summer, I give my customers large bags full of basil leaves, at least four times the amount you get in a nasty plastic tray from the supermarket.

Types and varieties

There are plenty of varieties of basil to chose from but I tend to stick to three or four types. Sweet basil can't be beaten as the standard for a pasta meal. Neapolitan or Lettuce Leaf basil has, as its name suggests, large leaves, which makes harvesting a quick job. Rubin or Red Ruffles basil are deep purple varieties that add colour to salads. Cinnamon basil has a lovely tangy flavour. There are many other varieties that are fun to try: find your own favourites or those best suited to your purpose, and stick to them.

Soil, site and rotation

Because basil needs warmth to do well in this part of the country I always put it in a nicely composted polytunnel bed. As it doesn't take up much room I can easily rotate it around the tunnels.

Sowing and planting

I sow basil seeds in mid March, in modules in a propagator at a temperature of 18–21°C. Any earlier and they will be ready to transplant before it's warm enough in the polytunnel. Once they're 4–5cm tall I plant them in the prepared bed at 30–45cm intervals. Some varieties are quite bushy and you should allow plenty of space between them to give lots of ventilation to prevent moulds.

If you do decide to plant any outdoors pick a sheltered, fertile site. Ventilation will not be a problem and they will benefit from being planted closer together.

I plant any left over plants amongst my tomatoes, inside and out, as they are a good companion plant helping to keep whitefly at bay.

Food, water and mulch

As I add plenty of compost to the bed before I plant my basil, it does not need feeding while it is growing. However, they do need frequent watering or they run to seed earlier than necessary. I don't mulch basil to start with because I like to keep an eye on how moist the soil is. Once the plants begin to reach their peak, though, the leaf canopy is too dense for my irrigation sprayers to penetrate effectively so I mulch with grass mowings or straw. Later in the season, wetting the leaves encourages moulds so the mulch helps, and if you need to water keep it to the roots only.

Seasonal care

Basil needs little care during the season although if you see any signs of the plants bolting, nip the flower shoots out. This encourages the plant to put its energy into producing leaves. If the plants are too close together then remove some of them to give adequate ventilation.

Succession and continuity

Leaves can be picked from the plants throughout the growing season. The only way to prolong the season is to grow basil in heat. A few plants in pots and kept on your kitchen windowsill will give you basil for a few extra weeks at the end of the season when the polytunnel crops have finished. Cinnamon basil tends to last longer than most other varieties.

Problems

Aphids may trouble young plants so make sure they don't suffer through lack of water. However, slugs will devastate young plants if given a chance so try to keep the soil surface dry during the early stages of growth. Covering with clear plastic bottles early on protects them from slugs and snails but make sure you remove the tops of the bottles so that there is some ventilation.

Harvest, storage and sale

It's essential that basil is picked in the right way, to encourage the production of more leaves. A basil plant grows up and produces side shoots from between the stem and stem leaves, in much the same way as tomato plant. Wait until a shoot has one or two pairs of leaves then pinch out the growing tip. More shoots will develop from between the stem and leaves. By picking the plant in this way you inhibit the flowering process and encourage leaf production.

Basil leaves don't store well. If you are selling them, pick them in the coolest part of the morning and keep them somewhere cool. If you pick all the leaves into a basket or box you can spray them thoroughly with cool water before putting them in plastic bags and sealing.

Basil can be dried but the best flavour is retained if you freeze it. To dry basil, lift the whole plant at the end of the season and hang somewhere warm for a month or two. To freeze, pick as many leaves as you can and blend in a food processor until you have a paste. I sometimes add a teaspoon of water to help it along. Keep adding the leaves as they reduce. Freeze the paste in ice cube trays. The cubes can be added to pasta and other dishes during the winter when basil is expensive in the shops. Even though it has been frozen the taste of fresh basil is quite amazing.

Profit and efficiency

I usually give my customers a bag of basil every other week, particularly if I don't have enough salad to go round. Basil does not take up much space in the polytunnel but is highly rated by my customers and giving them plenty will keep them happy.

Hints and tips

Keep the plants somewhere warm, preferably covered, but space the plants well for ventilation.
Frequent watering will prevent bolting.
Careful picking will give greater yields.
Use as a companion plant to keep whitefly off your tomatoes.

Celery Leaf

In terms of growing celery leaf is very similar to parsley, but the flavour is definitely of celery. Once the plant has bolted the flavour is even stronger, very good in soups. I use the leaves mainly in salad bags particularly later in the season when there is less greenery around. The stalk is useful as an alternative to celery.

Types and varieties
There is just one type, called celery leaf.

Soil, site and rotation
See parsley.

Sowing and planting
Celery leaf seed is very small and needs light to germinate. Sow on the surface of the compost and keep it damp during germination. Once the seedlings are big enough, prick them out into seed trays and grow on until they are big enough to plant out.

Food, water and mulch
See parsley.

Seasonal care
See parsley.

Succession and continuity
See parsley.

Problems
Celery leaf has yet to suffer from any problem in my experience. However, if grown in abundance carrot root fly or celery diseases may affect it.

Harvest, storage and sale
Use the stalk and leaf in salad bags. If you give your customers information sheets then suggest that the stalk be used in place of celery in soups, stir-fries etc.

Profit and efficiency
Celery leaf is not what I'd call a profitable crop, but it is relatively easy to grow. As a constituent of salad bags and an alternative to celery it is definitely worth growing.

Hints and tips
Don't cover the seed with compost as it needs light to germinate.

Chervil

I occasionally add chervil to salad bags. It has a light, aniseed flavour and can be used in soups, stews, sauces, and salads and as a garnish.

Types and varieties
There are two varieties. Chervil is quite delicate and has fern type leaves. The leaves of plain chervil are straighter and longer.

Soil, site and rotation
Chervil is a biennial, needing to be started every two years, but I have found that it tends to seed itself. It can tolerate light shade and is very hardy so it does well in a perennial herb bed amongst taller herbs like rosemary and chives.

Sowing and planting
Sow seed in modules in the spring and plant out in early summer. Once established the bed will continue to crop for many years.

Food, water and mulch
Chervil is generally an easy plant to look after and needs no special attention. Remember that it favours moist ground so try to water it during dry spells.

Seasonal care
Cut back flowering shoots to provide continuity.

Succession and continuity
See above.

Problems
None.

Harvest, storage and sale
Use in salad bags.

Profit and efficiency

This is an easy herb to grow as it readily reseeds itself. It adds variety to salads and can be put in boxes as one of the more 'unusual' herbs.

Hints and tips

Plant chervil where the bed can remain undisturbed for several years.

Chives

Chives are one of my favourite plants. Once established they provide abundant oniony flavour for omelettes, salads, pasta dishes etc, and flowers that are a real treat. They set seed freely and provide you with little chive plants every year, which some people seem to find annoying but I find a great boon to gardening. To me chives is the ideal plant: it looks after itself, seeds itself, is pretty, is tasty, and has no pests.

Types and varieties

Most people only know the variety of chives that has pinky/purple flowers. There is also a variety called garlic chives that produces a flatter leaf and has a distinctive garlic flavour.

Soil, site and situation

Being a tall spiky plant, chives can easily be grown amongst other plants in a perennial herb bed. Chives are said to thrive in damp places.
I have a few plants in one of my polytunnels so that I can start picking leaves early.

Sowing and planting

Chives are easily grown from seed. It is also easy to split an established clump, so find a gardening friend or neighbour who has one, dig up part of it and replant it in your garden.
Chives are perennial and so there is no need to resow once you get started. Some people say that the flavour gets less strong the older the plant, but I've had a plant in my polytunnel for eight years and it still tastes pretty strong to me.

Food, water and mulch

Generally speaking, chives need no attention and will look after themselves all season.

Seasonal care

See below.

Succession and continuity

Chives die back in the winter so I grow some in one of my polytunnels where it provides me with an early picking of leaf and flower for my own use.

The plants tend to flower in May and June. If you want a fresh crop later in the year, cut a couple of the plants down to 5cm in June and they'll grow fresh leaf later in the year.

Problems

None yet, though it can be affected by rust, a yellowy-orange powder on the leaves. If it gets bad, dig the plant up and throw it away. Restock with fresh seed or new cuttings.

Harvest, storage and sale

Use the leaves and flowers in salads. Small bunches can be made up using elastic bands and put in boxes or sold at market stalls. Be generous with them as people love them and they are easy to grow.

Profit and efficiency

Another salad bag crop that is worth its place in my garden as, once established, it needs little or no care at all. It is easy to harvest and adds variety to boxes.

Hints and tips

Cut a plant or two back in May and you will get fresh leaf for salads within a month or two.
The flowers attract bees.
Create new stock by division.

Coriander

Many people have a great fondness for coriander, others absolutely hate it. I'm in the former category and so are lots of my customers. As a result, I grow as much as I possibly can and try to get two cuts off each sowing.

Many gardeners tell me they can't grow coriander, but what they really mean is they can't grow it without it bolting before they've had a decent harvest from it. As long as a few simple techniques are adhered to, a good harvest can be achieved.

Types and varieties

I only know of two types of coriander seed, Cilantro A for seed production and Cilantro B for leaf production – I use Cilantro B for both and the seed seems to be fine for cooking.

Soil, site and rotation

In my experience, coriander readily bolts in conditions that are too hot and/or too dry. For this reason

I grow most of my coriander outside and pay particular attention to the moisture of the soil it grows in. However, I have grown it undercover and left it to self-seed. This gives an early harvest and when it flowers it attracts hoverflies into the polytunnel to eat aphids.

Coriander is an umbellifer so I grow it in the umbellifer, or root, section of the rotation. The soil needs only to be tilled and rotovated before sowing. For some reason I tend to grow it in the same bed as parsley, it seems to go well there and gets the attention that it needs. It is also one of the few herbs that needs quite a lot of space so I devote a whole bed to these two plants.

Sowing and planting

Always sow coriander seed direct. Never transplant it as the shock will make it bolt. Make a drill about an inch deep and sow thickly, cover and water. Rows should be about 30cm apart. If the weather is dry water the rows before the seedlings emerge.

Food, water and mulch

Coriander plants don't need any additional feeding but they do need plenty of water to prevent them from bolting. Continue to water throughout the growing period whenever the weather turns dry. If you keep to this watering method you should get at least two cuts. To prevent slugs feasting on it do not mulch.

Seasonal care

Attention to watering and weeding is necessary, but not much else. It isn't necessary to thin the rows as you need the thickness of growth in order to harvest efficiently.

Succession and continuity

I make three sowings a year, the first in April as the ground begins to warm, another in early May and another in June. This gives me fresh coriander to eat and sell from June to September. If I'm really switched on, a sowing under cover in July will keep me going even later although it won't tolerate cold and is unlikely to last much beyond October.

As coriander seed is expensive to buy I always leave a few plants to flower and save my own seed for sowing the following year and for culinary use.

Problems

I have never had much of a problem with slugs eating my coriander but I know many gardeners who have. I grow rows of coriander in the same bed as parsley, which is very susceptible to slugs, so I do police the area quite closely. I do not mulch the parsley and coriander bed, or the one on either side. I also try and keep the bed as dry as possible while the plants are establishing. On a small scale you could keep the young plants dry with cloches, removing them later.

As well as attracting hoverflies, coriander seems to deter red spider mite. When I have grown coriander beneath my cucumber plants I haven't had any problems with red spider mite. I really need a few more years before I am sure it works but it certainly seems to. It has been suggested that the smell of the coriander plant puts the mites off.

Harvest, storage and sale

Harvesting coriander is time consuming on the first cut but quick on the second. For the first harvest, pick the biggest individual stalks and leaves and tie with an elastic band. If you can keep the bottom of the stalks in water and mist the tops with a spray before packing they will be, and look, much fresher when they arrive at their destination. On the second harvest, cut the plant with a knife about 10cm above ground level and continue as for the first cut. If you leave a few of the stalks that appear to be bolting and let them flower you will be able to collect the seed for sowing next year.

The seed is collected by pulling up the mature plants when they are dry and hanging them upside down in a dry airy shed for a couple of weeks. Rub the seed heads between your hands onto a large sheet and then keep in a paper bag somewhere dry until the following year. This should give you plenty of seed for sowing and eating.

Profit and efficiency

Again, it is the variety that is added to the boxes by growing coriander that makes it profitable. It does require a lot of watering but you can increase its efficiency by only harvesting each crop once, by the knife method.

Hints and tips

Always sow direct and don't transplant.
Keep well watered once established.
Beware of slugs.
Allow some plants to flower and run to seed.

Dill and Fennel

I grow dill and fennel to add to salads where they contribute a delicate, aniseedy flavour as well as attractive fronds. Dill and fennel are very similar in looks but dissimilar in terms of their growth. Both seed themselves readily but fennel dies down over winter and regrows from the root each year. It will grow up to, and sometimes over, a metre and a half tall and should not be mistaken for bulb fennel (a vegetable) although their top fronds are almost exactly the same and can be used to the same effect. Dill is more feathery, has a delicate flavour and will only grow from seed.

Types and varieties

Dill and fennel are both members of the umbellifer family and there are a number of varieties of each. Of dill, the varieties Sari and Fernleaf (a dwarf variety) are less inclined to bolt than others so are good for leaf production. Fennel comes in two colours, green and bronze. Bronze fennel does add a good dose of colour to a salad.

Soil, site and rotation

I grow fennel plants in the perennial herb bed. They are also useful dotted around the garden as the flowers attract hoverflies.

Dill is sown directly, in ground that becomes available in the polytunnels and sometimes outside.

Both require well-drained soil and a sunny position.

Sowing and planting

Try and sow dill directly to prevent it from bolting too quickly. If it is left to seed, it will germinate and grow in the soil around the original plant for the following year.

Fennel can be sown in modules and transplanted, and once it is established it will seed new plants on a yearly basis.

Food, water and mulch

Dill and fennel don't require any particular feeding although dill does need frequent watering. I don't mulch them as dill isn't very slug tolerant and fennel doesn't really need it.

Seasonal care

Keep well weeded.

Succession and continuity

Fennel can be picked throughout the season. If you want fresh new growth then chop a couple of plants down and they will resprout with fresh fronds.

For a continuous crop, dill must be sown three or four times in succession, until midsummer.

Problems

Dill can be attacked by slugs but has few other problems.

Fennel is prone to aphid attack in dry springs. It can be an early indicator of green aphid populations so keep an eye on it to alert you to further problems in the other areas of your garden.

Harvest, storage and sale

Both these herbs are only used in salad bags so should be picked fresh on the day. Dill does wilt quickly so try and pick in the early morning and then keep it covered with damp paper or with its stems in water until packing.

Profit and efficiency

Fennel and dill are not commercially profitable herbs, but they add to the diversity of the salads I grow and the garden as a whole. Dill is more sought after than fennel, particularly by restaurant chefs.

Hints and tips

Easy to grow but watch out for slugs on dill.

Lemon Balm

Just rubbing a leaf of lemon balm releases the strongest smell of lemon you can imagine. It seems ridiculous to use imported lemons for flavourings when we have a native herb that does the same job. I add it to salad bags, use it to make a good herbal tea and to give a lemon flavour to many dishes.

Types and varieties

There is only one type and it is a perennial.

Soil, site and rotation

I have lemon balm everywhere. It is mostly in my perennial herb bed but it seeds readily and can be found all over my house garden. It spreads by root growth too and can get out of control.

Sowing and planting

The easiest way to get lemon balm is to beg a rooted cutting or clump from a neighbour or friend, or buy a small plant. Once this has established you won't need much more. If you want to grow it from seed, sow the tiny seeds in modules in the spring and then transplant to pots in the summer. They can be planted out the following spring after which they will be ready for use.

Food, water and mulch

Lemon balm seems to thrive on neglect. However, it does like a moist soil so either mulch or keep well watered if your soil is light or sandy.

Seasonal care

I cut around the base of the plant in the winter to stop it spreading.

Succession and continuity

It continues successfully of its own accord but I cut back a few plants in the summer when they start to flower, to get fresh growth for the autumn.

Problems

Its vigour is its greatest problem, but on the plus side it is very attractive to bees.

Harvest, storage and sale

Pick the fresh shoots down to where the leaves start to deteriorate and add them to salad bags. Don't pick any flowering shoots as they will be bitter.

Profit and efficiency

Lemon balm is not profitable but it is easy to pick in the spring to add to salads.

Hints and tips

Use instead of lemons to flavour a wide range of dishes.
Cut a plant back in summer to get fresh growth for autumn.

Lovage

This is not a herb I use a lot because its flavour is so strong, but it is very good in soups, creamy pasta sauce and mushroom dishes. The main reason I grow it is because it is so tall, probably the tallest plant in my garden, and it produces a mass of umbelliferous flowers that attract masses of hoverflies.

Types and varieties

There is only one and it's called lovage.

Soil, site and rotation

Remember to take account of its height as it will shade anything on its north side quite dramatically. It is a perennial and will die back in winter but once established it's there to stay.

Sowing and planting

Lovage is easily grown from seed. See parsley for details.

Food, water and mulch

Since I planted my two lovage plants I have largely ignored them.

Seasonal care

Lovage is vigorous enough to take care of itself.

Succession and continuity

The plants die back in winter and emerge in spring of their own accord. Pick the leaves as you want them.

Problems

I have yet to discover a problem that affects lovage and it is a beneficial plant to have in the garden. It produces a huge array of umbelliferous flowers in mid summer, attracting hoverflies. After the flowers there are loads of seeds that attract birds in the autumn. Having a healthy bird population in the autumn means that you are likely to have a healthy bird population in the winter, and they will help clear up unwanted pests.

Harvest, storage and sale

Lovage has such a strong flavour that the amount one plant produces would be enough to feed a small town all year. If you want to appreciate its flavour during the winter save some seed and crush them into or onto whatever you are eating or cooking.

You can add lovage to salad bags but be wary as its scent will probably over power any other herb in the bag.

Profit and efficiency

Not profitable as such but it is beneficial in the garden.

Hints and tips

Plant where it won't shade other plants – the north side of your garden or up against a hedge is a good idea.

Mint

If you have a kitchen garden you must grow garden or spear mint, if only to flavour your new potatoes. There are many other mints too, which are good to add to salad bags.

Types and varieties

Spear or garden mint is the right type for mint sauce and for flavouring new potatoes. There are other mints that are useful for teas, such as peppermint and water mint. Apple and pineapple mints make a nice addition to salad bags.

Soil, site and rotation

Mint doesn't seem to require any particular soil or site but it does prefer moister ground. Mint is grown in my perennial herb bed because it spreads so readily. If you want to contain it and grow large amounts, use an old bath or other such container. Be sure to leave the plug out to allow drainage, and don't let the soil dry out in hot weather.

Sowing and planting

Take a cutting with a bit of root from a friend's plant. This will grow and spread rapidly in the first year and later on you will have difficulty containing it.

Food, water and mulch

Keep watered in dry weather but otherwise it needs little care.

Seasonal care

If mint becomes invasive cut it back and pull out roots in the winter. The other plants in the herb bed can generally stand up to it so I tend to let it do its own thing. When the top shoot is pinched out, new shoots will grow out from the stem making it a bushier plant.

Succession and continuity

Keep cutting the shoots during the spring and summer and it will continue to produce for most of the year, although it does die back in harsh weather in the winter.

Problems

Mint can get rust but if it is kept well watered this doesn't tend to be a problem. The flowers attract bees and butterflies.

Harvest, storage and sale

Fresh shoots are picked and added to salad bags throughout the season, and extra sprigs are added to the boxes in early summer with the new potatoes.

Profit and efficiency

It is essential for cooking and to add to salad bags and once you have a plant or two established it doesn't require much attention.

Hints and tips

Grow in containers if you don't want it to run wild in your garden.

Oregano, Sweet and Pot Marjoram

These are lovely herbs, particularly good in pasta and pizza dishes. They are easy to grow once established.

Types and varieties

I use Greek oregano because it is a perennial and has a good flavour. It has a woody stem that sends out soft green shoots, ideal to add to salads throughout the summer. Sweet marjoram is very aromatic and is an annual whereas pot marjoram has a milder flavour and is a perennial.

Soil, site and rotation

Anywhere light and open where you can leave them to grow for several years. I grow them in the perennial herb bed and polytunnels.

Sowing and planting

Marjoram and oregano can be grown from seed but I must admit to buying the odd plant now and then. The plants can be divided at the roots in spring and autumn and this will give bigger and better plants much more quickly than by growing from seed.

Food, water and mulch

Add compost around the base of the plants in spring and keep watered in hot, dry weather.

Seasonal care

Keep well weeded and they will sprawl over the ground.

Succession and continuity

Cut back when the plants start to flower and more fleshy green shoots will appear through the season.

Problems

None.

Harvest, storage and sale

Pick two or three shoots per salad bag or make up bunches to sell in boxes and on market stalls. The leaves tend to wither more quickly than most woody herbs so it is wise to keep their stems in water. The flowers of marjoram can be used in salads as well as the leaves.

Profit and efficiency

As with many of the other herbs it is most useful in salad bags so it isn't profitable as such. However it is valued by my customers and sells well before the more highly favoured basil arrives on the scene.

Hints and tips

Grow one or two plants in a polytunnel for early cuttings.

Parsley

Parsley is a biennial umbellifer and is therefore very similar to plants such as carrots, parsnips, fennel and coriander. It can suffer from the same pests but generally it is a fairly easy crop to grow and my customers appreciate it.

Types and varieties

There are three main types for leaf production. Moss (or curly) parsley is the most popular probably only because it is the one most people recognise. French parsley is becoming more popular as more and more chefs recommend it for its flavour, which is much stronger than the curly type. Its leaves are flat. Italian parsley is also flat leafed but much bigger than French parsley.

Hamburg Parsley is grown for the parsnip-like root that can be used to flavour soups and stews. The flavour is a blend of celery and parsley.

Soil, site and rotation

I always sow parsley in the root or umbellifer section of my rotation. It seems to grow well without any additional soil treatment but I would recommend a sunny site. You will need a fine tilth because the seed are very small. Parsley doesn't like an acid soil so add some lime and/or plenty of compost if necessary.

Sowing and planting

Parsley seeds are quite small and, like carrots and parsnips, take a long time to germinate. You can pre-germinate them if you want, to get them going more quickly. I grow parsley both indoors and out, to prolong the season.

For my indoor crop I start a small tray of parsley in the propagator in February and harden it off in the polytunnel. Prick out the tiny seedlings into seed trays or modules and grow on until they are big enough to plant out in the polytunnel. This will give you a good crop of parsley by June and several smaller pickings before then.

For the outdoor crop sow rows of parsley in early April or as soon as the soil is warm enough. If you cover the soil in advance with cloches or clear plastic it will warm more quickly so you can start your seeds earlier. Sow the seed in drills up to 30mm deep and cover very lightly, leaving an indentation in the soil. Cover the bed with clear plastic, which will warm the soil and help the seed to germinate. Once the seedlings have emerged remove the plastic and the tiny plants will be protected from the elements because they are in a dip below the soil level.

Parsley seedlings are very attractive to slugs, so now I more often raise plants under cover and plant out in early April.

Food, water and mulch

Parsley has a large root system so it requires little attention once it gets going. However, make sure it gets enough water in the first month. If the weather is particularly dry through the summer give it some water. I don't bother to mulch it as the canopy is usually dense enough to keep weeds at bay.

Seasonal care

Hand weed when the plants are establishing to prevent any competition.

Succession and continuity

Growing parsley indoors and out will give you a crop all year round. My indoor crop is usually ready for full harvesting by the time I start selling in June and then the outdoor crop starts in July. Covering the outdoor crop in the autumn will keep it cropping for another few weeks.

Some books recommend that you sow a crop in the autumn to over-winter. I never bother with this because I can harvest parsley all year from my spring sowings.

Problems

Parsley is a member of the umbellifer family and can be attacked by carrot root fly. As we don't eat the root (apart from Hamburg Parsley) this is not of great concern. The most carrot root fly can do is to weaken the plant making the leaves turn yellow and uninviting. It never attacks all my plants so I ignore the affected ones and leave them where they are. I have the feeling that if I removed them any carrot root fly about will move over to the healthy plants and I would lose more.

I try to leave some parsley plants to go to seed during the summer following their harvest, inside and out, because being an umbellifer their flowers attract hoverflies, which eat aphids.

Harvest, storage and sale

Harvesting parsley isn't too time consuming. Aim to pick about eight stalks of the largest leaves and wrap an elastic band around them. Don't try and store parsley before sale unless you can keep the stems in water: they will wilt quickly.

Although I sell bunches of parsley in my boxes, one of the main advantages of growing the curly variety is that you can put it in the top of a salad bag. It looks attractive and pads out the bag, stopping the contents from settling into a dense and heavy mass, which often makes the softer lettuce leaves go slimy.

Profit and efficiency

Despite being slow to start, if you can get plants growing early on the leaves will be welcome in early salads. Being easy and quick to harvest and providing greenery later in the year are added bonuses.

Hints and tips

Avoid slug damage by growing transplants for your outdoor crop.

Use parsley in salads to add bulk and when you don't have enough parsley to make up bunches.

Rocket

Rocket is so popular now that it deserves it's own section. I used to hate rocket because of it's strong flavour. I found that I grew to like it when I started to grow it myself and picked the best leaves to munch on as I gardened. I am now such a convert that I like to eat the leaves once the plant has bolted and the flavour becomes even stronger. It is also extremely easy to grow and can be sold independently from salad bags if you have a surplus.

Types and varieties

Salad Rocket is the usual variety and the one I normally use. It has been developed for salad production with a milder taste whereas the variety Wild Rocket has a much stronger flavour.

Soil, site and rotation

Rocket belongs to the brassica family but it doesn't seem to suffer from brassica type pests other than flea beetles. A fairly fine tilth is needed and a sunny site. I grow most of my rocket in the polytunnels where flea beetle damage is minimal although growing outside under fleece can prevent this problem.

Sowing and planting

Sow from March (under cover) until September/October. It isn't necessary to transplant but sow a seed every 1cm in drills 20cm apart and you will get a fairly thick row which is well ventilated.

Food, water and mulch

A composted bed is all that is required and adequate watering during the main stage of growth.

Seasonal care

Keep weeded and avoid letting the soil dry out as this will make the plant bolt.

Succession and continuity

Sow areas every two to three weeks and you will get fresh rocket all season. It will also stand in the winter under cover. Once it has bolted you can continue to pick the leaves but they have a much stronger flavour. It will also readily seed itself so if you have spare ground, let it flower and within a month or two you will find fresh rocket leaves growing.

Problems

Flea beetles. Grow rocket under cover, either indoors or under fleece and flea beetle damage will be minimal.

Harvest, storage and sale

It is most efficient to let the rows grow to about 20cm in height and then cut with scissors. Picking individual leaves is time consuming but lessens the number of sowings you will have to make. The leaves wilt fast in hot weather so try to pick in early morning. Either add leaves to salad bags or fill a small bag with the leaf if you have a surplus.

Profit and efficiency

It is one of the easier and more reliable salad leaves to grow and is very popular.

Hints and tips

Keep covered to prevent flea beetle damage.

Rosemary and Sage

Rosemary and sage are similar in that they are quite woody shrubs with a very strong aroma. Sage has a stronger flavour and tends to be more straggly than rosemary but both are worthwhile providing fresh, green, pungent leaves nearly all year round.

Types and varieties

Sage has green, purple, variegated, pineapple (not a true sage), painted and Spanish varieties but I stick to the common green type. The other varieties are good for winter salad bags. Rosemary varieties differ in the shape of their flower, their growing habit, and their hardiness. Try Mrs Jessup's Upright, if you can find it, for its hardiness.

Soil, site and rotation

They tend to grow anywhere but prefer full sun and should be placed in the perennial herb bed. Alternatively grow them in pots around the garden and outside the kitchen door.

Sowing and planting

Sage is easy to propagate from cuttings. In May take woody stems with fresh top-growth and push them into some sandy soil. Leave them to take root.

Growing rosemary from seed is difficult. Take 15cm cuttings between June and August and put in a jar of water where they will develop small white roots. Move to a pot of poorish soil for the winter and plant out the following spring.

Food, water and mulch

Once the cuttings are established they need little attention.

Seasonal care

Cut back any untidy branches in the winter.

Succession and continuity

As long as you remember to start new sage plants every few years you should have a continuous supply of fresh sage.

Problems

None so far but be careful of wind damage.

Harvest, storage and sale

Cut sprigs in the autumn and winter to add to boxes. Sage flowers are edible and can be used in summer salad bags.

Profit and efficiency

Both are particularly useful in winter when vegetable boxes and market stalls need a bit of interest. They are profitable for this reason alone. Different varieties of sage add interest to boxes in the colder months.

Hints and tips

Add the flowers to summer salad bags. Remember to start new plants regularly. Grow Rosemary from cuttings rather than seed.

Salad Burnet

I grow this herb because it has an amazing cucumber flavour and stays green throughout the winter. It seems to just keep growing year after year once it is established so it needs very little work.

Types and varieties

Just the one.

Soil, site and rotation

Salad burnet is a native of chalk downlands so prefers a limey and free draining soil. If your soil is not like this add plenty of compost to the bed.

Sowing and planting

Sow the seed in modules in the spring. When the plants are big enough either plant directly into the bed or into pots to grow on. Site it in the perennial herb bed and near the kitchen window. Established plants can be divided so beg a section or two from a friend and you will get a good crop much more quickly.

Food, water and mulch

Adding compost each year as a light mulch will keep the roots moist and well fed.

Seasonal care

It isn't necessary to do anything during the season although if you want fresh growth later in the year you can cut the plant back to remove any flowers.

Succession and continuity

Salad burnet will start to flower in the early summer and must be cut back if you want tender leaves. Once it has flowered, the leaves tend to get tough and bitter. You can pick the leaves for most of the year, apart from the few coldest months in the winter.

Problems

None.

Harvest, storage and sale

I use the leaves mainly in salad bags during the spring and late in the season when there are few other green leaves about. They add a good cucumber taste to salads before the cucumbers become available.

Profit and efficiency

Profitability is negligible but it looks particularly nice and you don't need very much to add to a salad.

Hints and tips

Cut back plants when flowering to produce tender new shoots.

Savory - Summer and Winter

Savory is known to be excellent for keeping black fly away from broad beans, rather than any culinary use. I find this difficult to believe as black fly is so persistent and virulent, but it's worth a try. It does attract hoverflies and bees to the garden.

I have yet to grow savory successfully and am storing it up as one of my experiments.

Types and varieties

Summer savory is an annual and tastes a little like sage. It is also particularly good eaten with broad beans, making it the ideal companion plant. Winter savory is basically the same but it is a perennial and has a stronger flavour. Winter savory can be used in soups and stews as well as dried.

Soil, site and rotation

Summer savoury prefers a fairly rich, moist soil whereas winter savoury will thrive in poor, well drained soil. Both prefer a sunny position.

This herb is mainly used with broad beans and can be sown between the rows in the spring. Thus it moves around the rotation with the beans. In my experience it doesn't grow as quickly as broad beans so it is best to sow it early in pots and then plant out between the rows when you sow the broad beans.

Sowing and planting

Sow in drills 1cm deep between the rows of broad beans or sow in pots under cover earlier in the spring and transplant to the broad bean bed when they are grown. If you are growing savory separately from the beans you should thin the plants to one every 15cm in rows 30cm apart.

Food, water and mulch

As for broad beans.

Seasonal care

You can get two crops from savory by cutting it back once the flowering stem has emerged.

Succession and continuity

Grow both varieties and you will have savory all year round, apart from a few months in the spring. You can even get a crop throughout these months if you sow a little winter savory under cover.

Problems

It is said to keep black fly away from broad beans, and it attracts hoverflies and bees to the garden.

Harvest, storage and sale

It can be put in salad bags during the broad bean season.

Profit and efficiency

Negligible, unless it makes a significant difference to the beans!

Hints and tips

Reputed to repel blackfly from broad beans.
Enhances the flavour of cooked broad beans and is said to go well with peas and potatoes.

Sorrel

This is one of my favourite herbs because it has a very sharp flavour and grows almost without attention. It is delicious added sparingly to salads but it comes into its own when cooked with fish. It is perennial and is available for most of the year, particularly if you have the odd plant under cover. It has a high vitamin C content.

Types and varieties

There are three varieties. Buckler leaved sorrel has small succulent leaves, spreads to give ground cover and has the best flavour of all the sorrels. Sheep sorrel is too bitter for my liking and can be dangerous due to its high oxalic acid content. Garden or common sorrel has large leaves and so is easy to pick for sale.

Soil, site and rotation

I have a few plants in the perennial herb bed and a couple in the polytunnel.

Sowing and planting

Sorrel is quite easy to grow from seed and you need only do this once as the plants will multiply themselves. It is easy to take root sections to plant up if you want more plants. If you are growing a lot of plants space them 45cm apart as they do get quite big.

Food, water and mulch

A dressing of compost around each plant every year is enough to keep them healthy, and watering in dry weather will prevent bolting.

Seasonal care

Sorrel will run to seed during the early summer particularly when it is hot and dry but simply cut back the flowering stems and the plants will put out new leaves.

Succession and continuity

Leaves can be picked all through the year if you have a few plants under cover.

Problems

Slugs will nibble sorrel but presumably they don't like the taste as they never do serious damage.

Harvest, storage and sale

Harvest as you would other salad leaves. They will wilt quite quickly during the summer so try to pick in the early morning and keep them cool and moist. This particular herb does sell well to restaurants.

Profit and efficiency

Large leafed sorrel is good for early salad bags and being a perennial plant that needs little attention it is definitely worthwhile growing for sale.

Hints and tips

Buckler leaved sorrel has the best flavour and is the prettiest.

Tarragon

Tarragon can be used as a flavouring for chicken, fish and potatoes, or to make herb vinegar. Personally I don't like the flavour much when it is used in cooking but as a raw addition to salads I absolutely love it. I grow enough to give my customer's a sprig or two in their salad bags every now and then through the summer.

Types and varieties
There are two varieties, Russian and French. It is said that French tarragon has the finer flavour but the Russian is a much hardier plant and survives better in our climate. I have a Russian plant outside where it always does well and a French plant inside – it was new last year and is still alive despite freezing conditions.

Soil, site and rotation
Tarragon is a perennial that regrows from the same rootstock every year. It needs light, warmth and a well-drained soil. It can grow quite tall during the season so if you are growing a lot you will need to site it where it won't shade out other herbs or plants.

Sowing and planting
Seed of French tarragon is difficult to get hold of so give in and buy a plant or two. Russian tarragon seed is more readily available but I would tend to buy plants of that too because it is a lot of effort to grow from seed if you only want a couple of plants. The plants take a year or two to establish but once they get going they produce a lot of leaf. New plants are easy to raise from cuttings taken from an established plant in the spring.

Food, water and mulch
Water well during dry spells but don't mulch the plants as they are prone to slug attack when they start to grow in the spring.

Seasonal care
None.

Succession and continuity
Once the plants have gone to seed I leave them alone. I have never cut it back to see if it shoots out new leaves but you could try this if you want a longer season.

Problems
Tarragon is prone to slug attack when the plants are small and when their first shoots emerge in the spring. To prevent damage and to encourage early growth cover with a glass or plastic cloche to keep

the ground dry and to give the plant a protected and warm environment in which to start.

Harvest, storage and sale
Pick three or four long sprigs to add to a salad bag.

Profit and efficiency
The profit in tarragon is negligible but it should be regarded as one of the herbs that adds value to your boxes or market stall. It is a particularly popular herb with restaurant chefs.

Hints and tips
Buy in plants if you only need one or two.
Take cuttings for new plants.

Thyme

This is another of the woody herbs that I add to the boxes later in the year when the summer herbs have finished. It is good for tea and flavouring, particularly in stews and roasts.

Types and varieties
There are several varieties that you can grow. I grow common thyme. I love creeping thyme, which gives off a great aroma when you tread on it but it is too fiddly to pick for sale. Other varieties include variegated, lemon, mastic and broad-leafed.

Soil, site and rotation
Thyme needs an open position in a well-drained soil and should be placed in the herb bed with other perennials. Dotting the plants around the garden is worthwhile too as their flowers attract bees and hoverflies. It prefers a limey soil.

Sowing and planting
I have grown thyme from seed quite easily but you can also propagate by cuttings or dividing established plants.

Food, water and mulch
As with other herbs, an annual dressing of compost and plenty of water during dry spells is usually enough.

Seasonal care

None, apart from a hair cut in the winter.

Succession and continuity

Continues to produce all year. It is said that the plants lose their flavour after three or four years and that they should then be renewed. I've found that a good short back and sides every year keeps them going.

Problems

None, and the flowers attract beneficial insects.

Harvest, storage and sale

Take three or four sprigs and tie with an elastic band. It keeps fresh much longer than more leafy herbs. As thyme is such a small herb you can tie in some sage as well to make it look a bit bigger.

Profit and efficiency

Negligible. In terms of boxes, a bunch really adds something. Selling small bunches of thyme on market stalls is worthwhile considering how easy they are to pick and how long they keep fresh.

Hints and tips

Give the plants a good trim in the winter.
Try growing different varieties for taste and interest.

Soft Fruits

Introduction

grow soft fruit mainly for my own consumption. If I have a surplus it goes into my veggie boxes where it is always appreciated. If you are growing soft fruit just for yourself I suggest you aim to grow as many different types and varieties as you can.

With careful preparation and helpful weather conditions you could be picking soft fruit for most of the year. Forced rhubarb comes first in March, followed by a crop of strawberries from the polytunnel in April. After that there are outdoor strawberries, then raspberries, black/red/white currants, gooseberries, hybrid berries and blackberries. You could finish with autumn cropping raspberries, and if these are grown in pots and moved indoors before the frosts they can be kept going as late as December. Add to that your own apples that will store between Christmas and March and in theory you can be self sufficient in fresh and stored fruit all year round. In reality, you must be very committed to get this sort of production.

I must confess to managing to pick only about half of the soft fruit on my bushes and store just the odd box of apples. Still, I keep trying. If I have the time I freeze surplus soft fruit and make my own jams. There is a lot of pleasure to be had from eating blackberry and apple pie, in the depths of winter, with fruit from your own plot.

Most soils are fine for soft fruit. Chalky soils are the exception – they tend to lock up iron causing poor growth with yellowing leaves. If you have a particularly chalky soil then a seaweed fertiliser will help. If your soil is acid you can add lime to bring the pH nearer to neutral, and you have the advantage of being able to grow blueberries and cranberries which thrive on an acid soil.

Your fruit bushes will be kept healthy with a regime of good feeding and regular pruning. An application of potash in the form of a comfrey mulch or the occasional addition of wood ash will be much appreciated.

To cage or not to cage

Siting your soft fruit is important. Birds attack most soft fruit as soon as it begins to ripen and strip the buds from currants and gooseberries during the winter. If you use nets to protect your harvest, you have to struggle with them every time you want to pick anything. If you are growing soft fruit on a large scale in order to sell the fruit, the only really efficient way of protecting your crop, and subsequently harvesting it, is to grow it all under a fruit cage over which a net can be draped for most of the year.

When growing soft fruit on a small scale, entirely for your own consumption, a more sustainable answer is to dot your soft fruit around the garden and net each bush. This creates diversity and should limit pest and disease problems, but it is quite a lot more work. You can also let tall weeds grow up through the foliage to hide the fruit from birds.

Grapes, figs and the more exotic fruits are not discussed here because I have no experience of them, preferring to grow fruits that are naturally inclined to our climate. I have not included tree fruits as they warrant more space than this book allows.

Blackberries and Hybrid Berries

When I first started growing and selling vegetables I harvested wild blackberries to fill up the boxes I sold in Bristol. This was time consuming work but customers loved them. Nowadays you can get varieties that have huge fruits and are very prolific, so I grow my own and don't have to walk miles to pick them.

Hybrid berries are usually a cross between raspberries and blackberries. The most common are tayberries and loganberries. However, there are many more varieties and if you choose carefully you can get crops from late June through to early October.

These types of berries have several advantages. They flower between May and July avoiding most of the frosts, the birds tend not to take as many as they do of other soft fruits and the range of flavours is wide (if you are prepared to be adventurous with your varieties). The problem with them is the hassle of providing some sort of support for them to grow up.

Types and varieties

I grow the blackberry Fantasia because it has big and tasty fruit. This cuts down the picking time considerably as each berry is double the size of the wild ones. If you want a dense and vigorous plant then choose Himalaya Giant, which can also act as a windbreak. The fruits, however, are sharper than Fantasia and are best used for cooking.

There are several thornless varieties, but it is said that in breeding out the thorns the flavour has been impaired. In other words, you have to earn the flavour you get from a blackberry with the odd scratch. One thornless variety worth thinking about is Loch Ness. This plant has less of a sprawling habit with canes that tend to stand upright, needing little support. I haven't tasted it myself but if it saves putting up a fencing structure then it must be worth investigating.

Of the many different varieties of hybrids, loganberries, tayberries and sunberries are always reliable. If you have an acid soil (less than pH 5.5) then you might want to consider growing blueberries. Boysenberries favour sandy soils. Other types include the hildaberry, marionberry, silvanberry, tummelberry, veitchberry, and youngberry.

Remember that blackberries and hybrid berries can be very vigorous so choose the varieties that fit your size of garden or the area you have available.

Soil, site and rotation

This all depends on the type of berry you want to grow. Blackberries tend to grow well on all soils except dry and chalky ones. They can tolerate a bit of shade and poor drainage. Some of the hybrid berries may need a particular soil type so check with your supplier. As with most fruit, the better the soil and site the better the result.

If you don't have room to grow berries in full sun then try growing them at the edges of your garden where there may be shade but there will be plenty of room. Think about placing particularly vigorous varieties in areas where a windbreak is needed.

Planting

All of these berries will need some sort of support, which needs to be erected before planting the young stock. I use 2.5-3m fencing posts supported with struts and placed about 5m apart. I stretch fencing wire between the posts to tie the plants to. You can attach the wire to existing walls and fences but it must be at least 2m high to accommodate these plants. If you have to use deer fencing round your plot this makes a perfect support. It is tall enough for the plants to ramble over, and will be hidden into the bargain.

Plants can be bought either pot grown or as bare rooted canes. The latter are ideally planted in November or December, although they can go in anytime up until the end of March - weather permitting. Container grown plants can go in anytime of the year.

To prepare the ground slice the turf off an area about 60cm square and dig a hole a good spit deep. If you have heavy soil, fork the bottom then put the turf upside down in the bottom. Add a layer of well-rotted FYM or compost and some bonemeal. Plant the young stock about 8cm deep and refill the hole with the soil. Depending on the variety, you will need to space them from 2.5 to 4.5m apart. Leave 2m between rows. The variety Loch Ness only needs to be spaced every 1.5m, another string to it's bow. Shortening the main stems to about 30cm above the soil level after planting promotes good growth in the first few years. It may seem drastic to cut back the main shoots but it does work. Mulch the plants in March, with any material you want. I use black woven plastic, which keeps the weeds down but lets the water through. To peg it down, use hoops of fencing wire pushed through into the ground.

Food, water and mulch

A top dressing of composted FYM can be added but my theory is that if they grow quite happily in the wild without it they can grow quite happily in my garden without it. If you want to add FYM and you have put plastic down as a mulch then you will need to lift the plastic and repeg it afterwards. You will get better crops if you water the plants during dry spells in the summer when the fruit is swelling.

Seasonal care

Blackberries produce fruit on new growth from the previous year and also on old growth. It is quite complicated to keep track of how old the stems are so I tend to take out most of the old growth and rely on the new growth for my fruit. If you train the first year's growth in one direction this will fruit the following year. You can then train that year's new growth in the opposite direction and see what to cut out easily. Another method is to train the plants in a fan shape. Train the new growth inside one

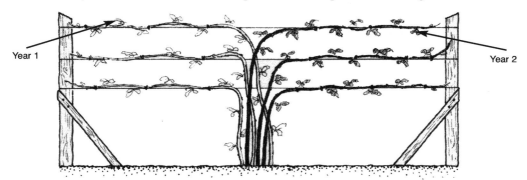

Year 1

Year 2

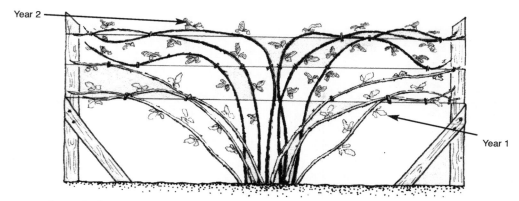

Year 2

Year 1

year and outside the next, for ease of pruning. This method is said to give a good yield. Pruning and training should be done between December and February.

You also need to cut out any dead or damaged shoots, at any time, and tie in new shoots as they grow. The various hybrids have slightly different training and pruning needs depending on their type. For example, the loganberry is a cross between a blackberry and a raspberry and will fruit only on the shoots that grew in the previous summer, a little like raspberries.

Succession and continuity

The blackberry season is more dependent on the weather than anything else. Most blackberries fruit in August and September and if you combine them with other soft fruits then succession isn't really a problem. The same applies to hybrid berries to a certain extent, but by their very nature as hybrids some will crop a bit earlier.

Problems

Blackberries don't seem to have any problems apart from their thorns: if these bother you opt for a thornless variety. Being tolerant and vigorous they can go without any form of added fertility.

The hybrids are more likely to have problems as they have other fruit types in their make up. Having the hardy blackberry in them will help but they can get problems associated with raspberries (*see Raspberry Problems page 223*).

Getting new plants

This couldn't be simpler. During the summer months dig a hole and bury the end of a shoot about 15cm down, pegging it down for good measure. The buried tip will produce roots and you can cut it away from the main plant in the winter, to grow on the following year.

Harvest, storage and sale

It really is best to pick and pack this type of fruit on the same day because they soon begin to go soggy.

Pack the fruit into punnets – cardboard ones if you can get them. Put the punnet in a plastic bag to contain any spills should it tip over, and place it on top of the vegetables in the box. Obviously plastic bags aren't sustainable either but squashed berries in amongst the other vegetables are unpopular with customers.

Profit and efficiency

As blackberries and hybrid berries tend to crop in the most productive months of the season they aren't really necessary for filling up the boxes. I find that sometimes it is worth leaving out a crop like onions and replacing them with a berry of some sort. The price difference, weight for weight, between berries and onions is huge but onions will store whereas the berries are perishable. Storing the onions to sell later also saves money on buying in crops to sell in the lean times.

Hints and tips

Make sure you tie in the new shoots and keep the bushes under control.
Berries like these will grow without added fertility provided your soil is OK.

Blackcurrants

Everyone seems to like blackcurrants. In terms of selling, blackcurrants are possibly the easiest fruit to organise, you simply cut the stems that they grow on and put them directly in the box – pruning and harvesting in one fell swoop. The major downside to blackcurrants is they do need netting to protect them from birds, although they always come second on the avian menu to redcurrants.

Types and varieties

The older varieties, such as Laxton Giant and Wellington XXX, tend to flower quite early so they can be prone to damage from frost, but they are sweet enough to eat fresh. I grow the variety Ben Lomond, late flowering, resistant to mildew and it always crops heavily. Most varieties crop in July and you can get ones that are ready later, but by August and September there are plenty of different fruits around.
The dwarf plant Ben Sarek is good for restricted space and has in-bred frost and mildew resistance, cropping in mid July with large fruits.
The jostaberry, which is a cross between a blackcurrant and gooseberry, is a very vigorous plant with big fruits and resistance to mildew. Sadly it doesn't taste quite as nice as a true blackcurrant.

Soil, site and rotation

Blackcurrants need an open and sunny site. Their flowers can be frosted easily so getting the bushes in the right position is quite important.
The ground that they are planted in should have had a good quantity of compost or FYM added, together with some bonemeal. They will tolerate a wetter, heavier and more alkaline soil than most soft fruits but obviously, the nearer you can get to a rich, moist loam with a pH of 6.5 the better.

Planting

Whether you are buying either bare root or container grown bushes, they will normally be two years old with four to six shoots. This age is ideal because any younger and they will take too long to establish. Three-year-old bushes are likely to suffer a growth check when they are transplanted, adding to the length of time before you get a crop.

It is best to plant bushes in November, but February will do. Start by digging a hole 15cm deep and 30cm wide. Add some well rotted FYM then plant the bushes, spreading their roots out, refilling with soil and treading them in. Plant them so that the soil just covers the fork at their base, as new growth will come through from beneath the soil. It might feel odd to plant them this deep but it does work and you won't kill the plant.

The best spacing is 1.5 to 2m apart to give you space to get around the plant. Smaller varieties like Ben Sarek can be spaced as little as 1.2m apart while large varieties such as Laxton Giant will need 1.8m. Jostaberries need at least 2m. The branches should all be pruned to about two or three buds above the soil level. They won't produce any fruit in the first year, and not a great deal in the second year but as the bush gets larger and more established you will find that it crops well.

Food, water and mulch

In the first two years you don't need to worry about adding any extra food because there should be enough available from the initial planting. After this I add compost or FYM and bonemeal in the spring every other year. Under this regime the fruits never seem to suffer despite the general advice that blackcurrants are nitrogen hungry. If you have a poor sandy soil you will need to be vigilant with your feeding programme.

Mulching is necessary from the start and if the bed isn't weed free cover with a layer of plastic, cardboard or newspaper. I prefer newspaper as it lets water through, but you must cover it with straw or grass mowings to stop it blowing away in the wind.

Seasonal care

Blackcurrants fruit on the new branches that grew in the last season as well as on two year old wood, and less so on three year old branches. This means you must take out any branches older than this. You can tell which are the oldest branches because they have much darker bark. Pruning the old branches really close to the ground will encourage younger shoots to grow up. To make sure that the bush does not get too crowded prune to an outward facing bud. It is even worth pruning out new growth, particularly any branches that are growing at a low angle. The weight of the fruit will drag the branches down onto the ground encouraging moulds etc. Pruning should be done between November and the end of February.

If you have early flowering varieties cover the bushes with fleece in April to protect the flowers from frost. To keep birds off your crop net the bushes from June until they finish cropping. Keep the plants well watered in a dry summer for a good crop.

Succession and continuity

It is possible to get blackcurrants cropping from early July to September with a careful choice of variety, but there is so much fruit available after July that it doesn't seem worth it. If you're growing for restaurants it might be worth considering. You could even try growing a dwarf variety pots in the polytunnel for a really early crop. Blackcurrant bushes can last up to 15 years before their yield begins to drop.

Problems

Birds are the worst problem for blackcurrants so it is important to net the bushes from June onwards. In a harsh winter there is a tendency for bullfinches to strip the buds from the branches so you may need to net from December onwards. This is when a fruit cage comes into its own.

Big bud mite is the next worst problem. These are microscopic and carried by the wind and other insects in the late spring. Once they get inside the bud they make it swell and by the summer the buds have shrivelled and fallen off. The mites are responsible for carrying the reversion virus that makes the whole plant quite sick, preventing the leaves from forming properly and damaging the buds. The only effective way to control big bud is to pick off and burn the affected buds in winter. If the plant is badly affected, dig it up and burn it. The anthocoris bug preys on big bud mites so these should be encouraged.

Blackcurrants can also suffer from American mildew, leaf rust, grey mould and red spider mite, but usually only in poor years. Keeping your plants healthy and well pruned should help to prevent these problems. Remember that if your fruit bushes are dotted around the garden, any problems that occur are less likely to spread to all of them.

Getting new plants

Propagation is so easy that you will never need to buy bushes unless you wish to grow a different variety. Take any new shoots from a healthy plant and cut them to about 20cm long. Bury them 15cm apart in a seedbed, with 5cm showing above ground. Tread the soil down well. By the following November you should have nice young plants with two or three shoots and good roots. Thin the new bushes to 30–45cm apart and let them grow on for another year before planting out in their final position.

The only problem with this method is the risk of passing disease and pests such as big bud mite on to the new plants. If you want to be risk free I would advise buying new, certified stock.

Harvest, storage and sale

Harvesting blackcurrants individually is painstaking, even if they are for your own consumption. If you are harvesting for yourself and aren't worried about bruised fruit, place an old sheet under the bush and just shake it vigorously. This saves a lot of time and energy.

Alternatively wait until all of the fruit on a branch is ripe then harvest it all in one go. As mentioned above, I cut off the branches with the ripe fruit on and put the whole lot in the vegetable box, or take them indoors to strip at leisure. Be careful, though, to leave enough branches to fruit on the following year.

Customers are always pleased to see blackcurrants in their veg boxes, and I expect they would also be popular at farmers' markets.

Profit and efficiency
Blackcurrants are profitable if you don't spend hours picking them; cutting the branches is the most efficient way of selling. Being a perennial, once the plants are established they will crop without all the annual ground preparation that many crops require, and they don't need a lot of care during the growing season.

Hints and tips
Cut branches with the fruit on for sale.
Keep well watered as the fruits ripen.

Cape Gooseberry

Cape gooseberries, also known as physalis, Chinese lanterns or Golden berries, are not what I think of as soft fruit. The berries are encased in delicate little paper-like husks and their unique flavour is very sweet and tart all at once. The plants look a little like deadly nightshade with potato shaped leaves and furry purple stems. The delicate, pale yellow flowers grow from a tiny stalk between the stem and leaf axil. However, they caused quite a stir when I sold them in my veggie boxes.
They belong to the solanaceae family and are perennial, and easy to grow from home-saved seed. They are only likely to survive our winters if you grow them under cover, where they can grow up to 2m tall.

Types and varieties
Cape gooseberries are physalis, and there are several varieties available, which can be confusing. The one you need is Physalis peruviana. Luckily all the seed companies sell it as plain Cape gooseberry.

Soil, site and rotation
Cape gooseberries crop best under cover although an adequate harvest can be had outside in a good season. They need a fertile, well-drained soil but other than this they don't seem to have any special requirements. They are so similar to tomatoes that I automatically grow them in the tomato part of my rotation.

Sowing and planting
Sow seeds in modules in March or April, depending on whether they're going to end up inside or out. When they are large enough to transplant set them out next to a tall cane or pole. If you are planting them outside then it is best to give them some protection either with a cloche or a fleece tent for the first month, to harden them off.

Food, water and mulch

Treat them much as you would tomatoes, feeding them with comfrey once a week after the fruits have started to set, although if they are outside they should only really get this luxury once every two weeks. Providing a mulch will help to stop their roots from drying out.

Seasonal care

You can limit the height of the plants by pinching out their growing tips at about 45cm. This will encourage the plants to send out more side shoots. If they are grown outdoors it will also help to stop them getting beaten about in the wind.

At the end of the year, the plants can be cut down to just above soil level and covered with hessian sacks or fleece. If you are lucky they will regrow the following year.

Problems

This plant has never suffered when I have grown it but I imagine they are susceptible to the same types of pests as tomatoes, particularly whitefly and aphids. If you grow them in the tomato section of your rotation with marigolds they shouldn't have a problem.

Harvest, storage and sale

The fruits are ready to eat once the green lanterns have turned to a beige papery consistency and the fruits are very orange. Unlike most soft fruit they will keep for a couple of weeks once picked but if you are selling them then the fresher the better. They don't require any special techniques for storage other than to be kept dry.

When selling Cape gooseberries in veggie boxes it seems only fair that you should tell your customers what they are and how to eat them. The first time I put them in the boxes I forgot to do this. Nobody said a word, apart from one person who knew what they were and was really impressed. If you have a surplus, restaurants will probably snap them up as decoration to their dishes, or they make a particularly good jam.

Profit and efficiency

Cape gooseberries are particularly profitable if you can sell them as delicacies to restaurants. Finding out what to charge for them is another matter. Sometimes you will see them in supermarkets or specialist greengrocers and can price them accordingly.

In vegetable boxes, cape gooseberries are a bit of a garnish, brightening everything up and adding quite a lot of interest. They do not add great deal to the boxes and in this case are not especially profitable.

Hints and tips

Grow Cape gooseberries as you would tomatoes.
Tell your customers what they are and what they can do with them.

Gooseberries

Gooseberries are big fruit that are easy to freeze and more profitable to sell than a lot of soft fruit because they don't bruise and they aren't too time consuming to pick. On the negative side, picking them is always painful. Another advantage is that the fruit isn't generally attacked by birds, although the buds can be in the winter.

Types and varieties

There are plenty of varieties available but consider ones that are resistant to American mildew. When choosing your plants, select ones with the longest legs – the longest main stem from roots to where it branches out – as this will make them easier to manage. Bushes with an upright habit will save your back a little when picking.

I grow two varieties, Whinham's Industry, which has red fruits and will tolerate shade and a heavy soil, and Jubilee, which is a green skinned variety with good disease resistance and large fruits.

Soil, site and rotation

Gooseberries will grow in semi-shade but prefer full sun. Avoid frost pockets and exposed sites. It is important to give the sprawling varieties a wide spacing, a gap of 1.5m is best. This is because you will need to get around the bushes and the closer they are, the more the thorns will shred you and your clothes.

Planting

Choose two-year-old bushes when buying and prepare the ground as for blackcurrants. Do not plant the stem below ground level because gooseberries, unlike blackcurrants, grow from the framework of the bush above ground: it should really be treated more like a small tree.

After planting, cut back the branches to an upward facing bud if it is a sprawling variety. If it is upright variety prune to an outward facing bud. This will give you a framework for pruning once the bush has become established.

Food, water and mulch

Gooseberries do need a lot of potash. Mulching with comfrey leaves or adding wood ash in the winter every three or four years will keep them happy, particularly on soils with a low clay content. Otherwise, treat the same as blackcurrants.

Seasonal care

Gooseberries need to be pruned twice a year to keep them in good shape. Major pruning work should be done between November and March. You need to aim for a goblet shape so that you can see the fruits that need picking and so that they will get enough sun to ripen them. To achieve this it is neces-sary to prune out the centre of the bush, particularly of upright varieties, pruning to outward facing buds. Cut the leading shoots back by half their length and reduce any side shoots to about 5cm.

You need to aim for about ten main branches maximum per bush. In late June, if growth has been vigorous, cut back each side shoot to four or five leaves. This helps with picking and can be effective in keeping down aphids, which tend to congregate on new shoots.

Succession and continuity

Gooseberry plants, like blackcurrants, won't fruit in their first year but after that they come into full production.

The gooseberry season isn't very long. You can extend it by picking fruit for cooking as early as June, leaving some berries on the bush to ripen to eat fresh. This has the added benefit that those that are left will get more food, water and light and therefore grow much bigger. You can also extend the season by growing different varieties but most do tend to crop in July.

Problems

My worst problem with gooseberries is American mildew. This periodically affects the bushes according to the season and how well the plants are pruned. It affects the shoots of the bush first, forming a white mould that gradually reaches the fruits and turns their skins brown. The best way to avoid bad outbreaks is to keep to the twice a year pruning regime, giving the bush plenty of breathing space. Avoid over-feeding as mildew is also encouraged by too much nitrogen. Keeping the plants well watered during dry spells will help, as will choosing a variety that has some resistance to the problem.

An important pest is the gooseberry sawfly. It is the caterpillar that does the damage. They are pale green with many black spots so are easy to identify, and they eat around the edge of the leaf, quickly making each stem look very bare. There is a tendency for them to start in the centre of the plant so take care to check here carefully. Outbreaks tend to be in mid to late spring, but can still occur later in the season. The only really effective way to control it is to inspect the underside of the leaves for the little clusters of eggs and pick them off or squash them. Alternatively spray with derris, but frankly by the time you have sprayed each leaf you may as well have just picked the eggs off.

As with blackcurrants, red spider mite may be a problem. The best predators are anthocoris bugs, which will be killed if you spray with derris.

Aphids can also be a pest, introducing disease and causing severe leaf distortion. You can pray with a soft soap to kill the aphids although this is a fiddly job. It might be worth just waiting for the late June pruning to reduce the problem if it isn't too bad.

Getting new plants

Treat them in a similar way to blackcurrants. In November take 30cm cuttings and strip off all the buds except for the top four. Stick the stripped bit in the ground, leaving the buds showing at the top. The following year, either thin the plants or plant them out to slightly wider spacing, and prune to make the goblet framework. By the second year the bushes are ready to go into their permanent positions.

Harvest, storage and sale

Harvesting gooseberries early, from late May onwards, gives fruits for culinary use, but leaving them until they are ripe is best. You can tell when they are ripe by squeezing them gently and they will give a bit under the pressure.

If you are harvesting them for sale, put them in plastic bags and seal. As the fruits are more robust than other soft fruit you won't need to inflate the bag to protect them. They can be picked the day before sale.

Suggest recipes to customers, as gooseberries are often tarred with the same brush as beetroot. People have often only eaten them once, as children, and they were too bitter, or undercooked. They need to be cooked to a pulp, with adequate sweetener added and then blessed with copious amounts of thick cream and custard to make delicious gooseberry fool.

Profit and efficiency

Being large and blessed with a firm skin, gooseberries take less time to pick and require less care than other soft fruits. In terms of profit, they don't command such a high price as the dark soft fruits but as a perennial crop they are worthwhile.

Hints and tips

Choose different coloured varieties for interest in the veggie box.
Keep the plants well pruned allowing lots of ventilation between individual branches and around the bushes.

Melons

I grow melons almost every year. When they get lots of attention, they provide me with more fruit than I can eat and some of my customers may be lucky enough to get one in their box. However, more often they are neglected so I only get a few fruits. However many (or few) I get, they are always delicious.

The origins of melons are in the cucurbit family – they are very closely related to both cucumbers and squashes.

Types and varieties

There are four types of melon. Cantaloupe melons tend to be round or oval with green, pink or orange flesh. The skin of musk melons looks like it is covered with a net and the flesh is similar to that of a cantaloupe. Honeydew melons are oval with yellow or green skin and white or pale green flesh. There are also water melons, which I have tried to grow but without success.

I tend to grow either Ogen or Sweetheart F1, which are cantaloupe varieties, because they are really the easiest, hardiest and least trouble.

The different varieties will crop at different times, with early, mid season and late ripening fruits.

Soil, site and rotation

Grow melons under cover, in a polytunnel, greenhouse or cloche, as they need warmth to grow and ripen. However, they do need dry conditions and will probably do better in a greenhouse than in a polytunnel. I wouldn't recommend growing them under cloches outside unless you live in the warmest parts of Great Britain or you can predict that the season is going to be a baker.

Grow melons in the squash part of your rotation. They need a rich and moist soil, so prepare muck sinks as for courgettes. Build a frame to support the plants, as you would for cucumbers. Melons can be grown in the same polytunnel or greenhouse as cucumbers but you need to keep them separate: melons like it dry and cucumbers need it humid.

Sowing and planting

Propagate and plant melons as you would cucumbers. To grow melons outdoors under cloches, harden them off for at least two weeks before you plant them out.

Food, water and mulch

The muck sink provides all the nutrients that the melons need. The roots do need to be kept moist, but not wet. Like cucumbers, they are very susceptible to stem and root rot. Mulching is only really a good idea if you are growing melons outside under cloches.

Seasonal care

Melons require much the same cultivation as cucumbers, but with a much drier climate. Train the main shoot up the supporting frame until it reaches the roof, then nip the tip out. Train the side shoots along the diagonal strings and nip their tips out when they have six to eight leaves. Flowers will then begin to appear, and to get fruit you will need to pollinate the flowers by hand. This is really easy. The female flowers have an obvious swelling behind the petals, absent from the male ones.

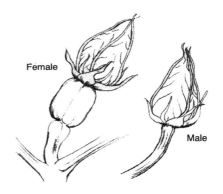

Female

Male

The male flowers are nearly always the first to appear. On a sunny day, pick a male flower and press it into a female flower. You can use the same male flower for up to three females. Alternatively, use a small paintbrush to pick up some pollen (very fine yellow dust) from the stamen of a male flower and brush this onto the stigma of a female flower. Don't pollinate too many fruits as the plant will only be able to support up to ten melons.

Succession and continuity

Individual melons ripen from July through to September. Indoor melons will ripen earlier and outdoor melons may struggle to ripen at all before the weather becomes too cold. You can achieve the longest season by growing a range of varieties.

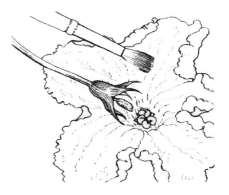

Problems

Melon stems and fruits are prone to rotting if the soil they are grown in doesn't drain freely or the air is too moist. Avoid problems by growing in dry and well-ventilated conditions.

Mildew can be a problem if the plants are short of water or nutrients, and there is insufficient ventilation. The other likely problem is wilt, a soil-borne disease that can be avoided by following a suitable rotation.

Harvest, storage and sale

When a melon is ripe the end furthest from the stem will give a little when gently squeezed. Also melons smell very strongly when they are ripe – just entering the greenhouse, your nose will tell you if one is ready. Melons don't ripen very much once they have been picked so leave them on the plant until they are ripe, or nearly so.

Once picked, you need to sell melons fairly quickly. They are a bit of a treat in the boxes, and customers are usually amazed! However, bear in mind that melons are expensive and an organic melon is probably worth twice as much as an ordinary one. A melon in the box makes up quite a lot of its value, so the box is likely to look rather meagre.

Profit and efficiency

To be honest, melons are not at all profitable. Each plant will give between five and ten good fruits, but they take as much space and effort as a cucumber plant. Unless you can sell your melons at a premium it is hardly worth growing them to sell. I grow melons for myself because I like them, and if I have a surplus I'm more likely to give them to friends than sell them.

Hints and tips

Grow under cover if possible.
Keep plants dry and well ventilated.
Hand-pollinate the flowers.

Raspberries

Raspberries can be a very lucrative crop. In terms of flavour they are one of my favourites. On the other hand, I never seem to get around to looking after them properly and they are a bit fussy for my liking. I neglect them in the summer and forget about them in the winter. But even when they are neglected they provide tasty fruit from June to November if you have a good selection of varieties, and a cropping lifetime of up to twelve years. As they flower late they avoid the spring frosts which tends to guarantee some sort of crop even in the worst of years.

Types and varieties

There are two types of raspberries – summer and autumn fruiting. Summer varieties fruit on last years growth, and autumn ones fruit on new stems. They require different cultivation methods.

I'm not sure what varieties I am growing because I inherited them when I bought the garden. The range we have gives us fruit from late June through to November. If I were renewing stock I would try and get varieties with disease and pest resistance. I might try a yellow variety such as Fallgold for a change.

Soil, site and rotation

The site you choose for raspberries is important. Although they are a woodland plant and tolerate shady conditions, they need plenty of sun for ripening the fruit. They also need shelter to avoid strong winds and plenty of water. As raspberries tend to flower quite late they will tolerate frosty sites better than other soft fruits.

Raspberries don't like lime and will do well on a slightly acid soil. Increase your acidity if necessary with annual applications of FYM. They do not like very wet or dry soil either so add plenty of organic matter to improve the soil structure.

If you are choosing summer fruiting varieties you will need to either erect some sort of structure to tie the canes into or grow them against a wall or fence. A post and wire fence, 2m high with three wires spaced 30cm apart, starting from the top, is ideal. Autumn fruiting varieties don't need any support apart from the odd word of encouragement. As mentioned earlier raspberries do need a bit of sun so if you are planting more than one row, make sure there is at least a 1.5m gap between each row.

Before planting your canes remove all perennial weeds. Raspberries grow new suckers from their wide and shallow root system, and you don't know exactly where they are going to come up. Therefore you cannot control weeds with a plastic mulch, so get them out before you start.

Planting

Planting summer fruiting raspberry canes is really best done in January. For some reason or other they just don't like being put in later. Dig a trench about a spit deep and two spits wide just beneath the supporting wires and fill with composted FYM and bonemeal. Refill the trench to about 8cm from the top. Place the canes in the trench, firm them in, then fill the trench with soil to the top. The new soil level should be the same as the old soil level mark on each cane. They should be planted about 30cm apart and cut back to about 30cm in height.

In the first year the canes will produce shoots. With summer fruiting varieties you will not get a crop until the second year. Autumn fruiting raspberries, planted in the late winter or early in the spring, will fruit in the first year.

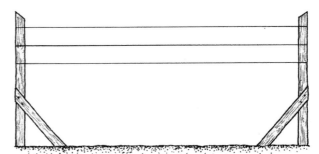

Food, water and mulch

Raspberries like a lot of water in the spring and summer so mulches are important, but not plastic mulches or new shoots will not be able to get up. The roots of raspberries grow wide and shallow so you need to mulch quite a large area. I put a thin cardboard or paper mulch on once the new shoots have emerged, and by the time next year's new shoots appear it has rotted down enough for them to grow through. Another good mulch is grass mowings, which will cover the ground widely and keep moisture in.

Seasonal care

Any dry spells during the spring and summer will reduce your raspberry crop so make sure you remember to water them. As the new shoots grow in the spring and summer you need to tie them into the fence as they are easily damaged by strong winds.

After the first year, cut the old canes back to near ground level when new shoots appear. In the second summer, cut out the canes that have fruited as soon as they have finished. With autumn fruiting varieties cut all of the canes to just above ground level in the spring. If suckers start to grow away from the supports or out of the bed, pull them out and chop them off the parent root.

Succession and continuity

To harvest raspberries from June to November and sometimes into December, grow a range of different varieties. If you grow a few autumn fruiting canes in large pots you can take them indoors in October and November and if the weather is warm enough, they will continue to crop until Christmas.

Problems

Bird damage can be a problem so you may have to net the plants as the crop starts to ripen. This is quite easy to do with summer fruiting varieties, just drape a net across the structure. The autumn fruiting varieties are more difficult to net because the canes tend to stick out all over the place. In practice, I never net any raspberries and just try to get there before the birds do.

Raspberries can be devastated by a virus that is spread by aphids. Once you have a virus then you basically have to scrap the crop and start again. Choosing a virus and aphid resistant variety will help, as will keeping the plants healthy and well watered during dry spells.

Raspberry beetle is another problem and it will soon eat the whole crop. It can also affect blackberries and hybrid berries. The first signs are the stalks dying back and dried up patches on the fruit just below the stalk. The actual pest is a small white grub and they can be controlled with derris if you have a serious problem.

Grey mould, or botrytis, can be a problem in wet summers but good ventilation and preventing overcrowding will help keep it at bay.

On chalk soils, raspberries can suffer from iron deficiency – cure the problem by feeding with a seaweed fertiliser.

There is a range of diseases that are specific to raspberries, including cane spot (purple spots with white centres), cane blight (canes die back in summer due to a fungal infection at the base of the canes), spur blight (dark purple patches around the buds of new canes) and raspberry rust (orange pustules on the leaves in spring and summer). These can all be prevented by choosing resistant varieties, not overcrowding your plants, avoiding over feeding and by good pruning.

Getting new plants

Where a new shoot is growing out of the ground, pull it up with its root and cut it away from the parent root with secateurs. Plant this shoot where you want it to grow. This should be done in October or November.

Harvest, storage and sale

The trouble with raspberries is getting them from the cane to the house and then waiting until supper before you eat them. My little boy never waits, they go directly from the cane into his mouth. I have never sold raspberries to my customers because we just like them too much.

If you do want to sell them, prepare them as for blackberries. If you are selling at a farmers' market then you do need to present them in punnets and although cardboard punnets are the most environmentally friendly, they always look nicer in white plastic punnets. Adding a little sprig of mint to each makes them look even better.

Profit and efficiency

If you can sell raspberries to restaurants and at farmers' markets they are worth a lot of money.

Hints and tips

Ensure good watering during dry spells.
Don't let them get overcrowded as this encourages disease.
Raspberries freeze very well and make delicious jam.

Red and Whitecurrants

To most adults, red and whitecurrants are just a bit too bitter to eat without adding sugar or honey. To most children, they seem to be as magnetic as strawberries. When the redcurrants are ready children happily pick them from the bush and eat them there and then.

In terms of selling they are probably the most delicate and fiddly of the soft fruit but their colour alone makes them worthwhile. Despite being a currant, they are treated more like a gooseberry than a black-currant in terms of cultivation. Although they aren't a favourite fruit of mine, I like them as plants because they are easy to manage and, being thornless, they are a pleasure to prune.

Types and varieties

There are several varieties of each red and whitecurrants. I have one variety, called Redstart, that has long strigs of currants and an upright look. Red Lake is a popular and reliable variety that has large fruits and good flavour.

Whitecurrants seem to crop slightly earlier. The variety White Versailles is popular because it has large, sweet fruits on long trusses in early July. The slightly later variety White Grape is very sweet but has a lower yield. Both are upright bushes that are easier to manage than those with a spreading habit.

Soil, site and rotation

Prepare the bed in the same way as for blackcurrants but add more bonemeal, as redcurrants will crop for up to 25 years. Like blackcurrants and gooseberries, they need a good deal of space and ventilation and although they will tolerate shade, they will do better in full sun.

Planting

Plant in the same way as gooseberries. Cut out any branches between the roots and 10cm above the soil level. Cut back the leading shoot to half its length and prune back any side shoots to one bud, preferably one facing outwards.

Food, water and mulch

As for gooseberries.

Seasonal care

The fruit is borne on spurs that are this season's growth. In the winter prune the whole bush as you would a gooseberry, keeping the centre clear for good ventilation and ripening. Prune each leading shoot by half and then prune all side shoots to about 5cm. You can prune in late June too, but as redcurrants don't suffer badly from pests I tend to ignore summer pruning.

Succession and continuity

The season is generally from July to August, with the white varieties ripening first.

Problems

Bird's love the bright red fruits and they will strip the buds in the winter, so grow the bushes in a fruit cage if you can.

Although redcurrants will succumb to some of the same pests and diseases as blackcurrants and gooseberries, they seem generally more hardy and much less prone to problems. I do have trouble with blister aphid, which sucks the sap from the leaves and turns them red. So far this hasn't affected the crop significantly, but if it does I will probably just prune out the top leaves, where the aphids are, in June.

Getting new plants

Follow the instructions for gooseberries.

Harvest, storage and sale

Harvesting red and whitecurrants is time consuming and a fiddle. The fruit is very delicate, so sell them in punnets with lids to protect them from damage in the veg boxes. Pick the strigs of currants and place them straight in the punnet. Due to time constraints I have to pick redcurrants the day before they are sold and it is important to leave them covered overnight, either with punnet tops or newspaper, to stop birds pinching them, unless you can store them inside somewhere.

Profit and efficiency

Not as profitable as other soft fruits because they take such a long time to pick but they are nice plants to cultivate and being so long lived (up to 25 years) they are worth the initial outlay.

Hints and tips

The colour of redcurrants attracts birds so they must be netted before the fruits begin to ripen. Children love red and whitecurrants raw and as they are such a good source of vitamin C they are worth growing for that reason alone.

Rhubarb

We tend to think of rhubarb as a fruit rather than a vegetable, but in fact we eat the stalk and rarely even see the fruit. It was eaten far more widely in the past because it filled the gap between the last of the stored apple crops and the first soft fruits of the early summer, in the days before aeroplanes zoomed crops around the world. Rhubarb contains a lot of oxalic acid which is why it makes your teeth go funny, so you should never eat too much of it.

Types and varieties

Rhubarb can be grown from seed or from crowns, which are sections off an established crown with a bit of root and a top shoot attached. The advantage of growing crowns is that you gain a season over plants grown from seed.
The normal seed variety is Glaskin's Perpetual, and this variety has the lowest oxalic acid content. The cheapest way of getting crowns is to find a neighbour or friend who already has a few plants and ask to take some crowns from their plants. Do this in January or February.

Soil, site and rotation

Rhubarb often gets shoved into a shady corner on poor soil, but it will do best in a well-prepared bed somewhere open but sheltered. Break the subsoil up well to provide good drainage and add compost.

Sowing and planting

Grow two or three crowns for your own use, and more if you want to sell rhubarb. I haven't grown it for sale but plan to grow thirty or forty plants once I have enough room. If you're raising plants from seed, sow very thinly 1cm deep in rows 75cm apart. Thin to 30cm apart and grow lettuce between them in the first year. You may need to thin the plants again the following spring. If planting crowns, cover with 2.5cm of soil and make sure they are 75cm apart each way.

Food, water and mulch

Once established, rhubarb likes an annual dressing of bonemeal and compost. Wait until the leaves have died down at the end of the season then completely cover the plant. Mulch the crowns well with straw during the summer and there will be little need to water them.

Seasonal care

If flower buds appear, remove them so that the growing energy goes into the stems and not the flower.

Succession and continuity

Leave the plants in their first year if they are grown from crowns, and for two years, preferably, if they are grown from seed.

To get the earliest rhubarb, force it by putting a black bucket or drum over it with a brick on top. A large black tree pot with holes in is ideal or maybe three tyres with a sheet of plastic with a 15cm hole in it in between the top two. The black plastic will warm in the sun, encouraging the young shoots up toward the light at the top. Tender stems will be ready to harvest in April. After harvesting leave the cover off and more stems will grow up for use in May and June. If you're growing them in tyres, simply remove the plastic sheet.

Stop harvesting after July so that the plants have some time to build up energy in their roots before the winter. Each plant can crop for up to 15 years.

Problems

Crown rot is a bacterial disease that simply makes the plant rot. It's best to dig the plant up and throw it away and start afresh with some new crowns. Avoiding crown rot is easy, just site your plants somewhere well drained and with plenty of ventilation.

Harvest, storage and sale

Harvest young and tender stems, but no more than half the plant or you will pick it to death. Literally pull the stems up, take off the leaves that are poisonous (particularly to aphids – *see Pests and Diseases page 73 for making a safe spray*) and stew, make into crumble or sell. The stems will store for a few days if kept cool.

Profit and efficiency

Being a perennial and early crop rhubarb is profitable if you can spare the room. It is available in May and June when other crops are thin on the ground. It is one of the vegetables I would recommend for a box scheme even though I haven't grown it for sale myself.

Hints and tips

Plant crowns rather than seed.

Don't exhaust the plant by cutting too much or too late in the year.

Strawberries

Strawberries are so popular they are becoming boring. These days, foreign imports are available nearly all year round but their flavour is generally far inferior to the sun ripened, home-grown fruit. Strawberries aren't too difficult to grow and if grown indoors will provide some delicious fruit early in the season.

Putting these fruits in the boxes I sell is always a good move but I must admit to eating most of them and making strawberry jam and ice-cream with the rest. I don't really have enough plants to bear to part with any of my crop, and strawberries are often ready before I start selling my boxes, such a shame for my customers!

I grow my strawberries through plastic. I never water them and I hack them about mercilessly at the end of the year and they still seem fine. The same plants have been cropping for four years without any noticeable loss of vigour. I'm giving them one more year just because I like to be different and I don't rely on them for selling. Then I will start another strawberry bed.

Types and varieties

There are three types of strawberries worth growing, each for different reasons. The obvious and most popular one is the summer fruiting type, which fruits from late May to late July (earlier under cover). The plants will last for three or four years. The Remontant or mid-season type fruit from late summer to early autumn but the plants last for only two years and tend to be more susceptible to mildew and moulds and crop less heavily. Alpine strawberries fruit all year, but only for one year. There is a fourth type, day neutral strawberries, which don't flower according to day length so they will fruit almost continuously. However, the yield drops considerably in their second year so they should be treated as annuals, and the flavour is said to be very poor.

Choosing a variety is really up to you but if you can, go for ones that are mildew and disease resistant. I grow Honeoye for its early start in late May and its resistance to botrytis, and Cambridge Favourite - a little later but full of flavour.

Soil, site and rotation

Strawberries like to be in the sun for ripening, but ventilation must be good and siting them out of frost pockets is essential unless you are going to cover them during cold periods. This is particularly so with the summer fruiting varieties. A slightly acid soil suits them best and they like a lot of organic matter, whatever type of soil you have. It is important to rotate the strawberry bed to keep down disease: try to fit it in your rotation so that each time you start a new bed it is somewhere different.

Planting

Strawberry beds should be planted in August or September to crop the following year. Alpine varieties can be planted in April or May.

To start a bed, dig in a barrow load of compost or well-rotted FYM together with about a kilo of bonemeal (for the phosphorous that strawberries particularly like) to each square metre.

A weed free bed is essential so either grow the plants through plastic or keep a mulch, preferably of straw, on the bed all year round. Space the plants at 45cm intervals in rows 60cm apart. Make sure the roots are spread out widely as they are quite shallow rooting plants and need to have a lot of room. If you are not planting through plastic you can make a wide, shallow hole with a small mound in the middle. Rest the crown of the plant on this mound and spread the roots out around the mound before refilling with soil. Be careful not to bury the crowns or they will rot, but equally don't plant them too shallowly or they will be lifted out of the ground by frosts.

If you are planning to grow strawberries for sale in a box scheme, allow one strawberry plant per vegetable box to provide each customer with a 250g punnet. This is for one variety over a period of two to three weeks but you will need more plants if you want to extend the season.

Food, water and mulch

If you add enough compost to your soil before you plant the strawberries and your soil is reasonably fertile, you won't need to add any extra food for the 3 or 4 years that the plants are in the ground. Watering is essential during dry weather but if grown through black plastic then this is less important. However, as my strawberries are grown through plastic I never water them and I don't put straw down. I do not want to encourage slugs, which will happily chomp away on the fruits, particularly if the weather is wet.

Seasonal care

Strawberries flower early in the season when frosts are still likely, so protect with fleece in cold weather. Make sure that the fleece is removed during wet weather or the reduced ventilation will encourage moulds.

In the autumn the plants need to have a good haircut, removing all the runners and leaves 7 or 8cm above the crown.

Succession and continuity

I grow three types of strawberry, two summer fruiting and an alpine. You can lengthen your season by growing a Remontant, or mid season strawberry. An alpine variety will keep you going if you want strawberries just for yourself.

If you grow an early variety under cover they can provide a crop in late May/June when other crops are scarce. To get a harvest as early as April, grow a few plants in pots and keep them undercover through the winter and spring.

Problems

Grey mould or botrytis is about on a par with bird damage in terms of problems. The bird problem is easy, just net the crop as soon as the fruits begin to ripen. Laying a net across the crop is adequate but putting in some stakes that will raise the netting a little is better. Put jam jars on top of the stakes to stop the netting from tearing.

To prevent grey mould, which develops as a greyish fuzzy mass on the fruits, keeping the plants well ventilated and dry is important. If it is a particularly wet season cover the plants with cloches to keep the plants dry and help the fruit ripen whenever the sun replaces the clouds. Cutting out affected leaves and fruits will help reduce the problem.

Getting new plants

Strawberry plants reproduce themselves by sending out runners, the ends of which will root in the ground and start a new plant. This is the quickest and easiest method of getting plants. All you have to do is peg a runner, still attached to the plant, into a pot of compost mix in July. It will root in the pot and in late August you can cut the runner from the parent plant and transfer the new plant to a newly prepared strawberry bed.

Harvest, storage and sale

Strawberries are always a winner with customers. If you are growing them to sell it is best to harvest them on the day of sale as they deteriorate quite quickly once picked.

Profit and efficiency

As the plants last for up to four years strawberries are quite an efficient crop to grow. They are easy to sell to restaurants, at farmers markets and in box schemes, quite profitably.

Hints and tips

Keep the plants well ventilated.
Net to stop bird damage.

Introduction

If you have a kitchen garden you probably hope that you will be able to grow enough vegetables to supply your table. If you grow too many you can give them away, store them or make them into something with a longer shelf life, such as chutney. If you still have a surplus, the temptation is to sell it. Once you start selling vegetables, people will ask for more, and more, until eventually you are growing vegetables specifically to sell.

My introduction to growing vegetables to sell was not as gradual as this. I was growing for my own use when I decided that I wanted to set up a business. I was inexperienced at growing vegetables on a large scale so it took me a few years to reach the point where it provided me with a living.

Although I have the opportunity I have resisted the temptation to expand. I know that if I did my life would change from being a gardener tending crops to a manager sitting indoors with a telephone and computer. As it is, I can grow enough vegetables for my customers and sell them quite comfortably, as well as leading my own life away from the garden. I hope to always be able to garden the way I do but believe that this is only possible if I listen to nature's wisdom and don't expect the huge income that most of modern society demands.

Expansion does go on in my head, though. I continually look out for and think about better ways to garden. As well as supplying my box scheme I now teach how to grow vegetables.

Although my livelihood is entirely derived from selling vegetables, I do not feel that I am a born sales-person. I am often tempted to give things away rather than demand a reasonable price for what I have to sell. As I have become more experienced at running my box scheme I have become less concerned with satisfying everyone's needs. I am confident that I provide a good service: people can buy into it or not.

There are a number of outlets for your vegetables, and you must decide which is best for you. You can sell at your farm gate or at farmers' markets, to wholesalers or restaurants, or via a box scheme like I do. My experience with box schemes is reflected in these chapters on selling. Whichever way you sell your vegetables remember that your business depends upon satisfied customers, so listen to their comments and respond to them where necessary.

Finding and Keeping Customers

There are people out there who already understand why local selling initiatives are a good thing: these people will be your best customers. There are also a lot of people who only understand a little of the politics behind local food. They don't understand why they should support local growers and will be difficult to keep as customers. Arguments about food miles, genetic engineering, organic growing, environmental benefits etc might help, but in the end it will be the quality of the product that you are selling that will convince them.

Getting customers

To get people to buy your vegetables you are going to have to do some sort of marketing. Advertising your box scheme in your local paper can bring in customers, and libraries, community centres and local surgeries might display your poster on their notice boards. More targeted advertising, directed at people who are already aware of environmental issues, is likely to be more successful. Try local environmental groups, or ask if you can display your poster at natural health centres. Being opportunistic can pay off. Selling your vegetables at farmers' markets is a good way of finding regular customers. Give out information about your drop off points, and people might decide that a regular box would be more convenient than visiting the market. Once you have a few people who are interested in your scheme it doesn't take long for word to get around. I never advertise and I still get new customers enquiring every other week, even at times when I'm not selling.

Beware of taking on too many customers too quickly. Start by growing enough for only half the customers you eventually want to supply and make sure you give them a good deal. Better to turn a few people away from your scheme than over-stretch yourself and disappoint your existing customers. Once you have a satisfied customer you will have their loyalty for years to come. Remember that one of the arts of a good gardener is patience.

If you are setting up your box scheme in competition with other growers you are unlikely to be making any friends. There is another box scheme operating in the same area as mine, but we have come to an amicable agreement. We have divided up the area and when a potential customer approaches either of us we advise them to go to the other scheme if it is closer or more convenient. There are enough customers in the area for both of us.

Customer awareness, communication and information

Next to the quality of your produce, keeping your customers well informed is probably the most effective way to keep hold of them as customers. Encouraging them to comment if they have a problem with anything can make the difference between a loyal customer and a lost one. In my experience, any customer can show signs of impatience if they are not given information on why some crops fail. If they understand why you have run out of their favourite vegetable they are likely to stick with your substitutes. Be honest and let them know if you have made a mistake.

I still have customers that have been buying my vegetables since I started growing them on a large scale. That is nine years of commitment. Many of these customers have children who have been eating my produce for all that time. They know where their vegetables come from and have visited the garden, usually on open days. They are always particularly interested in the frog ponds in the polytunnels and the gigantic pumpkins, but they get to see what goes on. They know that a real person is growing the vegetables they eat and they see that the garden is teeming with wildlife. They like seeing funny shaped carrots and they are amazed when you eat a flower in front of them. These children will probably try to eat organic vegetables in the future, and some will buy their vegetables through a box scheme or at a farmers' market. That is education.

Open days and garden tours

Having an open day is extremely useful. Many of your customers will be keen to see where and how their food is being grown. June is usually the best month to invite visitors. Vegetable gardens look most abundant and beautiful at this time of year, even if the weather lets you down. If you fit your open day in before you start selling, your customers will start the season with an image of where their vegetables have grown. They will still remember it in the depths of winter, when your garden may look anything but beautiful and abundant.

Where I grow my vegetables we have a joint open day. There are tours of the animals, vegetable gardens and the other farm enterprises. We put on a barbecue lunch and organise competitions like 'guess the weight of the pumpkin'. It is all good fun and teaming up to organise the day makes it much less effort for everyone. If your garden is isolated or if you just want to concentrate on the vegetables, it's probably a good idea just to have an open afternoon.

Giving a tour of your garden can be rather daunting, particularly the first time. You need to know what you are going to say. Make a simple list of the main points of how you grow your vegetables. This will be enough of a guide, because no matter how knowledgeable they are, people always ask questions. And if they don't, ask them if they've got any questions. They are bound to have things they want to know or they would not have come on the tour in the first place. Walking round the garden will give you prompts as well. I only need to walk a few paces before I have seen something I can talk about: gauge how interested your audience is before you go into too much depth.

How long your tour lasts is up to you, depending on your confidence and the interest of your audience. I give my customers anything from 20 minutes to an hour depending on their level of interest. If I am doing a specific tour for people interested in setting up their own gardens I usually keep talking for an hour and a half. For anyone who wants to know more than that, I run a weekend course on growing vegetables for sale, once or twice a year.

Growing Vegetables for Sale

K nowing what to grow and when to grow it to supply your customers can appear rather
daunting to the new grower. The simple answer to this is nature does it for me. Crops each
have their own season, becoming available at different times of the year. To sell vegetables for
a living I control this process to a degree, by growing a succession of crops and by extending
the season for crops where possible by growing under cover at the beginning and end of the year.

Succession is very important for running a successful box scheme. I have included details of succession
for individual crops in the A–Z section. I have also compiled the information into a table (*page 259*).
This shows when to start growing each crop and when I would normally expect to harvest them.
Knowing how much to grow comes with experience. The table shows how much ground is needed to
grow the vegetables to supply my box scheme, which caters for around 75 customers. These figures are
very rough, and may not be replicated by a different gardener in a different garden. However, it is a
good guide to start from, and if you want to grow more simply multiply up what I do.

Crops that look good

Supermarkets have a lot to answer for. They have convinced the public that vegetables should look perfect to have any value. Marks and Spencer were the first supermarket-type food seller that only allowed
perfect vegetables onto their shelves, and other supermarkets followed. This has led to an ingrained idea
that vegetables should look pristine, which they do not when they are grown under ordinary and sustainable conditions.

I do still come across customers who remember the old days, when cutting the bad bits out of potatoes
was just part of peeling them. Many people are becoming aware that a real vegetable isn't perfect, just as
a real person is never perfect. They do not all need to be the same shape and size, and bits of soil and
the odd hole are OK.

So, what do my crops look like? Fresh, of course, which means vibrant, colourful and full of flavour. I
try my best to harvest everything as near to sale as possible, so they are as fresh as possible. I arrange the
vegetables in boxes to look attractive, making sure that the most colourful vegetables and any flowers
can be seen. Not only do fresh vegetables look good though; their flavour is far more in tact than any
vegetable you are likely to buy off a shop shelf.

Harvesting

Some vegetables deteriorate quickly once they have been harvested, particularly in the summer, and care must be taken to keep them fresh.

I harvest all leaf crops as early in the morning as I can, on the day they will be sold. They are cool and crisp at this time and won't wilt nearly as quickly as those picked in the middle of the day when the sun is high. Once a salad has been picked, it must be stored somewhere cool and still. This could be under a hedge or in a cool shed. Spraying them with cold water now and then, or standing bunches of leaves or veg in buckets of water, will also help.

Root crops also need to be harvested early in the morning, if you are leaving the tops on. They do look much more attractive like this, particularly carrots, but it is only fair to tell your customers that they keep much fresher with the tops removed.

As soon as I can I take my harvest to my packhouse, which is cool, and pack the vegetables into the boxes. The boxes stay in the packhouse until I am ready to leave, and are only in the van for up to half an hour, unless I'm going to Bristol which takes an hour.

Days when I am out delivering boxes are very busy, and I make good use of the days in-between by harvesting crops that keep well. Vegetables like peppers, aubergines and tomatoes can be picked the day before selling, but any sooner and they will lose their shine. Potatoes are nicest on the day they are dug, but it is unrealistic to expect to be able to dig them on sale days. Their flavour and texture will keep well for a couple of days in a sack. Peas and beans are also time-consuming to harvest and pack, and I often pick them late in the afternoon on the day before sale. As long as they are kept cool they are fine. Some vegetables, such as cucumbers and courgettes, need to be harvested when they are ready, however busy you are. I whiz round the garden early and I store them in a polystyrene box in the packhouse, where they will keep for several days in very good condition. The trick is to make sure that the produce has been cut when it is cool and damp and the polystyrene will keep it in that condition.

In the middle of the summer, particularly in August, I sell a lot less because so many of my customers are on holiday. I have learned a few tricks over the years to try and avoid surpluses. Courgettes and runner beans are the vegetables that I need to watch, and I pick them smaller than usual to avoid the possible glut. The customers that aren't on holiday get particularly tender baby veg.

As autumn approaches not only are crops changing but it is cooler during the day. It becomes less critical to harvest early in the morning. Leaf crops are still harvested on the day of sale, but there is no longer any need for an early morning dash. Crops such as onions, carrots, garlic and potatoes will be in store if they have not all been sold, whilst crops such as squash are being harvested and ripened for storage. Autumn crops, such as leeks, celeriac, Jerusalem artichokes and parsnips, will all keep quite happily for a day or two in the cool weather, and should be dug and packed on the non sale days.

As the winter weather comes on the picture changes again. Keep an eye on the weather forecast and if frosts are on the way, dig any vegetables you plan to sell before they are frozen into the ground.

Salad bags

I always put a salad bag in my boxes in the summer and as often as I can in the winter. As well as generating a good proportion of my income, they are one of the reasons that my customers stay loyal to me. On the downside, picking enough salad for 100 or so salad bags every week becomes extremely tedious. Summer salad bags contain a combination of lettuce, rocket, rape salad, landcress, sorrel, nasturtium leaves, herbs and flowers. I put chicories, oriental leaves, winter lettuce, lamb's lettuce, claytonia, rocket, herbs and cress into winter salad bags. When I am short for the bags I add leaves of wild plants and weeds. Plants that are suitable include wild ransoms, dandelion, jack by the hedge (mustard garlic), fat hen and chickweed. Try to always include flowers, they are the crowning glory of salad bags. I regularly add the flowers of nasturtium, violets, elderflower, chive and borage. Lavender, red clover, chicory, marjoram, pot marigold, rosemary and sage flowers can also be used.

When you pack the leaves and flowers into the bags, make sure that there is plenty of space. If they are over-packed they are likely to go slimy. Including a frilly type of lettuce, frizzy endive or moss parsley adds volume and air, reducing the slime factor.

Once the season is underway and you are madly harvesting, it is easy to forget to sow more salad beds. Make sure that you keep up a regular supply throughout the season.

Buying in Vegetables to Sell

I grow about two-thirds of the vegetables I sell. These are the ones that I enjoy growing and the ones that are profitable to grow on a small scale. The remainder I buy in from wholesalers. Most years I produce all of the vegetables that I sell between June, when I start selling my boxes, and the end of September, barring shortfalls and crop failures. Bear in mind that by September I have been working flat out for six months and I'm beginning to want to take things a bit easier. My enthusiasm begins to wane and buying in vegetables allows me to wind down a bit. In October about half of the vegetables I sell are bought in, by November the figure rises to 70%. For my last boxes, the week before Christmas, as much as 85% is bought in.

Availability, prices and what I have in the garden determine what I buy in each year. Every year I have one crop that somehow doesn't go as I planned. Last year it was parsnips, and I had to supplement my harvest by buying them in. I would normally sell parsnips in October, but I substituted them with leeks in the boxes and waited until November when the price dropped to start buying them in. Being able to mix and match the vegetables I put in the boxes means that surpluses are never wasted and minimises the amount of vegetables that I have to buy in.

Vegetables that I don't like growing on a large scale

There are some vegetables that I happily grow for my own use but for one reason or another I don't grow them on a large scale. I prefer to buy them in, and I have explained the reasons below.
Asparagus fruits at a time of year when I'm not selling boxes. I grow a small patch for myself.

Brussels sprouts I will not grow for sale. I used to grow them but one winter my fingers were permanently frozen and I realised that there were better things to do in life. I now buy them in and alternate them with other brassicas during the winter months. I am happy to grow them for my own use.

Celery is fiddly in its early stages. It takes a long time to germinate and needs pricking out into modules. Later it needs transplanting and a close eye kept on watering to prevent the stalks from becoming hollow. If you leave it too long before harvesting it 'goes over' and isn't very nice to eat. Far too much trouble for my liking. It is not always available from the wholesalers but I buy it in when it is, particularly during the winter.

Valuable Vegetables

Fennel is an occasional crop for me. It has a tendency to bolt as soon as your back is turned so when I have the patience to keep an eye on it I have a go. It is often available at the wholesalers but usually imported, so I limit the number of times I add it to the boxes. It's a bit of a 'treat' vegetable.

Globe artichokes require a lot of space and effort for a small return. Salsify and scorzonera are crops that I have grown in the past but my customers weren't impressed. If you are keen to sell them, give your customers plenty of information about what they are and how to cook them.

Annual spinach is grown for mixed salad bags and my own use but I rarely sell it as a vegetable because it takes so long to pick.

Sprouting broccoli, spring cauliflowers and spring cabbages are all ready in the months when I'm not selling. I do grow them for myself.

Winter brassicas, such as cauliflowers, calabrese and cabbages, require a lot of land and cabbages in particular are quite cheap to buy in. If I grew them I would have to worry about caterpillars.

Vegetables that aren't profitable on a small scale

During the spring and summer months, potatoes, carrots, onions and brassicas are relatively expensive, and I grow enough to fill my boxes. As autumn arrives the prices of these vegetables begin to fall, and they fall to such an extent that it really isn't worth my while growing them any more. With the space that I have available I cannot compete with large-scale growers who can keep their costs low. So I grow enough potatoes and onions to see me through to October and my carrots usually last into November. I buy in brassicas for the autumn and winter because I do not have space to grow the numbers that I need.

I could educate my customers in the economics of vegetable growing, and sell them maincrop vegetables that I have grown. My prices would have to be far higher than I charge for vegetables from the organic wholesaler. I know that my vegetables are already relatively expensive and asking my customers to pay even more would stretch their generosity too far. Making people aware of just how cheap their food is in this country is the role of the politician, and I am a gardener.

Where to buy vegetables and how to be sure they are OK

Most of the vegetables that I buy in come from a wholesaler. Apart from the wholesaler I have two local suppliers of vegetables. Like me they aren't registered as organic growers, but I know that their understanding of organic principles is thorough and I trust them implicitly. My customers trust me and know that I won't buy vegetables from anyone I don't have confidence in. When I don't have enough for the boxes myself I supplement them with vegetables from these growers, which gives them an outlet for their vegetables at a reasonable price.

There are other local growers who could supply me with the basics such as potatoes, carrots, onions and brassicas. It is probably time to start supporting them, although it will mean a more restricted range of vegetables in my winter boxes. If I explain to my customers they are more than likely to be very understanding.

Finding other organic growers can be difficult. The Soil Association will sell you a list of registered organic growers in your area. They can also provide a list of registered wholesalers.

Buying wholesale

Organic wholesale prices are often higher than conventional retail prices. I have never bought a 25kg sack of organic potatoes for less than £6.50, yet when I drive past the local shop I see them selling a sack of conventional potatoes for as little as £2. This is really galling. I wonder that conventional farmers can afford to grow potatoes at all if they are sold so cheaply at a retail outlet.

I get a weekly price list from the wholesalers. This shows how much, for example, 12 Savoys cost (about £6). I work out the unit cost (50p), add my own costs (about 25p) then add this figure (75p) to my weekly lists of what vegetables are going to which drop off point.

Anything that comes in a batch has to be shared out amongst my customers so that I don't lose money by having too many left over. For example, if I allocate a Savoy cabbage to each of my medium boxes for a Tuesday but there are only ten such boxes, I will have two spare. These will either be put in another type of box (large or small) or kept until the following day to supplement another box. Keep careful records or you might find that one customer has had a Savoy for the last four weeks and wants a change! This can all become a logistical nightmare.

If you plan carefully and can use an occasional vegetable from the garden to fill gaps, it is nearly always possible to make a profit on anything brought in. The advantage of a complicated system, with a range of drop-off points each with different box requirements on different days, is that you can swap crops around. Again, it is the diversity of the system that keeps it healthy.

Selling Vegetables

f you want to sell your vegetables decide which approach would suit you best. You can sell your vegetables at farmers' markets, or to restaurants, wholesalers or to the public at your farm gate. I sell my vegetables via a box scheme, and this is reflected in the coverage that I have given them here.

Box schemes

My box scheme runs on a no choice system, which allows me to grow a range of vegetables and sell most of them. If I allowed people to choose what vegetables they wanted I would get completely bogged down in the logistics and paperwork. I would not be able to sell the less popular crops, which would be a shame. Most of them are unpopular because they haven't even been tried, people don't know how to cook them or, most commonly, they remind people of school dinners. In practice I find that once my customers get used to having no choice they begin to welcome it. They enjoy the challenge to cook what they have been given instead of spending ages trying to decide what to buy and how to cook it.

Packaging

The whole point of box schemes is to encourage people to buy and eat food that has been produced in a sustainable system. They get vegetables that are in season and have been grown locally. The packaging is not over-done and the box is returned to be used again. Apart from the box there are a couple of plastic and paper bags, the odd elastic band and perhaps a punnet. Imagine the mountain of packaging that you would have to throw away if you bought the same vegetables from a supermarket.

When I started using boxes to sell my vegetables, I could not afford to buy sturdy boxes so I used the old wooden apple boxes which green grocers throw out. The problem was that my customers didn't return them. When I had enough money I bought some plastic stacking boxes and charged a deposit on them. If my customers didn't return the box to the drop off point, they had to pay another deposit. This worked fairly well and my customers got into the habit of returning the boxes. I have been able to go back to using the old wooden apple boxes, but with my name and 'please return' written on them in large black letters, and they usually come back.

The small boxes of vegetables that I sell are actually not boxes at all, I deliver the vegetables in used supermarket carrier bags. My customers give the bags to me during the selling season so they are being re-used, sometimes several times over before they end up in landfill.

What you will need to pack your vegetables

You will need some sort of packing area, ideally somewhere that is cool in the summer and dry in the winter. A simple corrugated tin shelter is adequate as a packhouse, but it is not ideal for winter storage of vegetables when frost and vermin will be a problem. I am lucky to have a stone barn for my pack-house. It is cool in the summer and relatively frost free in the winter.

In my packhouse I have benches to put my boxes on to fill, a large storage box for winter vegetables, a pallet to store sacks of bought in vegetables and a set of scales. After a while you get a feel for how much vegetables weigh and the scales are used only as a guide. Onions and garlic hang from the beams. I use two sizes of plastic bag to pack crops, 25 x 30cm for salads and 18 x 23cm for basil, tomatoes and peppers. I occasionally use larger plastic bags, to wrap chunks of squashes and pumpkins. A tool to seal the plastic bags is very useful. I use two sizes of paper bags, 18 x 18cm and 23 x 23cm, for peas, French and runner beans and Brussels sprouts. Bunches of spinach, radish, beetroot or carrots are held together with elastic bands. During the autumn and winter months packing vegetables can be a bit of a bore and I find a wind-up radio particularly helpful.

Packing the boxes

You are responsible for making the vegetables in your box look appealing. You put a lot of effort into making sure that everything is fresh, so don't spoil it by leaving it in a thick coating of mud. Brush any soil off the vegetables, but don't wash them or they will deteriorate rapidly.

When I pack the boxes I put the potatoes, carrots, onions and roots in the bottom. Softer things, which I do not want to bruise, go in next. These are the peas, beans, courgettes, tomatoes and peppers, which can add colour to the box. I put leaf crops such as cabbage, spinach and salad bags on the top. Adding flowers to the salad bags and putting them in the boxes so that the flowers are visible always makes the box look attractive. In the winter when there aren't any flowers, place a red chicory leaf, dried red chillies or a coloured herb such as purple sage on the top.

Box sizes and quantities of vegetables

I sell three sizes of vegetable boxes, small, medium and large. They are designed to cater for different sized families but it is impossible to say exactly how many vegetables any one family will eat. The small box is designed to feed one or two adults who don't eat many vegetables or eat out a lot. The medium box is based on a family of two adults and two children, but if this is a vegan or vegetarian family they are likely to need the large box. These are designed to feed two adults and four children.

When I get an enquiry about my boxes and which one to choose, I usually suggest they start with the one that matches their family size. If they find it too much or not enough, they can change to a different size. I have one customer who has a medium box all to herself every week yet I know other customers that find the small box sufficient for two adults.

The quantity of vegetables that you put in the boxes is determined by price rather than weight. See the Money chapter (*page 245*) for information on pricing vegetables. The prices of the boxes remain the same throughout the season but the weights differ quite dramatically between summer and winter. The summer boxes contain fewer root type vegetables and more leaves, and the picture reverses in the winter. When there is no leafy, bushy crop to sell the boxes will look a bit 'thin'. Growing a crop of perpetual spinach under cover ready for the winter months will keep the boxes looking full and green at a time when it is difficult to get any colour out of the garden.

When I start selling in June, vegetables are a little on the sparse side. My customers understand this and accept that they will get a smaller box than usual because there's not much to go round.

Supplying variety

My customers do not have the option to choose what they get in their box, but I try to make sure that everyone has different vegetables each week. I aim to give them no single vegetable more than once every two weeks, apart from the staples potatoes, carrots, onions and salad.

My box system is very flexible and can soak up surpluses and shortfalls very efficiently. What goes in the boxes depends on what is available. I alternate leaf crops such as spinach, Swiss chard and cabbage in the summer, and in the winter I try and use cabbage, kale or spinach every week. Sometimes I only have enough calabrese for ten boxes, so my customers at one drop off point get that, the next drop off point gets cabbages, and the next spinach. The next week I make sure that a different group gets the calabrese.

All this involves making numerous lists every week. I assess what I have cropping in my garden, what is about to crop and what is just finishing. I need to know what goes in the boxes for each drop-off point every week, and refer back to them to avoid repetition.

Growing vegetables does not always go entirely to plan and there are times that I have a surplus of one particular vegetable. If this happens I explain the situation to my customers via a newsletter. Generally they are very accommodating. Last year I had a surplus of leeks. As soon as I realised that I had too many I let everyone know that they would get leeks every week, and nobody seemed to mind.

Collection or drop off points

Once I have my boxes all packed up, I must deliver them. I do not take them to each customer individually, but take them to collection, or drop-off, points. This saves a great deal of time, fuel and effort. The drop-off points are usually a private house, or sometimes an office, central for a group of customers to collect their boxes.

The organiser at each drop off point takes the orders every week and rings them through to me a few days before delivery. They are usually available for an hour or two in the afternoon on the day of delivery, to collect money and returned boxes from customers and to organise the orders for the following week. In return I give each organiser 10% of my total sales. At one drop off point I leave the vegetables in a garage and the money is posted through the letterbox so the organiser doesn't even need to be there. My packhouse is another drop-off point; my customers leave a cheque in a tin and come and collect their boxes whenever they want.

Obviously my drop-off points are very valuable to me, but because I have several I am not dependent on any one. This makes my business fairly stable. I have noticed that the drop-off points enjoy their responsibilities for the growing season but appreciate the break between Christmas and June. When I ring them up though they are always keen to start again.

I deliver on Tuesdays, Wednesdays and Thursdays. This allows me time to harvest the vegetables and pack the boxes in the morning. On Tuesdays I make up and deliver roughly 25 boxes to two drop off points. On Wednesday I deliver 12 to 15 boxes to two drop off points, and leave the same number for collection in my shed. On Thursdays I deliver about 25 boxes to one drop off point in Bristol, my farthest point. The number of orders doesn't vary very much apart from during school holidays and August, when lots of people go away.

Christmas boxes

My last box of the year is in the week before Christmas, and every year 90% of my customers want a Christmas box rather than an ordinary one. I make sure that a Christmas box includes parsnips and Brussels sprouts, but the main difference is in the treats that I add to the vegetables. As ever it is dependent on what is available, but I try to include clementines and Kiwi fruits, and anything from avocados to dates to chestnuts. A few sprigs of holly finish it off.

Newsletters

I usually send 4 or 5 newsletters to my customers each year. The first is a welcoming newsletter at the beginning of the season. The second tells people how the season is going. The autumn newsletter lets my customers know about the change from summer to winter vegetables and invites them to an open day. The winter newsletter includes the prices of vegetables available to buy in bulk, and news of Christmas boxes.

Sometimes I put a recipe in the newsletter, an explanation of why I have had to include or exclude certain vegetables, or just a reminder of why buying vegetables from me is such a good idea.

Farmers' markets

Selling vegetables at farmers' markets comes second to box schemes for me. I like the markets because they are bringing communities back together and rejuvenating towns. Also they are a really good way of raising public awareness of your veg boxes.

One of the main reasons that I don't sell at farmers' markets is that it takes such a lot of time. I would have to start very early in the morning getting vegetables ready and loading the van. After driving to the market and setting up I would need to man the stall for between four and eight hours. There is no guarantee that I would sell anything, then I would have to pack up and take anything left over home. And you will need to cough up for the cost of the stall - this varies but tends to be about £20 a pitch. This takes an awful lot of time, when I could be getting on in the garden, or better still, living my life. My box scheme suits me better.

Restaurants and farm gate sales

Selling to restaurants can be a good source of income but it can be very time consuming. Most restaurants like to have their produce delivered, they often want the best looking vegetables, and don't like to pay more than wholesale rates. There are exceptions to this but generally I have found my box scheme is a better bet.

Farm gate sales are another option. Using an honesty box means that you don't have to sit waiting for passers-by, but there is no guarantee that all your vegetables will be sold.
I used to sell vegetables direct from my garden and it took a lot of time. I ended up going down to pick a bunch of spinach for a passer-by several times a day. I didn't mind but they always wanted to chat for half an hour as well. I do like chatting but I wasn't getting any gardening done. With the box scheme I see each of my customers maybe once every six months, and that is plenty to keep in contact.

Money

Getting started

When I teach people about setting up box schemes I always say that you need £2500 to get started, as an absolute minimum. I would need to spend £10k to buy the assets that I have built up over the last nine years, and that does not include the goodwill of the business. Obviously these figures are singular to my situation, but unless you buy in to an established business, setting up the growing area and customer base does take time and money.

When I started growing vegetables for sale I managed to get an Enterprise Allowance, which gave me guaranteed cash income every week for a year. I made a small loss in my first year but this has grown to a third of my sales being profit and living expenses, yet I still have a relatively small business. I started with a quarter of the customers I now supply. I have a slightly larger garden than I started with but I need do no more work than I did in the first year.

Pricing vegetables

I have become so used to pricing up my boxes every week that I hardly think about it any more. I know what I have to put in the box in terms of variety and quantity for it to achieve its value.

How I price my vegetables may seem a little arbitrary. For example, potatoes have a weird pricing structure. They are incredibly heavy yet in the winter they are just about the cheapest vegetable you can buy. The early potatoes I grow are worth quite a lot of money but I don't charge my customers any extra for them. A few years ago first early organic potatoes were selling for £2 per 500g in June. At these prices my £5 box would have had little value left for anything else. I balance out the price over the whole year, selling them very cheaply in the summer and relatively expensively in the winter.

Salad bags are the other end of the scale – they are probably one of the most expensive vegetables you can buy but they weigh very little. They are a lot of work to produce, requiring regular sowings and picking of each of the components. If my salad bags were sold in a supermarket they would probably cost two or three times the price of an ordinary supermarket salad bag. I cost them at £1.99 for a 25 x 30cm bag. I pack over 900 salad bags a year, bringing in over £1500 a year.

In the past I have gone into supermarkets to compare conventional and organic prices. My prices nearly always fell somewhere between the two. It would be nice to charge the higher, organic prices but the deal with my customers is two-way. Firstly, my customers don't get any choice in what they get in their boxes. I rely on them to buy the boxes as they are so I can sell most of the vegetables I grow with very little wastage. Secondly, they put up with my season that only runs for six to seven months of the year. Thirdly, I wouldn't pay £2 for 500g of potatoes myself even though I know that in terms of sustainability they are worth that, if not more. Again, we come back to the same argument that food is far too cheap.

Do not compare your prices with a high street chain greengrocer, because their vegetables are so cheap you will get really depressed. Your customers are buying vegetables from you because of all the additional benefits you offer.

Pricing boxes by distance

Five of my drop-off points are within a six mile radius of my garden (one of them is in my garden!). I deliver to two of them on Tuesdays and two on Wednesdays. I also deliver boxes to Bristol, an hour away. This involves considerably more time, fuel and costs, so I charge more for the boxes.

I am often asked why I continue to take my vegetables to Bristol when it is so far away. My Bristol customers were my first customers and they have remained loyal for 9 years, providing me with what I think of as my bread and butter income. Many of these customers have children who have grown up eating my vegetables, and they have an understanding of how food is grown and where it comes from. I believe that this education is very important and I repay their loyalty by remaining loyal to them.

Keeping records

Accounting takes time but it has to be done. It takes about an hour a week to record sales and expenditure and process cheques. Every six months or so I write up my accounts on ledger paper, ready to send to my accountant at the year-end. This usually takes a day or two, and I save it for when it is pissing down outside.

Earning a living

How much income does my box scheme generate? It varies from year to year, depending on how much effort I put in and the sort of lifestyle I have. I can give a rough idea but must stress that running a box scheme is very individual, and the income will vary accordingly.

A typical turnover from a 75 box a week scheme running on 1.5 acres is about £12k. From the information in the Growing for sale Table 1, I have estimated the amount of income I receive one week in four, giving an average annual turnover of between £12K and £13K. This figure rises when I add miscellaneous sales. This includes selling surpluses such as pumpkins at Halloween and bulk orders of potatoes, carrots and onions, and income from farmers' markets. These sales take the turnover to between £14k and £15K. My expenditure, which includes bought in vegetables, rent, van costs, fuel, telephone, seeds, materials etc, can range from £9k to £10k, leaving me with a profit of roughly £5k. I stress that it is very variable and it really is up to the individual as to how much they take out of the business and how much they plough back into it.

The following table gives an idea of weekly income from June to December 2001.

June – 2 weeks sale @ £342 per week = £684
July – 4 weeks sale @ £510 per week = £2040
August – 5 weeks sale @ £462 per week = £2310
September – 4 weeks sale @ £514 per week = £2056
October – 4 weeks sale @ £491 per week = £1964
November – 5 weeks sale @ £434 per week = £2170
December – 3 weeks sale @ £462 per week = £1386

246

Labour and Help

What you get out of your garden is directly related to what you put in. It takes a great deal of time, effort and thought to grow large quantities of vegetables to sell. I could run my garden and business on my own if I worked long hours every day of the week and farmed my son out to childcare. I don't want to: I want to spend time with my son and have a life apart from my garden and business. I also want other people to be involved. I like to teach people how to grow and sell vegetables, and to see them appreciate just how good it is to be a gardener. There is great satisfaction in working outside and nurturing life beyond your own. I like working with people in the garden, almost as much as I like working in the garden on my own.

Help

Start by deciding if you need, or want, help. You may want occasional help for one-off jobs like fencing or harvesting, or you may want help just through the growing season. Whatever you need, you must know what you want and who's in charge, and be organised.

Apprentices

Every year I take on an apprentice for the duration of the growing season. The benefits of having an apprentice are threefold. I need help, I like having people to work with and I want more people to grow vegetables.

When I take an apprentice, my principle aim is to teach them how to grow vegetables sustainably. My next objective is to show them how I sell the vegetables and how I run my box scheme. Lastly, I want apprentices to experience the good and bad sides of growing vegetables. When the rain is teeming down and the runner beans need to be picked, you have to get on with it. When the sun is shining on a bright spring morning, the birds are singing and we are sowing modules of spring onions, life is good. At times like this I point out to my apprentice that most people are sitting in offices in front of computer screens or with a telephone attached to their ear. The good aspects of being a gardener are soon very apparent.

I provide my apprentice with simple accommodation, as many vegetables as they can eat and pocket money. I ask them to be available for 30 hours a week from Monday to Friday. Once they have settled in I give them responsibilities such as watering and opening and shutting tunnels when necessary, so that they get an idea of how to think about the garden and the plants in it.

Apprentices can be employed all year round if need be but I find that the growing season is enough. It is often wet and dark for the rest of the year and the garden and I both need a rest. Having an apprentice living in your space and working with you full time can be a very intense experience and you have to be very laid back to accommodate them. A separate living area and cooking facilities make the relationship much easier.

The advantage of apprentices over occasional workers is that they stay with you for the season. They get to know you and your garden quite well. After a while they know where things are and how to do things. If you have a new helper each weekend it can get boring trying to explain everything to each of them.

Wwoofers and volunteers

Wwoofer stands for Willing Workers On Organic Farms. The organisation that places them on farms is called Wwoof. Wwoofers want to learn about organic farming and are keen, short-term helpers, usually staying for a weekend or a week. They often have city/town jobs and like to get away at the weekends, doing something active and learning at the same time. Wwoofers come in all guises and the questions they ask are always different. Volunteers are effectively the same thing but on a pre-arranged time scale. It is nice to have people coming to work for short periods of time and it can be arranged for busy times. You need to provide accommodation and food so make sure you have room available in your house. Remember that their lifestyle is probably very different from yours, particularly if they spend a lot of time behind a desk. While you might exist on a quick sandwich for lunch, your helpers might need a break and something more substantial.

A word of warning: if people are coming for a weekend you must plan to spend most of the time working with them, answering questions and socialising. By the end of the weekend you can feel more exhausted than if you'd done the work yourself. On the other hand, it is a good way of involving people in your garden, in the knowledge that they will be gone within 48 hours!

Casual workers and swapping time

I sometimes employ people from the Local Exchange Trading System (LETS) if I need extra help for specific jobs like fencing and picking vegetables. If you have a LETS then use it. You can charge for some or all of your box sales in LETS.

Swapping time with other gardeners in your area is good fun and makes daunting jobs much more manageable. Not only will you make friends with people with a common interest, you can swap gardening tips. Many jobs can only be done by two people, but any job is much nicer done with a companion in half the time.

Insurance

As a business you need to have public liability insurance if anyone is going to even walk round your garden. If you have anyone working for you, paid or voluntary, then you need to have employer's liability insurance. If someone injures themselves on your land they can sue you, and if you don't have insurance you (and possibly they) won't have a leg to stand on.

Appendices

Polytunnels

Siting polytunnels

Once you have got your new or second-hand polytunnel you need to choose a site for it. Factors that need to be taken into account are the direction of the sun, the direction of the prevailing wind, the heaviness of your soil, the slope of the site, surrounding structures or plants that may shade the tunnel or rob the beds of moisture, and aesthetics.

Placing a tunnel with the ends facing east and west will be warmer in the winter and hotter in the summer than a tunnel that has its ends facing north and south. This is because the sun will be hitting the whole length of the tunnel for most of the day. Although this is only a matter of degree at the height of summer and in the depths of winter, during the spring and autumn these few degrees can make all the difference. It can be argued that the light is more evenly distributed in a tunnel placed with its ends facing north and south, but where polytunnels are useful in extending the season the east west orientation is better.

When it comes to ventilation, the orientation and the slope of the ground are important. Where I garden the prevailing winds are from the west. Three of my tunnels are sited SW to NE and one is NW to SE. The first three are well ventilated as they get a good flow of air through them from the wind. The last tunnel is right in a hollow so it doesn't really matter where the wind comes from. It is the plants in this tunnel that tend to suffer most from moulds and mildews. On the other hand, you're not doing yourself any favours if you site your polytunnel on top of a hill. If you can site your polytunnel with a slight slope from end to end you will encourage ventilation. This is because as the warm air rises and escapes at the top end of your polytunnel fresh air will naturally be pulled in.

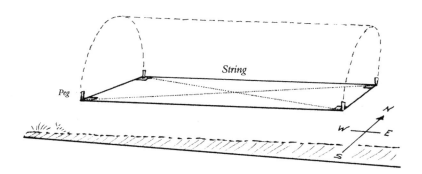

Erecting polytunnels

Laying out

When you have chosen a suitable site, mark up the ground so that your polytunnel will be square and orientated in the desired direction. The best way to do this is to carefully measure out the sides and ends. Use your eye to make sure the tunnel is square and a compass to check the orientation. Mark the four corners with pegs. Once the tunnel is in more or less the right place you can check that the structure is perfectly square by running strings diagonally between corners. Once these strings are equal in length, your structure will be square. Check again that the side and ends are the same length. Leave the marker strings in place to use as a guide for putting in the grounding tubes.

Grounding tubes and hoops

The next thing to do is to put in all the grounding tubes that will hold the hoops in place. Starting from the same end, this is simply a case of measuring the distance between each one, usually 1.75 - 2m apart. If you have a clay soil then they can just be whacked in and the soil will keep them in place. On a lighter soil you may need to embed the tubes in concrete to keep them in place. Each hoop can then be placed in the grounding tube and attached to the central ridge pole that keeps the side hoops together. Try and get this ridge pole as straight as possible. Lastly you will need to fix any struts to the end hoops, and sometimes middle ones.

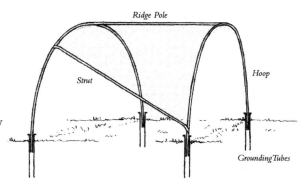

250

Door or end frames

Now you need to fix the end frames to the last hoop. These frames will hold the door and any ventilation openings. Also the plastic sheet that covers the polytunnel will be anchored to the frame. I always build my own doors and frames but you can buy them. Make sure the wood is treated, preferably with a non toxic, wood preserver.

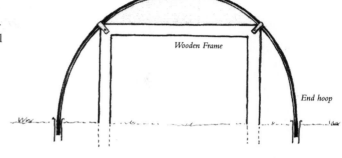

You will also need to dig a trench around the outside of the frame. This should be about one spit away from the grounding tubes, about one spit deep and one wide. The purpose of this trench is to anchor the plastic. A good way of keeping weeds down inside the edges of the polytunnel is to lay black plastic between the trench and the grounding tubes. This will stop weeds growing in the most inaccessible area of the tunnel and will save your a lot of work and a wet back.

Fitting the cover

Choose a warm, still day to cover the polytunnel. Organise any helpers you can get, four people is usually enough. Lay out your sheet of plastic next to the tunnel and let it warm for half an hour in the sun. Allow half the tunnels width as extra at each end. While you are waiting for the plastic to warm, fix anti-hot-spot tape to the outside of the hoops. This will stop the metal hoops getting hot in the sun, which makes the plastic go brittle and rip more easily.

When the plastic has warmed, slide it over the frame until there is the same amount on each side. The first area to attach is the piece that fits to the top of the doorframe. The plastic should be wound round a batten and nailed to the inside top of the door-frame. Then take the other end and pull it as hard as you can and batten and nail it to the top end of the other door frame. Starting from the middle hoop and with two people on each side, push the plastic into the trench with your boot (preferably wellies as they don't tear the plastic) whilst the other person shovels the soil back into the trench.

Batten nailed to inside of door frame

Both parties should work towards the same end of the polytunnel at the same rate and this will help keep the plastic evenly taut. If there are only two of you keep changing sides as you work from the middle to the end. When you reach the end, wrap the plastic around a batten and nail it to the inside of the doorframe. This is quite tricky because the plastic will ruckle where it goes round the corners. Don't worry about these ruckles. As long as the plastic is as taut as possible it won't alter the performance of the tunnel. Then go back to the middle to work to the other end.

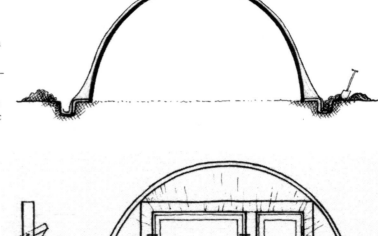

You now have a sheeted poly-tunnel with no doors. There are a variety of types of door. If they will be used mainly for

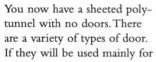

ventilation they can be swing type windows or roller blinds of plastic. I have easy access doors at either end of my tunnels for daily use and they are wide enough to fit my two-wheel tractor and wheelbarrow through.

Maintaining polytunnels

Keeping polytunnel covers clean means greater light transmission which means better growing conditions for your plants. As the tops of polytunnels are difficult to reach I tend to just clean the north sides of my tunnels, using a sponge mop. Although it's not a nice job it's easiest to clean the tunnels when it rains because you then have instant rinsing. The worst thing about this job is that water runs down the mop handle and up your arms into your armpits.

Mending tears and holes in the plastic sheet will increase its length of service and lessen heat loss.

Building your own Propagator

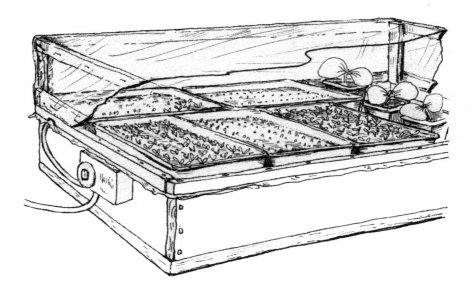

It really isn't very difficult to build your own propagator and depending on it's size, you can save a lot of money and have one that lasts for years. The one pictured below has already lasted nine years and shows no signs of wear and tear at all. For one the same size you will need:
- 2cm thick plywood or chipboard measuring 1m x 60cm for the base
- 4 pieces of 15cm wide floorboard to make the sides (2 x 60cm and 2 x 1m long).
- 4 battens for the top edge
- A piece of thick plastic (builders plastic will do) which will fit across the bottom and up the sides
- Two 25kg bags of sand and a piece of plastic to fit on top of the sand.

– 4m long soil cable and thermostat with a 30cm rod
– A handful of 5-7.5cm nails.
– For the lid – roofing battens and clear polytunnel plastic

Firstly fix the floorboards together in a rectangle and attach to the plywood base. Lay the plastic on the inside and batten it down on the top edge. Fill the box with sand to a depth of 10cm and moisten it. Lay the soil cable on the sand, a little like the element of an electric kettle, making sure that it isn't touching or too close to itself (turning it on so that it warms up will make it more pliable).

Next drill a hole through one end of the box, just above where the soil cable lies, and push the thermostat rod through. Attach the thermostat block to the outside of the box. Cover the soil cable and thermostat with a 5cm thick layer of damp sand. Cover the sand with the other piece of plastic, which will stop the sand from drying out. The soil cable should be connected to the thermostat box. This ought to be quite easy if you follow the instructions that should come with the thermostat.

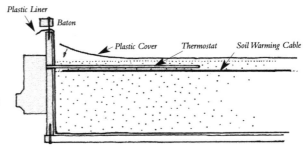

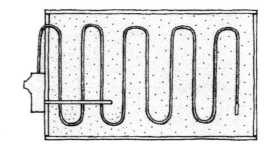

Your propagator is now ready to be used, but I also have a cover for mine. It gives the trays and modules just that little bit extra protection and warmth. Mine is literally some roofing battens nailed together with a piece of polytunnel plastic stapled to it.

Average Monthly Costing and Content of Boxes

Start of selling in June, only small boxes available

Size of box	Small	
Cost of box	£5	
Vegetables	**Quantities**	**Prices**
Potatoes	1kg	£1.00
Salad	Bag	£1.75
Broad Beans	500gms +	75p
Cucumber	Half	40p
Spring Onions	Bunch	75p
Spinach	Bunch	75p
As near box price as possible		£5.40

July starts with large, medium and small boxes available

Size of box	Small		Medium		Large	
Cost of box	£5		£7.50		£10.00	
Vegetables	**Quantities**	**Prices**	**Quantities**	**Prices**	**Quantities**	**Prices**
Potatoes	1kg	£1.00	1.5kg	£1.50	2kg	£2.00
Salad	Bag	£1.75	Bag	£1.75	Bag	£1.75
Broad Beans	500gms +	75p	750gms	£1.00	1kg	£1.50
Cucumber	Half	40p	Whole	75p	Whole	75p
Celery	One	50p	One	50p	One	50p
Toms	375gms	75p	375gms	75p	500gms +	£1.00
Calabrese			2 small heads	75p	2 heads	75p
Carrots			Bunch	75p	Large bunch	75p
Onions			3 Medium	40p	4 Medium	50p
Fennel					2 bulbs	75p
As near box price as possible	**£5.15**		**£8.15**		**£10.25**	

Typical week in August, low sales due to holiday season

Better value for money as surpluses appear						
Size of box	Small		Medium		Large	
Cost of box	£5		£7.50		£10.00	
Vegetables	**Quantities**	**Prices**	**Quantities**	**Prices**	**Quantities**	**Prices**
Potatoes	1kg	£1.00	1.5kg	£1.50	2kg	£2.00
Salad	Bag	£1.75	Bag	£1.75	Bag	£1.75
Cucumber	Half	40p	whole	75p	Whole	75p
Onions	3 Medium	40p	3 Medium	40p	4 Large	50p
Spinach	Bunch	75p	Bunch	75p	Bunch	£1.00
Garlic	Bulb	50p			Bulb	
Celery	Plant	70p			Plant	
Basil			Bag	50p	Bag	50p
French Beans			500gms	£1.00	500gms	£1.00
Courgettes			500gms	75p	500gms	75p
Beetroot			Bunch of 4/5	75p	Bunch of 6/7	90p
Runner Beans					500gms +	£1.00
As near box price as possible	**£5.50**		**£8.15**		**£10.15**	

Valuable Vegetables

September, the holiday season is over, crops begin to change

Size of box	Small		Medium		Large	
Cost of box	£5		£7.50		£10.00	
Vegetables	**Quantities**	**Prices**	**Quantities**	**Prices**	**Quantities**	**Prices**
Potatoes	1kg	£1.00	1.5kg	£1.50	2kg	£2.00
Salad	Bag	£1.75	Bag	£1.75	Bag	£1.75
Shallots	2 clusters	50p	3 clusters	75p	3 clusters	75p
Red Cabbage	half	50p	whole	75p	whole	75p
Courgettes	500gms	75p				
French Beans	500gms	£1.00				
Garlic			Bulb	50p	Bulb	50p
Runner beans			500gms	£1.00	750gms	£1.25
Tomatoes					500gms	50p
Beetroot			Bunch of 4/5	50p	Bunch of 6/7	60p
Carrots			500gms	50p	500gms	50p
Watercress			Bunch	75p	Bunch	75p
Calabrese					1 head	75p
Spinach					Bunch	75p
As near box price as possible	**£5.50**		**£8**		**£10.85**	

October, crops begin to take on winter flavour

Size of box	Small		Medium		Large	
Cost of box	£5		£7.50		£10.00	
Vegetables	**Quantities**	**Prices**	**Quantities**	**Prices**	**Quantities**	**Prices**
Potatoes	1kg	80p	1.5kg	£1.20	2kg	£1.60
Carrots	500gms	50p	600gms	60p	750gms	75p
Onions	3 medium	30p	4 medium	40p	5 medium	50p
Garlic	Bulb	50p	Bulb	50p	Bulb	50p
Salad	Bag	£1.75				
Beetroot	Bunch of 3/4	60p				
Cauliflower	One small	£1.00	One large	£1.15	One large	£1.15
Parsnip			500gms	85p	750gms	£1.25
Kale			Bunch	50p	Bunch	75p
Pumpkin			750gms	80p	1kg	£1.00
Alfalfa			Bag	80p	Bag	80p
Pepper					One	75p
Cucumber			Half	35p	Half	35p
Turnips					250gms	50p
Rosemary			Sprig	25p	Sprig	25p
As near box price as possible	**£5.45**		**£7.40**		**£10.15**	

November, much more bought in produce although still a lot of crops from storage and garden

Size of box	Small		Medium		Large	
Cost of box	£5		£7.50		£10.00	
Vegetables	**Quantities**	**Prices**	**Quantities**	**Prices**	**Quantities**	**Prices**
Potatoes	1kg	80p	1.5kg	£1.20	2kg	£1.60
Carrots	500gms	50p	600gms	60p	750gms	75p
Calabrese	One head	75p			Two heads	£1.50
Leeks	2 medium	75p	3 medium	£1.00	4 medium	£1.25
Garlic	Bulb	50p	Bulb	50p	Bulb	50p
Celeriac	One small	75p	One small	75p	One large	£1.00
Onions			4 medium	40p	5 medium	50p
Squash			750gms	75p	1kg	£1.00
Artichokes			500gms	50p	500gms	50p
Salad			Bag	£1.75	Bag	£1.75
Parsnips					500gms	85p
Cabbage			One	50p	One large	75p
Spinach		75p				
As near box price as possible	£4.80		£7.95		£11.70	

December

Size of box	Small		Medium		Large	
Cost of box	£5		£7.50		£10.00	
Vegetables	**Quantities**	**Prices**	**Quantities**	**Prices**	**Quantities**	**Prices**
Potatoes	1kg	80p	1.5kg	£1.20	2kg	£1.60
Carrots	500gms	50p	600gms	60p	750gms	75p
Onions	3 medium	30p	4 medium	40p	5 medium	50p
Alfalfa	Bag	80p	Bag	80p	Bag	80p
Garlic	Bulb	50p	Bulb	50p	Bulb	50p
Swede	One	50p	One	50p	One	50p
Turnips	250gms	50p				
Brussels sprouts	500gms	£1.00	750gms	£1.50	750gms	£1.50
Salad			Small bag	£1.25	Small bag	£1.25
Kale			Bunch	50p	Bunch	50p
Squash			500gms	50p	750gms	75p
White cabbage	Half	25p			Whole	50p
Celeriac					One	75p
As near box price as possible	£5.15		£7.75		£9.90	

If you would like a complete breakdown of the contents, price, number and delivery routine and income from box sales for the year 2000 send a large s.a.e. to eco-logic books or email your address and we will forward an Excel spreadsheet with the information.

Timetables of plantings for Succession

Crops grown in modules, pots and trays for transplanting

Month	Vegetable	Variety	Container	Quantity	Where it grows	Transplant time	When crops	Quantity crops
February	Parsley	Moss curled Plain	Module 24 Cell	1 Module	Polytunnel Outside	April	May - May	Salad bags
	Summer cabbage	Greyhound Spitfire F1 Stonehead F1	Seed Tray	1 Tray 1 Tray 1 Tray	Outside	Mar - April	June - Aug	90 heads
	Calabrese	Corvet F1	Seed Tray	2 Trays	Outside	Mar - April	June - Aug	10 boxes/wk
	Spring Onions	White Lisbon	Module 40 Cell	2 Modules	Polytunnel	Mar - April	May - July	80 bunches
March	Lettuce	Little Gem Salad Bowl Marvel of 4 Seasons	Module 40 Cell	1 Module 1 Module 1 Module	Polytunnel	April	April - June	Salad bags
	Celery	Celebrity Solid White	Module 60 Cell	1 Module 1 Module	Outside	May	July - Aug	120 heads
	Celeriac	Giant Prague	Module 60 Cell	2 Modules	Outside	May	Oct - Mar	120 roots
	Tomato	Sungold Tigerella Big Boy	Module 40 Cell	20 Cells 10 Cells 10 Cells	Polytunnel	April	May - Nov	10 boxes/wk
	Peppers	Bell Boy F1 Cono di Torra Banana Supreme	Module 40 Cell	20 Cells 10 Cells 10 Cells	Polytunnel	April	July - Nov	10 boxes/wk
	Chillis	Thai Hot Dragon Firecracker	Module 20 Cell	10 Cells 10 Cells	Polytunnel	May	Aug - Nov	Variable
	Aubergine	Vista F1	Module 10 Cell	10 Cells	Polytunnel	April	Aug - Oct	Home use +
	Spring Onions	White Lisbon	Module 40 Cell	4 Modules	Outside	April	June - Aug	160 bunches
	Cucumbers	Delta Star Birgit	Pots	5 Pots 5 Pots	Polytunnel	April	May - Nov	100/wk
	Melons	Sweetheart Ogen	Pots	5 - 10 Pots	Polytunnel	April	Aug - Oct	Home use +
	Lettuce	Lollo Rossa Cos	Module 60 Cell	60 Cells 60 Cells	Outside	May	June - Aug	Salad bags

continued

Crops grown in modules, pots and trays for transplanting

continued

Month	Vegetable	Variety	Container	Quantity	Where it grows	Transplant time	When crops	Quantity crops
	Kohl rabi	Purple Delicacy	Module 40 Cell	40 Cells	Outside	April - May	June - Aug	40 heads
	Basil	Sweet	Module 40 Cell	20 Cells	Polytunnel	April	June - Sept	50 boxes/wk
		Neapolitan		10 Cells				
		Red Ruffles		10 Cells				
April	Spring Onions	White Lisbon	Module 40 Cell	2 Modules	Outside	May	Aug - Sept	80 bunches
	Tomatoes	Red Alert	Module 40 Cell	20 Cells	Outside	May	July - Oct	75 boxes/wk
		Tornado F1		20 Cells				
	Courgettes	Patriot F1	Pots	20 Pots	Outside	May	July - Oct	50 boxes/wk
		Gold Rush		20 Pots				
	Squash	Butternut	Pots	10 Pots	Outside	May	Sept - Dec	35 boxes/wk
		Acorn		10 Pots				
		Vegetable Spaghetti		10 Pots				
		Uchiki Kuri		10 Pots				
		Sweet Dumpling		10 Pots				
		Crown Prince		10 Pots				
	Pumpkin	Golden Nugget	Pots	10 Pots	Outside	May	Sept - Dec	10 boxes/wk
		Tom Fox		10 Pots				
		Mammoth		5 Pots				
	Sweet corn	Sweet Nugget	Module 40 Cell	10 Modules	Outside	May	Sept	25 boxes/wk
	Runner beans	Scarlet Emperor	Pots	200 Pots	Outside	May	July - Oct	60 boxes/wk
August	Lamb's lettuce	Large leaved	Module 40 Cell	3 Modules	Polytunnel	Sept	Nov - Mar	Salad bags

Crops grown in seed beds
(under cover, either cold frame or tunnel)

Month	Vegetable	Variety	Transplant Time	Where it grows	When it crops	Quantity it crops	Amount of ground
April	Brussels sprouts	Early Half Tall	June	Outside	Oct - Mar	Home use +	1m x 10m
		Rampart F1					
		Braveheart F1					
	Kale	Nero di Toscano	June	Outside	Aug - Mar	10 boxes/wk	1m x 15m
		Pentland Brig					
		Hungry Gap					
	Cabbage	Red Drumhead	June	Outside	Sept - Feb	10 boxes/wk	1m x 15m
		Best of All					
		Tundra					
	Calabrese	Shogun F1	May/June	Outside	July - Sept	10 boxes/wk	1m x 10m
	Leeks	The Lyon	June	Outside	Sept - April	50 boxes/wk	15m x 20m
		Musselburgh					
May	Cauliflower	Stella F1	June	Outside	Aug - Nov	5 boxes/wk	1m x 10m
		Snowcap					
	Sprouting Broccoli	Purple Sprouting	June	Outside	Feb - April	Home use	1m x 3m

Crops in polytunnels

Month	Vegetable	Variety	Month it crops	Seed/Transplant	Resow month	Extra protection?	Replaced by maincrop
March	Carrot	Early Nantes	June - July	Seed			August
	Beetroot	Boltardy	June - July	Seed			July
	Spring Onions	White Lisbon	June	Transplant			July
April	Aubergine	Vista F1	July - Oct	Transplant		Yes	
	French Beans	Purple Teepee	June - July	Seed	July		August
	Endive	Endivia Riccia P	June	Seed	June		July
	Peppers/chillis	Various	July - Oct	Transplant	July	Yes	
	Rocket		May - Mar	Seed	May - Sept		
	Cucumbers	Delta Star/Birgit	May - Nov	Transplant		Yes	
	Melons	Sweetheart/Ogen	Aug - Oct	Transplant		Yes	
	Tomatoes	Various	May - Nov	Transplant		Yes	
	Sweet corn	Sweet Nugget	Aug	Transplant			September
	Watercress		June - Dec	Seed			
May	Radish	French Breakfast	June - Nov	Seed	Sept		July
August	Perpetual Spinach		Oct - Sept	Seed			
	Carrots	Chantenay Red Core	Dec - Mar	Seed			
	Claytonia		Oct - Mar	Seed			
	Oriental salads	Red Mustard	Sept - Mar	Seed	Sept - Oct		
		Green Mustard					
		Mizuna					
		Mibuna					
		Pak Choi					
		Komatsuna					
		Green in the Snow					
		Chinese Cabbag					
	Chicory	Sugar Loaf	Nov - Mar	Seed			
	Lamb's Lettuce	Large Leaved	Oct-Mar	Seed			

Crops sown outdoors

Month	Vegetable	Variety	Month it crops	Seed type	Amount of seed	Resow months	Early protection?
February	Broad beans	Bunyard's Exhibition	June - Aug	Seed	8 packets	Mar - April	
	Garlic	Cristo	July	Clove	25 bulbs		
	Jerusalem Artichoke	Fuseau	Oct - Feb	Tuber	30 tubers		
March	Beetroot	Boltardy	July - Nov	Seed	10gms	April - June	
	Onion sets	Turbo	August	Sets	25kgs		
	Shallots		July	Sets	2kgs		
	First Early Pots	Premiere	June - July	Tuber	50kgs		Yes
	Turnips	Snowball	June - July	Seed	1 packet	April	
April	French beans	Cropper Teepee	July - Sept	Seed	8 packets	May - June	Yes
		Sungold			4 packets		
	Carrots	Nantes	July - Aug	Seed	10gm		
		Autumn King	Aug - Oct		10gm		
	Coriander	Cilantro B	July - Aug	Seed	10gm	May - June	
	Fennel	Argo	July	Seed	1 packet	May - June	
	Lettuce	Various	June - Oct	Seed	Many packets	May - Aug	
	Red Onion	Red Baron	July - Aug	Sets	5kg		
	Parsnips	Tender and True	Oct - Mar	Seed	2 packets		
		Avonresister			2 packets		
	Parsley	Moss curled	July - April	Seed	1 packet		
		Plain			1 packet		
	Peas	Greenshaft	July - Sept	Seed	1kg	May - June	
	Second early pots	Estima	July - Oct	Tuber	25kg		
		Marfona			25kg		
	Maincrop pots	Sante	Sept - Oct	Tuber	25kg		
	Perpetual Spinach		June - Nov	Seed	10gms		
	Swede	Marian	Oct - Mar	Seed	2 packets		
	Swiss Chard		July - Oct	Seed	2 packets		
May	Radish	French Breakfast	June - Sept	Seed	15gms	June - Aug	
June	Chicory	Various	Sept - Nov	Seed	Various		
	Endive	Various	Sept - Nov	Seed	Various		
	Radish	Mouli	Oct - Nov	Seed	2 packets		
July	Turnips	Purple Top Milan	Sept - Nov	Seed	4 packets		
September	Onions	Senshyu	June	Sets	3kg		
October	Garlic	Germidour	July - Aug	Clove	50 - 60 bulbs		
	Broad Beans	Aquadulce Claudia	May - June	Seed	4 packets		

Sowing and Harvesting Table

	Jan	Feb	Mar	Apr	May	Jun	Jul	Aug	Sept	Oct	Nov	Dec
Jerusalem artichokes	H	H/S								H	H	H
Broad beans		S	S	S	H	H	H	H				
French beans				S	S	S/H	H	H	H			
Runner beans				S			H	H	H	H		
Beetroot			S	S	S	S/H	H	H	H	H		
Brussels sprouts	H	H	H	S	S			H	H	H	H	H
Calabrese				S	S		H	H	H			
Carrots				S	S	H	H	H	H	H		
Cauliflower			H	S/H	H/S		H	H	H	H	H	
Celeriac		S	S	S						H	H	H
Celery		S	S	S			H	H	H			
Chicory						S	S		H	H	H	H
Claytonia	H	H	H					S		H	H	H
Courgettes				S			H	H	H			
Cucumber			S		H	H	H	H	H	H	H	
Endive				S	S	S	S/H	H	H	H	H	
Fennel				S	S	S	H	H	H	H		
Garlic		S					H	H		S		

Key: H = Harvest   S = Sow

continued

	Jan	Feb	Mar	Apr	May	Jun	Jul	Aug	Sept	Oct	Nov	Dec
Kale	H	H	H	S	S				H	H	H	H
Kohl Rabi			S	S	S	S	H	H	H	H		
Lamb's lettuce	H	H	H	H				S		H	H	H
Leeks	H	H	H	H/S	H				H	H	H	H
Lettuce			S	S	S	S/H	S/H	S/H	H	H	H	H
Marrows				S					H	H		
Onions			S	S			H	H				
Oriental salad leaves	H	H	H			S	S	S		H	H	H
Parsnips	H	H	H/S	S						H	H	H
Peas			S	S	S/H	S/H	H	H	S/H			
Peppers and chillis				S				H	H	H	H	H
Potatoes			S	S	S	H	H	H	H			
Pumpkins				S						H	H	
Radish					S	S/H	H/S	S/H	H			
Rocket					S	S	S/H	S	S	H		H
Shallots			S				H	H				
Annual spinach			S	S	H	S/H		H	H	H		
Perpetual spinach				S		H	S/H	S/H	H	H	H	
Spring Onions		S	S	S	S/H	S/H	H	H	H			
Sprouting Broccoli		H	H		S							
Squash				S	S					H	H	
Swede				S						H	H	H
Sweetcorn				S				H	H	H		
Swiss Chard				S			H	H	H	H	H	
Tomatoes			S	S		H	H	H	H	H		
Turnips			S			S/H	H		H	H		
Watercress				S		H	H	H	H	H	H	

Key: H = Harvest   S = Sow

Useful Organisations

Garden Organic
Charity promoting organic gardening and Heritage Seed Library
Ryton Organic Gardens
Coventry
CV8 3LG
Tel: 024 7630 3517
Fax: 024 7663 9229
Email: enquiry@gardenorganic.org.uk
Website: www.gardenorganic.org.uk

Ragman's Lane Farm
Runs courses on vegetable growing and selling, willow sculptures and growing, cider making and apple juice pressing, permaculture, sustainable land use etc.,
Lower Lydbrook
Glos
GL17 9PA
Tel: 01594 860244
Website: www.ragmans.co.uk

Soil Association
Charity promoting organic farming and growing.
South Plaza,
Marlborough Street,
Bristol BS1 3NX
Tel: 0117 314 5000
Email: info@soilassociation.org
Website: www.soilassociation.org

Permaculture Association
Charity promoting permaculture worldwide.
BCM Permaculture Association
London
WC1N 3XX
Tel: 0845 458 1805
Website: www.permaculture.org.uk

Centre for Alternative Technology
Anything you want to know on alternative technology
Machynlleth
Powys
SY20 9AZ
Tel: 01654 705905
Website: www.cat.org.uk

WWOOF UK
Working on organic farms
PO Box 2154
Winslow
Buckingham
MK18 3WS
Tel and fax: 01273 476 286
Website: www.wwoof.org.uk

Biological Pest Control Suppliers

Defenders Ltd
Occupation Road
Wye
Ashford
Kent
TN25 5EN
Tel: 01233 813121
Website: www.defenders.co.uk

The Organic Gardening Catalogue
Riverdene Business Park
Molesey Road
Hersham
Surrey
KT12 4RG
Tel: 01932 253666
Website: www.OrganicCatalog.com
Ask them for the bulk price list for discounts. If you are a member of Garden Organic you are also entitled to 10% discount from the catalogue.

Green Gardener
41 Strumpshaw Road
Brundall
Norfolk
NR13 5PG
Tel: 01603 715096
Website: www.greengardener.co.uk

Seed catalogues

The companies I favour are marked with an asterisk★.

★ The Organic Gardening Catalogue
Riverdene Business Park
Molesey Road
Hersham
Surrey
KT12 4RG
Tel: 01932 253666
Fax: 01932 252707
Website: www.OrganicCatalog.com
If you become a member of Garden Organic you can get 10% off your order on most items.

★ Simpson's Seeds
The Walled Garden Nursery
Cock Lane
Horningsham
Warminster
Wiltshire
BA12 7NQ
Tel: 01985 845004
Website: www.simpsonsseeds.co.uk
Comprehensive supply of tomato and pepper seed with lots more veg lines coming on stream.

★ Suffolk Herbs
Monks Farm
Coggeshall Road
Kelvedon
Essex
CO5 9PG
Tel: 01376 572456
Fax: 01376 571189
Website: www.suffolkherbs.com
Useful company which supplies a good range of chicories, lettuce, French beans, herbs etc

★ Tamar Organics
Cartha Martha Farm
Rezare
Launceston
Cornwall
PL15 9NX
Tel: 01579 371087
Website: www.tamarorganics.co.uk
Very friendly.

★ Edwin Tucker & Sons Ltd
Brewery Meadow
Stonepark
Ashburton
Newton Abbot
Devon
TQ13 7DG
Tel: 01364 652233
Website: www.edwintucker.com
Ask for specialist potato list and bulk price lists. Tend to be the cheapest.

★ Jennifer Birch
Garfield Villa
Belle Vue Road
Stroud
Glos
Tel: 01453 750371
Best supplier of garlic in the country.

★ Real Seeds
Brithdir Mawr Farm,
Newport near Fishguard,
Pembrokeshire
SA42 0QJ
Tel: 01239 821107
Website: www.realseeds.co.uk

D T Brown & Co
Bury Road
Newmarket
Suffolk
CB8 7QB
Tel:0845 3710534
Website: www.dtbrownseeds.co.uk

Samuel Dobies and Son
Long Road
Paignton
Devon
TQ4 7SX
Tel: 01803 696444
Website: www.dobies.co.uk

Association Kokopelli Organic Seeds
Website: www.terredescemences.com
Rare seeds and strange varieties.

Mr Fothergill's Seeds
Gazely Road
Kentford
Newmarket
Suffolk
CB8 7QB
Tel: 0845 3710518
Website: www.mr-fothergills.co.uk

Heritage Seed Library
Garden Organic
Ryton Organic Gardens
Coventry
CV8 3LG
Tel: 02476 303517
Website: gardenorganic.org.uk/hsl
Become a member of the Heritage Seed Library and you get rare seeds to try out for free. You will help support their work that preserves old and odd varieties.

S E Marshall & Co
Alconbury Hill
Huntingdon
Cambs
PE28 4HY
Tel: 01480 443390 or 0844 922 2899
Website: www.marshalls-seeds.co.uk

Suttons
Woodview Road
Paignton
Devon
TQ4 7NG
Tel: 01803 696321 or 0844 922 2899
Website: suttons.co.uk

Thompson & Morgan
Poplar Lane
Ipswich
Suffolk
IP8 3BU
Tel: 01473 688821
Website: www.thompson-morgan.com

Unwins Seeds
Alconbury Hill
Huntingdon
PE28 4HY
Tel: 01480 443395
Website: www.unwins.co.uk

Garden Equipment (bulk supplier)

LBS Horticulture
Stanroyd Mill
Cottontree
Colne
Lancs
BB8 7BW
Tel: 01282 873333
Website: www.lbs-group.co.uk

Northern Polytunnels
Stanroyd Mill
Cottontree
Colne
Lancs
BB8 7BW
Tel: 01282 873120
Website: www.northernpolytunnels.co.uk

Bibliography

Books

Any book by Lawrence D Hills and/or Joy Larkcom

The Self-Sufficient Gardener - John Seymour
Publisher - Corgi Books 1994

The New Organic Grower - Eliot Coleman
Publisher - Chelsea Green Publishing Co 1995

Composting with Worms - G. Pilkington
eco-logic books 2005

Back Garden Seed Saving - Sue Stickland
eco-logic books 2001

The Permaculture Garden - Graham Bell
Permanent Publications

The Seed Savers' Handbook - Jeremy Cherfas, Michel and Jude Fanton
Grover Books 1996

Pests and Diseases - Pippa Greenwood and Andrew Halstead
Dorling Kindersley 1997

Four Season Harvest - Eliot Coleman
Chelsea Green Publishing Co 1992

The Living Soil - E B Balfour
Universe Books 1975

Growing Unusual Vegetables - Simon Hickmott
eco-logic books 2003

Books in print are available from:
eco-logic books, Mulberry House
19 Maple Grove, Bath BA2 3AF
email: info@eco-logicbooks.com
web: www.eco-logicbooks.com

Magazines

The Kitchen Garden Magazine
Kitchen Garden Subscription Dept, Warners, West Street, Bourne, Lincs, PE10 9PH

The Organic Way
Garden Organic, Ryton Organic Gardens, Coventry, CV8 3LG

Permaculture Magazine
Permanent Publications, The Sustainability Centre, East Meon, Hants

Index

A Frame 15
American mildew 76, 218
anthocorid bugs 70, 73, 214, 218
ants 66, 98
aphids 66, 73, 76, 82
apprentices 247
Bacillus thuringiensis
66,73,95,182,241
basil 182,241,
beds 15, 35
beetroot 71
big bud 214
birds 214
blackberries 209
blackcurrants 212
blackfly 66, 99
blight 76, 82, 155, 175
bone meal 20, 34
Bordeaux Mixture 76, 155
boron 20
botrytis 75, 223, 228
brassicas 35, 41, 94
broad beans 97, 201
brussels sprouts 99
bunyip 15
cabbage 101
calcium 20
cane blight 223
Cape gooseberry 215
capping 18, 105
capsid 66 ,70
carabid beetles 71
carrots 78, 82, 105
carrot root fly 25, 82, 105, 162,
197
caterpillar 66, 70, 73, 95
catnip 66
cauliflowers 107
celeriac 108
celery 110
celery leaf 184

centipedes 70
Chafer grubs 67
chalk 18
chervil 185
chicory 112
chillies 148
chives 186
clamp 57
claytonia 113
click beetle 69
cloches 8, 51
codling moth 70
coldframes 46, 51, 260
comfrey 20, 31
comfrey liquid 32
compost 29
contours 15
copper 20
copper fungicide 76
copper sulphate 76
coriander 187
courgettes 37
cutworms 67
damping off 48
deer 75
derris 73
dill 189
dolomite 19, 20
double digging 14
downy mildew 137, 141
drying vegatables 57
ducks 69
earwigs 70
eelworms 82, 141, 155
elder leaf solution 73
endive 122
farm gate sales 244
Farm yard manure (FYM) 12, 28
farmers' markets 243
fennel 123
fertilisers 33, 34

fish meal 34
flame guns 64
flea beetles 67, 73, 96
fleece 25, 53
French beans 126
French parsley 196
frogs 71, 233
garden tours 233
garlic 138
garlic spray 74
gloves 26
gooseberry 217
gooseberry sawfly 218
green manures 39, 40, 42
greenhouse – see polytunnel?
ground beetles 71
gypsum 19
heating 26
hedge 8, 11
hedgehogs 71
hoes 33
hoof & horn 34
hoverflies 71, 82, 192
hybrid berries 209
insurance 248
iron 20
irrigation 59
Jerusalem artichoke 86
kale 94, 130
labels 24
lacewings 72
ladybirds 72
lambs lettuce 132
leafmould 33
leather jackets 8
leeks 134
lemon balm 191
LETS 77, 248
lettuce 135
lime 17, 19, 20, 29
lovage 192

magnesium 20
marjoram 194
marrow 138
mealybugs 73
melon 219
mesh 25, 53, 65, 73
mice 44, 45, 75
mildew 48, 75, 116, 212, 228
millipedes 68
mint 193
modules 24
moles 74
molybdenum 26
mowers 22
muck tea 29
mulch - for fertility 17, 31
mulch - to clear ground 14
mulch – weed control 37, 63
mulches - water retention 59
mushroom compost 33
netting 25
nettles 33, 72
nettle tea 20, 29
nitrogen 20, 29, 34, 40, 41, 81, 94
onion 140
oregano 194
oriental leaves 142
packing 241
parsley 195
parsnip 143
peas 145
peat 18, 48
peppers 148
pH 19
pH test kits 26
phosphorous 20
physalis 215
Phytoseiulus persimilis 73
Ploughing 13, 154
polytunnel 26, 46, 50, 53, 119, 249
potassium 20
potassium permanganate 76
potatoes 152
powdery mildew 121
pre-germinating 44

pricing 245, 246, 255
propagation 43
propagators 26, 48, 253
public liability insurance 248
pumpkin 138
Pyrethrum 73
Quassia 73
rabbits 74
rainwater 60
raised beds 16
raspberries 221
red spider mite 68
redcurrants 224
restaurants
rhubarb 226
rhubarb leaf solution 73
root trainers 24
rosemary 199
rotations 35
rotovator 21
rove beetles (Devils coach horses) 70
row-seeder 24
runner beans 159
rust 76, 135
sage 199
salad bags 142, 235, 241, 245
salad burnet 200
salsify 162
savory 201
scorzonera 162
seaweed 34
seed compost 48
seed saving 77
seed viability 78
seedbed 45, 63
shallots 140
shrew 72
slow worm 72
slugs 15, 68, 155
snails 69
soft soap 73
soil blocks 24
soil structure 17
soil tests 17, 19, 26
soil types 17
sorrel 202

sowing 43
spent hops 33
spiders - wolf 72
squash 167
staging 25
strawberries 228
strimmer 22
string 24
succession 44, 259
swede 170
sweetcorn 171
tansy 74
tarragon 204
thermometers 26
thinning 45, 46
thrips 69
thyme 205
tilth 45
toads 71
tomatoes 174
tools 22
tractor 13, 21
tractor - 2 wheeled 14, 21, 154
trays 23
turnip 178
tyres 53, 115, 157, 227
urine 29, 66, 98
vegetable boxes 240
vine weevils 73
wasps 72
water sources 11, 61
waterproofs 27
weeds 29, 31, 45, 63
weevils 69
wellies 26
whitecurrants 224
whitefly 69, 125, 176
wilts 76
wireworms 69
wood ash 34
woodlice 70
worm composting 31
wormwood spray 74
WWOOFers 248
zinc 20

eco-logic books

www.eco-logicbooks.com

eco-logic books is a small, ethically-run company that specialises in publishing and distributing books and other material that promote practical solutions to environmental problems. Those books that are still in print and mentioned in the book plus many others are available from our comprehensive website or catalogue. Other topics covered in the catalogue include:

- **Gardening and Organics**
- **Permaculture**
- **Composting**
- **Climate Change**
- **Self Reliance**
- **Food and Related Issues**
- **Keeping Hens and other Domestic Animals**
- **Smallholding and Farming**
- **Wildlife**
- **Trees, Woodland Crafts and Forestry**
- **Orchards and Fruit Growing**

- **Community Building and Construction**
- **Peak Oil**
- **Alternative Energy**
- **Urban issues**
- **Transition Towns**
- **Transport**
- **Money and the Economy**
- **Trade Skills**
- **Sustainabilty**
- **Radical Thinking and Managing for Change**

You can download a **FREE** mail order catalogue from our website

Eco-logic books, Mulberry House,19 Maple grove, Bath, BA2 3AF
Tel: 01225 484 472   Fax: 0871 522 7054

email: info@eco-logicbooks.com
web: www.eco-logicbooks.com